ISLAM, GENDER, CULTURE, AND DEMOCRACY:

FINDINGS FROM

THE WORLD VALUES SURVEY

AND

THE EUROPEAN VALUES SURVEY

ISLAM, GENDER, CULTURE, AND DEMOCRACY: FINDINGS FROM THE WORLD VALUES SURVEY AND THE EUROPEAN VALUES SURVEY

Edited by Ronald Inglehart

President of the World Values Survey Association and Professor of Political Science at the Institute for Social Research, University of Michigan

de Sitter Publications

INTERNATIONAL STUDIES IN SOCIAL SCIENCE

Series Editor

S. Ishwaran

VOLUME 4

Edited by Ronald Inglehart

ISLAM, GENDER, CULTURE, AND DEMOCRACY: FINDINGS FROM THE WORLD VALUES SURVEY AND THE EUROPEAN VALUES SURVEY

de Sitter Publications

Canadian Cataloguing in Publication Data

ISLAM, GENDER, CULTURE, AND DEMOCRACY: FINDINGS
FROM THE WORLD VALUES SURVEY AND THE EUROPEAN
VALUES SURVEY

Edited by Ronald Inglehart

ISBN 0-9698707-7-9

Volume 4 in International Studies in Social Science.
Print-ISSN 1497-9616
E-ISSN 1497-9624

de Sitter Publications
104 Consumers Dr., Whitby, ON, L1N 1C4, Canada

http://www.desitterpublications.com
sales@desitterpublications.com

ISLAM, GENDER, CULTURE, AND DEMOCRACY

Edited by Ronald Inglehart

ISLAM, GENDER, CULTURE, AND DEMOCRACY
Introduction

Ronald Inglehart[*]

This collection of articles presents findings from the World Values Survey (WVS) and the European Values Surveys (EVS). These surveys cover 78 societies, containing over 80 percent of the world's population; they extend over the full range of cross-national variation, including societies with per capita incomes as low as $300 per year, ranging up to societies with per capita incomes of more than $35,000 per year; and long-established democracies with market economies, as well as authoritarian states and ex-socialist states. These surveys make it possible to compare the values and beliefs of people in every major cultural region of the world, and they reveal large and coherent cross-national differences in what people want out of life.

The World Values Surveys grew out of a study launched by the European Values Survey group (EVS), which carried out surveys in ten West European societies in 1981; this project evoked such widespread interest that it was replicated in 14 additional countries. Findings from these surveys suggested that predictable cultural changes were taking place. To monitor possible changes, a new wave of surveys was carried out in 1990-91, building on findings from the first wave, but this time designed to be carried out globally. Successive waves of surveys were carried out in 1995-96 and 1999-2001. In every case, we work with colleagues from the given society, and in most cases these surveys are supported by internal funding.

The first three waves of these surveys covered most of the world's major cultural zones except for Africa and the Islamic region, where we were able to carry out only a few surveys in each region. In planning the fourth wave, the World Values Survey Association set a high priority on attaining substantially better coverage of these regions; and the 2000-2001 WVS includes eight African countries and ten predominantly Islamic societies (including three overlapping cases). As a result, we have an unprecedentedly broad range of Islamic societies, extending from Morocco to Indonesia, and this volume includes two articles analyzing Islamic worldviews. Another set of articles focuses on the relationship between culture and democratic institutions; and still another set of articles analyzes the changing role of gender in society—with considerable overlap between the three groups, providing an overall theme of *Islam, Gender, Culture, and Democracy*.

An Overview of Findings

The first three articles deal with the relationship between Islam and democracy. Interestingly, all three writers reach the same conclusion: that the Islamic religion

---

[*] President, World Values Survey Association. Correspondence to: Institute for Social Research, University of Michigan, 3067 ISR, Ann Arbor, Michigan, 48106-1248, USA.

is not, in itself, a significant barrier to the emergence of democratic institutions.

Mark Tessler inquires whether Islamic orientations help account for the fact that—despite the global trend toward democracy—not a single Arab country qualifies as an electoral democracy. Evidence from the World Values Survey indicates that Islam does not discourage the emergence of attitudes favorable to democracy. He finds little evidence, at least at the individual level of analysis, to support the claims of those who assert that Islam and democracy are incompatible. The reasons that democracy has not taken root in the Arab world must therefore lie elsewhere, perhaps in domestic economic structures, perhaps in relations with the international political and economic order, or perhaps in the determination of those in power to resist political change by whatever means are required.

Farooq Tanwir examines the implications of the fact that in October 2002, for the first time in Pakistan's history, a sizeable share of the population voted for religious parties. Many analysts interpret this as signaling the rise of a major fundamentalist religious movement. He suggests, that in large part, this phenomenon can be viewed as a protest vote, rebuking the major political parties' failure to provide solutions to Pakistan's poverty and misery. He finds that the Pakistani public attaches strong importance to religion and believes that its political leaders should believe in God. But a strong majority—fully 74 percent—rejects the idea that religious leaders should influence how people vote in elections. The Pakistanis are Islamic—but they do not want to be ruled by religious leaders.

Fares al-Braizat tests Fukuyama's claim that Islam is resistant to modernity (as indicated by liberal democracy and capitalism). His empirical test indicates that Islam does not seem to play a significant role in explaining democracy/authoritarianism. Instead, he emphasizes the importance of human development and the political opportunity structure in explaining whether a society is authoritarian or democratic.

Two decades ago, the authors of *Political Action* predicted that "unconventional political participation" would become more widespread throughout advanced industrial societies, because it was part of a deep-rooted intergenerational change. Ronald Inglehart and Gabriela Catterberg and examine subsequent trends in political action. Time series data demonstrate that the predicted change has taken place—to such an extent that petitions, boycotts, and other forms of direct action are no longer unconventional but have become more or less normal actions for a large part of the citizenry of post-industrial societies. This type of elite-challenging actions also played an important part in the Third Wave of democratization—but after the transition to democracy, most of the new democracies saw a decline in direct political action. They interpret this decline as a "post-honeymoon" period effect; in the long run, they expect that elite-challenging activity will move on an upward trajectory in most of the new democracies, as it has in virtually all established democracies.

Christian Welzel demonstrates that low corruption and high female representation among elites go together, and help make formal democracy increasingly effective. But the quality of elites is not an independent phenomenon. It is shaped by an underlying mass factor: rising self-expression values that shift cultural norms toward greater emphasis on responsive and inclusive elites. These self-expression values, in turn, are favored by economic development. These three components are linked through the logic of Human Development: (1) human resources, (2) self-expression values, (3) elite quality, and (4) effective democracy—all of which help to widen the scope of human choice.

Alejandro Moreno and Patricia Méndez examine attitudes toward democracy in Mexico, which finally made the transition to democracy in 2000. They find that the prevailing political culture in Mexico expresses comparatively low support for democracy, relatively high support for non-democratic government, low interpersonal trust, low levels of tolerance, and a strong emphasis on deference. Changes over time indicate that Mexicans have reinforced both democratic and non-democratic values in recent years: it would be premature to conclude that Mexico now has a stably pro-democratic political culture.

Renata Siemienska asks, "Are generational changes taking place in democratic attitudes in political values in long-established democratic countries, and ex-communist societies?" She finds that changes are taking place that tend to make the societies of the new democracies increasingly similar to those of the old democracies. Particularly large changes are occurring in Poland, where the youngest generation differs greatly from the older ones.

Previous research has found that men and women have similar levels of happiness in terms of life satisfaction. Ronald Inglehart demonstrates that significant gender-related differences in subjective well-being exist—but tend to be concealed by an interaction effect between age, gender, and well-being. Women under 45 tend to be happier than men; but older women tend to be *less* happy. The aspiration-adjustment model implies that despite their continuing disadvantages in income, status, and power, women today should show higher levels of subjective well-being than men. A global women's movement has been pushing for gender equality throughout the world, with some success, so that women's current achievement tends to be above traditional aspiration levels. But this is offset by a systematic tendency to devalue older women. This tendency is particularly strong in advanced industrial societies where women have made the most progress—but where the mass media and advertising convey the message that only young women are beautiful and devalue the social worth of older women.

Pradeep Chhibber examines the reasons why women in India do not participate in political life to the same extent as men. While a fair number of women turn out to vote, women have little representation in legislative bodies. He attributes the limited presence of women in legislative bodies to the fact that many women are still confined to the household. Even after controlling for demographic factors, only those women who have an identity that is independent of the household are likely to run for office. Similar patterns exist globally: women who have identities outside the household are most likely to be politically active.

Acknowledgements

For many of the countries examined here, the 2000-2001 WVS was the first time that their society had been included in a cross-national survey (and in some cases, such as that of Vietnam, the World Values Survey was the first representative national survey *ever* carried out in that country). We are grateful to the Bank of Sweden Tercentenary Foundation, the Swedish Agency for International Development, and the U.S. National Science Foundation for making these surveys possible.

We owe a large debt of gratitude to the following WVS and EVS participants for creating and sharing this valuable dataset: Anthony M. Abela, Q.K. Ahmad, Rasa Alishauskene, Helmut Anheier, W.A. Arts, Jose Arocena, Soo Young Auh, Taghi Azadarmaki, Ljiljana Bacevic, Miguel Basanez, Olga Balakireva, Josip Balobn, Elena Bashkirova, Abdallah Bedaida, Jorge Benitez, Jaak Billiet, Alan Black, Rahma Bourquia, Ammar Boukhedir, Fares al-Braizat, Augustin Canzani, Marita Carballo, Henrique Carlos de O. de Castro, Pi-Chao Chen, Pavel Campeanu, Pradeep Chhibber, Mark F. Chingono, Hei-yuan Chiu, Margit Cleveland, Russell Dalton, Andrew P. Davidson, Juan Diez Nicolas, Jaime Diez Medrano, Herman De Dijn, Karel Dobbelaere, Peter J.D. Drenth, Javier Elzo, Yilmaz Esmer, P. Estgen, T. Fahey, Nadjematul Faizah, Georgy Fotev, James Georgas, C. Geppaart, Renzo Gubert, Linda Luz Guerrero, Peter Gundelach, Jacques Hagenaars, Loek Halman, Sang-Jin Han, Mustafa Hamarneh, Stephen Harding, Mari Harris, Bernadette C. Hayes, Camilo Herrera, Virginia Hodgkinson, Nadra Muhammed Hosen, Kenji Iijima, Ljubov Ishimova, Wolfgang Jagodzinski, Aleksandra Jasinska-Kania, Fridrik Jonsson, Stanislovas Juknevicius, Jan Kerkhofs, Johann Kinghorn, Zuzana Kusá, M. Legrand, Noah Lewin-Epstein, Ola Listhaug, Hans Dieter Klingemann, Hennie Kotze, Noah Lewin-Epstein, Marta Lagos, Bernard Lategan, Abdel-Hamid Abdel-Latif, Carlos Lemoine, Jin-yun Liu, Brina Malnar, Mahar Mangahas, Mario Marinov, Felipe Miranda, Robert B. Mattes, Carlos Matheus, Mansoor Moaddel, Jose Molina, Rafael Mendizabal, Alejandro Moreno, Gaspar K. Munishi, Elone Nwabuzor, Neil Nevitte, F.A. Orizo, Dragomir Pantic, Juhani Pehkonen, Paul Perry, Thorleif Pettersson, Pham Thanh Nghi, Pham Minh Hac, Gevork Pogosian, Bi Puranen, Ladislav Rabusic, Angel Rivera-Ortiz, Catalina Romero, David Rotman, Rajab Sattarov, Sandeep Shastri, Shen Mingming, Renata Siemienska, John Sudarsky, Tan Ern Ser, Farooq Tanwir, Jean-Francois Tchernia, Kareem Tejumola, Larissa Titarenko, Miklos Tomka, Alfredo Torres, Niko Tos, Jorge Vala, Andrei Vardomatskii, Malina Voicu, Alan Webster, Friedrich Welsch, Christian Welzel, Toru Takahashi, Ephraim Yuchtman-Yaar, Brigita Zepa, Josefina Zaiter, and P. Zulehner.

For more information about the World Values Survey, see the WVS web sites http://wvs.isr.umich.edu/ and http://www.worldvaluessurvey.com. The European surveys used here were gathered by the European Values Survey group (EVS). For detailed EVS findings, see Loek Halman, *The European Values Study: A Sourcebook Based on the 1999/2000 European Values Study Surveys.* Tilburg: EVS, 2001. For more information, see the EVS website, http://evs.kub.nl.

DO ISLAMIC ORIENTATIONS INFLUENCE ATTITUDES TOWARD DEMOCRACY IN THE ARAB WORLD? EVIDENCE FROM EGYPT, JORDAN, MOROCCO, AND ALGERIA

Mark Tessler*

ABSTRACT

Research on democratic transitions and consolidation has emphasized the importance not only of structural factors, such as institutional reform and economic development, but also political culture. There are differing scholarly opinions about whether a democratic political culture can emerge in the Arab world, however. More specifically, there is disagreement about whether the Islamic attachments of ordinary citizens discourage the emergence of democratic attitudes and values. Against this background, the present study uses World Values Survey data from Egypt, Jordan, Morocco, and Algeria to assess the influence of Islamic orientations on attitudes toward democracy. Two separate attitudinal measures pertaining to democracy are dependent variables in the analysis. Independent variables include measures pertaining both to personal religious involvement and the role of Islam in political affairs. The results of this analysis, which are similar in all four countries, show that strong Islamic attachments do not discourage or otherwise influence support for democracy to any significant degree.

The Absence of Democracy in the Arab World

During the last two decades, democratic currents have swept across the developing and post-communist world. While democratic regimes were in the minority just a few years ago, electoral democracy is the predominant form of government among today's nation-states and guides the lives of more than half of the world's population (Karatnycky 2000). The Arab world, however, has been largely unaffected by this political revolution, which Huntington has called the "Third Wave" of democratization (Huntington 1991). According to Freedom House, not a single Arab country qualifies as an electoral democracy (Karatnycky 2000; Sivan 2000:70).

The 1980s and early 1990s did witness halting moves toward democratization in some Arab countries. Confronted with popular anger fueled by economic difficulties, government mismanagement and corruption, and the violation of human rights, a number of Arab governments enacted programs of political liberalization. For the most part, however, these reforms were part of a containment

*   Department of Political Science, The University of Michigan, Ann Arbor, MI 48104, USA.

strategy designed to increase regime legitimacy at a time when calls for political change were widespread. Accordingly, and not surprisingly given their strategic purpose, most of these democratic experiments were slowed or even abandoned during the 1990s. By the end of the decade, as Anderson wrote in 1999, the political landscape was littered with "the remnants of so many of the democratic experiments—from the spectacular crash and burn of Algeria's liberalization to Tunisia's more subtle but no less profound transformation into a police state, from Egypt's backsliding into electoral manipulation [and repression of Islamic movements] to the reluctance of Palestinian authorities to embrace human rights" (Anderson 1999:6).

This situation is acknowledged and lamented by Arab intellectuals as well as Western scholars. A Lebanese political scientist writes, for example, that unchecked authoritarian rule is "paving the way to a deep crisis in the fabric of society" (Khashan 1998:43-44). Similarly, according to a Jordanian journalist, "one of the leading sources of instability and political-economic distortion in the Arab world is the unchecked use of state power, combined with the state's whimsical ability to use the rule of law for its own political ends" (Khouri 2000). Against this background, intellectuals from thirteen Arab countries attending a December 1999 conference in Amman, Jordan, issued a final communiqué emphasizing the need for "greater political freedoms and intellectual pluralism" (Al-Farawati 1999). Their concern, in the assessment of still another Arab scholar, is that "Arab countries do not allow freedom of thought . . . Where necessary, their surveillance spares neither the telephone nor the mail, neither the fax nor the Internet" (Talbi 2000:62).

There are some partial exceptions to this depressing characterization. In Jordan, Morocco, Lebanon, Kuwait, and Qatar, for example, some would argue that there is continuing albeit uneven progress and that it is possible to have a meaningful debate about whether the glass is half full or half empty. In the Palestinian Authority, too, there have been accomplishments as well as setbacks in the struggle for democratic governance. Nevertheless, taken as a whole, the Arab world clearly stands apart from other world regions with respect to the authoritarian character of its governments and the limited influence of institutions and individuals working for democracy. This point is emphasized by the recent Arab Human Development Report (AHDR) of the United Nation's Development Program, published in 2002. The report observes that, as in the 1980s, political openings remain "heavily regulated and partial" and political systems "have not been opened up to all citizens." Thus, the report continues, "political participation is less advanced in the Arab world than in other developing regions" and, with understatement, "transfer of power through the ballot box is not a common phenomenon" (AHDR 2002, chap. 7).

Support for Democracy and the Influence of Islam

There is disagreement about the reasons for the persistence of authoritarian rule in the Arab world, just as there is uncertainty about the prospects for Arab democratization in the years ahead. Research on democratic transitions and consolidation has emphasized the importance of structural factors, such as institutional reform and economic development, and also political culture. Both have been discussed in relation to the Arab world. On the one hand, many scholars have emphasized the resistance of Arab leaders to power sharing and meaningful reform (Sivan 1997; Brumberg 1995; Korany 1994). A widespread popular perception in the region, according to the report of a Moroccan political scientist, is that the primary motivation of many Arab kings, sultans, and presidents "is to remain in power and protect their personal interests . . . [and as a result they often have] to defend themselves against their own people" (Bennani-Chraibi 1994:243). In the succinct assessment of a senior American analyst, much of the explanation for the political situation in the Arab world "lies in the fact that many Middle Eastern states have no greater enemy than their own governments" (Cordesman 1999).

Students of democratization also stress the importance of citizen attitudes and values, which are the focus of the present inquiry. Relevant orientations include both generalized support for democratic political forms and the embrace of specific democratic values, such as respect for political competition and tolerance of diverse political ideas (Rose, Mishler, and Haerpfer 1998:98). Thus, as summarized by one prominent scholar, a democratic citizen is one who "believes in individual liberty and is politically tolerant, has a certain distrust of political authority but at the same time is trusting of fellow citizens, is obedient but nonetheless willing to assert rights against the state, and views the state as constrained by legality" (Gibson 1995:55).

Some analysts suggest that these normative orientations may be a precondition for democratic transitions (Huntington 1993:13). Much more common, however, is the view that democratic values need not precede, but can rather follow, elite-led transitions involving the reform of political institutions and procedures (Rose 1997:98; Schmitter and Karl 1993:47). Indeed, according to this argument, attitudes and values conducive to democracy tend to emerge among the citizens of countries experiencing successful democratic transitions. At the very least, however, the presence of appropriate attitudes and values would seem to be necessary for democratic consolidation. As expressed by Inglehart (2000), "Democracy is not attained simply by making institutional changes through elite-level maneuvering. Its survival depends also on the values and beliefs of ordinary citizens" (p.96).

Evidence in support of this assessment comes from a number of empirical investigations. According to a recent study of Taiwan and Korea, for example, the consolidation of democracy requires that "all significant political actors, at both the elite and mass levels, believe that the democratic regime is the most right and appropriate for their society, better than any other realistic alternative they can imagine" (Chu, Diamond, and Shin 2001:123). A cross-national study in Latin America makes the same point: an important factor "that has contributed to the greater survivability of Latin American democracies revolves around changes in political attitudes, toward a greater valorization of democracy" (Mainwaring 1999:45). Thus, as Harik has noted with respect to the Arab world, "a democratic government needs a democratic political culture, and vice versa" (Harik 1994:56).

There are differing scholarly opinions about whether citizen orientations conducive to democracy can emerge and flourish in the Arab world. The influence of Islam is the focus of particular attention in this connection (Tessler 2002). This is due, in part, both to the nature of Islam and to the religion's political resurgence during the last three decades. Islamic law includes numerous codes governing societal relations and organization. It guides that which is societal as well as personal, corporate as well as individual (Esposito 1992:3-5). As Voll (1994) explains, Islam is a total way of life; it represents a worldview (p. 211). This is one of the reasons that popular support for Islamist movements and parties has grown significantly in recent years (Tessler 1997).

Amid these assumptions, there have long been debates about Islam's proper role in political affairs, including, more recently, its compatibility with conceptions of governance based on democracy, pluralism, and popular sovereignty. Some observers, particularly some Western observers, assert that democracy and Islam are not compatible. Whereas democracy requires openness, competition, pluralism, and tolerance of diversity, Islam, they argue, encourages intellectual conformity and an uncritical acceptance of authority. According to the late Elie Kedourie, for example, the principles, institutions, and values of democracy are "profoundly alien to the Muslim political tradition" (Kedourie 1994:5-6; Huntington 1984:208). Equally important, Islam is said to be anti-democratic because it vests sovereignty in God, who is the sole source of political authority and from whose divine law must come all regulations governing the community of believers. Thus, in the view of some observers, Islam "has to be ultimately embodied in a totalitarian state" (Choueiri 1996:21-22; Lewis 1994:54-56). Comparable assertions are sometimes advanced in debates about "Asian values," in which it is asked whether Confucianism's emphasis on consensus, order, obedience, and hierarchy is compatible with such democratic values as individual freedom and identity, diversity, competition, and political accountability (Wei-Ming 2000:266; Flanagan and Lee 2000:653; Welsh 1996; Zakaria 1994).

But many knowledgeable analysts reject the suggestion that Islam is an enemy in the struggle to establish accountable government. They point out that Islam has many facets and tendencies, making unidimensional characterizations of the religion highly suspect (Halliday 1995:116; Esposito and Piscatori 1991). They also report that there is considerable variation in the interpretations of religious law advanced by Muslim scholars and theologians, and that among these are expressions of support for democracy, including some by leading Islamist theorists (Abed 1995:127-128). Finally, they insist that openness, tolerance, and progressive innovation are well-represented among traditions associated with the religion, and are thus entirely compatible with Islam (Hamdi 1996; Mernissi 1992).

As the preceding suggests, one can find within Islamic doctrine and Muslim traditions both elements that are and elements that are not congenial to democracy; and this in turn means that the influence of the religion depends, to a very considerable extent, on how and by whom it is interpreted. There is no single or accepted interpretation on many issues, nor sometimes even a consensus on who speaks for Islam. As one study demonstrated with respect to Islamic strictures about family planning and contraception, different religious authorities give different advice about what is permissible in Islam (Bowen 1993). In addition, serious doubts have been expressed about the motivation of some religious authorities, particularly in connection with pronouncements pertaining to governance. As one Arab scholar asks, "Can democracy occur if the *ulama* or jurists have sole charge of legal interpretation? May not the *ulama*'s ability to declare laws compatible or incompatible with the teaching of the *shariah* lead to abuse? There are numerous examples of *ulama* manipulating Islamic teachings to the advantage of [undemocratic] political leaders" (Al-Suwaidi 1995:87-88).

Debates about the compatibility of democracy and Islam have for the most part focused on issues of theology, doctrine, and historical precedent. Much less has been said about how, or even whether, Islamic conceptions and attachments influence the political attitudes and values of ordinary citizens. Further, when implications about the political orientations of ordinary citizens *are* proposed, it is almost always on the basis on deductive reasoning and analogy. Despite a few recent studies, empirical evidence about whether and how Islam helps to shape the political views of Muslim Arab men and women is extremely rare. Indeed, empirical research concerning the political orientations of ordinary citizens in the Arab world is something that has generally been lacking (Anderson 1999:6-7; Tessler 1999; Hudson 1995). The availability of World Values Survey data, recently collected in four Arab states, offers an important opportunity to begin filling this gap. The analysis of these data will shed light both on the degree of popular support for democracy and on the validity of competing positions in on-going debates about whether or not Islam fosters anti-democratic attitudes among ordinary men and women in the Arab world.

Data and Method

Questions about the impact of Islamic attachments on the attitudes toward democracy held by ordinary Arab men and women can be usefully investigated with data from the World Values Survey (WVS). The four Arab countries in which the WVS has thus far been conducted are Egypt, Morocco, Algeria, and Jordan. Surveys in each country were carried out during the fourth wave of the World Values Survey, and the data were therefore collected between 2000 and 2002. As elsewhere, each WVS project was designed and carried out in close collaboration with scholars from the participating country. The present author helped to direct the WVS in Algeria.

While no subset of states is completely representative of the Arab world, these four countries provide a strong foundation for insights that may be generalizable to much of the region. Egypt, Algeria, and Morocco are the most populous Arab countries; Egypt and Algeria are republics while Jordan and Morocco are monarchies. Two of the countries have a legacy of French colonialism whereas in the other two Britain was the dominant imperial power prior to independence. Finally, two were in the socialist camp and had a socialist orientation during much of the Cold War and two have always been allied politically and ideologically with the Western bloc. This subset of countries does not include any of the Gulf Arab states, countries with small populations and substantial wealth that to a considerable extent have a distinctive political and cultural orientation. Nevertheless, overall, Egypt, Algeria, Morocco, and Jordan encompass between them the political, economic, and social environments in which the vast majority of the Arab world's citizens reside. Accordingly, if data from the four countries suggest similar conclusions, these are likely to shed light on the attitudes of Arab citizens elsewhere. Alternatively, should there be differences among the four cases, it will be possible to offer insights about the conditionalities associated with particular patterns and relationships.

Five items from the WVS interview schedule have been used to measure attitudes toward democracy. These items are:

> I'm going to describe various types of political systems and ask what you think about each as a way of governing this country. For each one, would you say it is a very good, fairly good, fairly bad, or very bad way of governing this country?

> V167.　Having a democratic political system

> I'm going to read off some things that people sometimes say about a democratic political system. Could you please tell me if you agree strongly, agree, disagree or disagree strongly, after I read each one of them?

> V169.　In democracy, the economic system runs badly

> V170.　Democracies are indecisive and have too much quibbling

> V171.　Democracies aren't good at maintaining order

> V172.　Democracy may have problems but it's better than any other form of government

Factor analysis was used to select these items from a slightly larger battery of questions pertaining to democracy. Factor analysis identifies items that cluster together and hence measure the same underlying concept, thereby increasing confidence in reliability and validity (Marradi 1981). Confidence is further increased, as is cross-national conceptual equivalence, by the similar pattern of factor loadings observed in all four countries. Two distinct sets of attitudes toward democracy were identified by factor analysis. One, reflecting the strong intercorrelation of items V167 and V172, concerns the degree to which respondents have a favorable attitude toward democracy. The second, reflecting strong correlations among the other three items, concerns the degree to which respondents believe there are important problems associated with democracy, regardless of whether or not they believe these make an alternative political formula more desirable.

The two sets of attitudes identified by factor analysis are the dependent variables in the analysis to follow. V167 and V172 have been combined to form an additive index measuring the first of these dimensions, support for democracy. V169, V170, and V171 have been combined to form an additive index measuring the second of these dimensions, significance of the perceived drawbacks associated with democracy. Table 1 shows the distribution of responses to each of the two indices and its constituent items for each of the four countries. The table shows, first, that in all four countries attitudes toward democracy are much more likely to be favorable than unfavorable. While the distributions are skewed in favor of democracy to a greater degree in Morocco and Egypt than in Jordan and Algeria, even in the latter two countries most citizens have a favorable, if not a very favorable, attitude toward democracy. Second, again in each case, there is considerable variation in views about whether there are important problems associated with democracy. On average, roughly one-third of the respondents agree or agree strongly that democracies are not good at managing the economy, maintaining order, and acting decisively. Other respondents disagree, or in many instances disagree strongly, that such problems are associated with democracy.

Factor analysis was also used to select items measuring attitudes and attachments pertaining to Islam and two distinct dimensions were again identified. One of these concerns personal piety and religious involvement and the other concerns the role in public affairs of religion and religious leaders. The measure of personal religiosity resulting from this analysis is an additive index composed of two items dealing with mosque attendance and participation in mosque activities. A question requesting a subjective assessment of personal religiosity and another asking about the importance of God had high loadings on the same factor. But while these loadings increase confidence in the reliability and validity of all items, the latter two were not included in the personal piety index because their response distributions were highly skewed and contained little variance. For example, on a 10-point scale ranging from not at all important to very important, the proportion of respondents selecting a 10, meaning extremely important, in response to a question about God was 81.6 percent in Egypt, 94.8 percent in

Algeria, 98.5 percent in Jordan, and 99.2 percent in Morocco. In the Egyptian case, another 14 percent chose an 8 or 9. This means that only with respect to mosque attendance and participation in mosque activities is there variance whose impact on political attitudes may be explored. With respect to religious conviction and personal piety, at least as measured by the World Values Survey, the virtual absence of variance obviates questions about the explanatory power of these characteristics.

Table 1.
Attitudes Toward Democracy in Egypt, Jordan, Morocco and Algeria

	Egypt	Jordan	Morocco	Algeria
V167 Having a democratic Government in this country is:	%	%	%	%
Very good	67.9	51.2	81.5	60.4
Fairly good	30.6	43.5	14.5	32.3
Fairly bad or bad	1.5	5.3	4.0	7.3
V172 Despite it problems, democracy is better than any other form of government	%	%	%	%
Strongly agree	63.6	39.1	77.3	48.5
Agree	34.1	51.2	18.6	39.9
Disagree or strongly disagree	2.3	9.7	4.1	11.6
Attitude toward democracy index	%	%	%	%
Very favorable	52.1	28.6	71.6	41.4
Favorable	45.7	61.0	24.0	47.3
Somewhat favorable	1.6	7.9	2.7	5.6
Not favorable	.6	2.5	1.7	5.7
V169 In democracy, the economic system runs badly	%	%	%	%
Strongly agree	3.1	7.4	15.1	9.2
Agree	15.0	25.1	20.7	22.0
Disagree	56.8	39.3	42.4	54.9
Strongly disagree	25.1	28.2	21.8	14.1
V170 Democracies are indecisive and have too much quibbling	%	%	%	%
Strongly agree	3.3	9.7	28.2	15.3
Agree	25.7	34.0	43.6	47.9
Disagree	53.4	35.4	20.5	29.7
Strongly disagree	17.6	20.8	7.7	7.1
V171 Democracies aren't good at maintaining order	%	%	%	%
Strongly agree	3.2	8.2	18.1	9.4
Agree	17.0	24.9	23.0	23.0
Disagree	55.6	37.3	40.1	51.8
Strongly disagree	24.3	29.6	18.8	15.8
Index of agreement that democracy brings problems	%	%	%	%
Strongly agree	2.6	7.6	17.9	11.7
Agree	16.5	27.0	28.6	28.0
Disagree	51.6	38.1	41.3	46.2
Strongly disagree	29.2	27.3	12.2	14.1

Two measures of attitudes toward the role of Islam in public affairs have been established on the basis of the factor analysis. One is an additive index composed of two intercorrelated items, and the second is a separate item that factor analysis indicates should not be combined with the others. The first two items, which load strongly on the same factor, ask respondents to agree or disagree with the following statements: "Politicians who do not believe in God are unfit for public office" and "It would be better for [this country] if more people with strong religious beliefs held public office." The third item, which asks respondents to agree or disagree with the statement "Religious leaders should not influence how people vote in elections," loads strongly on a separate factor. Also loading on the second factor is an item that asks whether religious leaders should influence government decisions. There is a great deal of missing data on the latter question, however, and thus, while its correlation with the other item asking about the political influence of religious leaders offers evidence of reliability and validity, it has not been used to construct an additive index in order to avoid excluding a large number of respondents from the analysis.

Table 2 presents the distribution of responses to the two sets of measures pertaining to Islam: personal religiosity, or mosque involvement, and also to both the two-item index and the remaining item pertaining to the role of Islam in public affairs for each of the four countries. Turning first to personal religiosity, the table shows a bimodal pattern of mosque attendance and involvement in all four countries. In each case, a significant proportion of men and women participate regularly and frequently and as many, if not more, participate rarely or "almost never." Responses are particularly polarized in Egypt and Jordan, but the pattern is similar in Morocco and Algeria as well. There is considerable, albeit less, variation in all four countries with respect to attitudes about the role of Islam in public affairs. The distribution in Egypt is skewed in the direction of giving a greater role to Islam, and to a lesser extent this is the case in Jordan and Morocco as well. The greatest diversity of opinion regarding the political role of Islam is found in Algeria where, for example, only one-third of the respondents agree or agree strongly that it would be better for the country if people with strong religious beliefs held public office.

Attitudes and attachments relating to Islam are the primary non-dependent variables in the present study, the goal being to determine whether and to what extent these orientations account for variance in the attitudes toward democracy held by ordinary citizens. In addition, however, a number of other non-dependent variables are included in the analysis for purposes of statistical control. These include age, education, sex, income, and residence, the latter referring to the size of the town in which the respondent lives. These variables have been selected both because they constitute important demographic characteristics and because research in other world regions has found that they are sometimes related to attitudes toward democracy (Bratton and Mattes 2001; Mishler and Rose 1999; Waldron-Moore 1999; Ottemoeller 1998; Mattes and Thiel 1998; Shin, Chull and

Table 2.
Religious Orientations in Egypt, Jordan, Morocco and Algeria

	Egypt	Jordan	Morocco	Algeria
V30 How often do you spend time with people at your mosque	%	%	%	%
Weekly	37.9	39.1	23.5	29.3
Monthly	19.5	18.3	10.5	10.2
Less		29.2	9.3	14.4
None at all	42.6	38.3	56.7	46.1
V185 Apart from weddings, funerals and christenings, about how often do you attend religious services	%	%	%	%
More than once a week	22.4	28.9	32.4	25.2
Weekly	19.8	15.2	11.8	18.6
Less	32.8	13.3	19.1	37.5
Never, practically never	25.1	42.6	36.7	17.7
Index of mosque involvement	%	%	%	%
Very high	24.9	41.4	29.8	33.8
High	17.4	2.3	5.0	6.4
Low	45.4	12.5	21.3	22.5
Very low	12.3	43.8	43.9	37.3
V200 Politicians who do not believe in God are unfit for public office	%	%	%	%
Strongly agree	73.7	73.9	66.5	53.5
Agree	18.5	12.3	15.3	21.5
Neutral		4.2	8.1	7.8
Disagree	2.6	2.4	4.2	8.2
Strongly disagree	5.2	7.2	5.9	9.0
Religious leaders should not influence how people vote in elections	%	%	%	%
Strongly agree	34.2	38.5	41.3	11.8
Agree	26.8	33.5	23.6	21.0
Neutral	2.9	7.2	22.2	20.5
Disagree	12.8	8.8	6.8	21.5
Strongly disagree	23.2	11.9	6.1	25.2
V201 It would be better for [this country] if more people with strong religious beliefs held public office	%	%	%	%
Strongly agree	53.2	30.3	30.6	13.8
Agree	33.7	31.4	22.8	20.4
Neutral	.8	6.6	18.7	19.0
Disagree	8.6	14.0	17.0	26.2
Strongly disagree	3.8	17.7	10.9	20.6
Index of attitudes about whether persons holding public office should be religious	%	%	%	%
Strongly agree	73.4	51.0	40.7	25.2
Agree	14.9	16.7	30.3	28.1
Neutral	8.7	21.8	17.4	26.1
Disagree	2.6	7.9	7.5	13.8
Strongly disagree	.5	2.6	4.0	6.8

Shyu 1997; Duch 1995; Seligson and Booth 1993). Finally, a measure of regime evaluation has been developed for inclusion in the analysis, again because several studies have found this to be a determinant of attitudes toward democracy (Chu, Diamond, and Shin 2001; Rose, Mishler, and Haerpfer 1998). The measure is an additive index composed of two highly intercorrelated items. One asks respondents how much or how little confidence they have in their national government. The other asks respondents how satisfied they are with the way officials of the national government are handling the country's affairs.

Findings and Conclusions

Tables 3 through 6 present regression analyses for Egypt, Morocco, Algeria, and Jordan, respectively. In each case, both the index measuring the degree to which attitudes toward democracy are favorable or unfavorable and the index measuring the degree to which respondents believe there are important problems associated with democracy are treated as dependent variables. The three measures pertaining to Islam, the five demographic variables, and the measure of regime evaluation are the non-dependent variables in these regressions.

Table 3.
Multiple Regression Showing the Influence of Islamic
Orientations on Attitudes toward Democracy in Egypt

	Favorable Attitudes Toward Democracy	Agreement that Democracy Brings Problems
Independent Variables		
Greater Mosque involvement	.036 (1.533)	.050 (2.056)*
Persons holding public office should be religious	.069 (3.184)***	-.026 (-1.141)
Religious leaders should not influence how people vote	.031 (1.447)	.041 (1.865)
Control Variables		
Positive evaluation of government leaders	-.004 (-.167)	-.107 (-4.768)***
Higher education	.107 (4.356)***	.034 (1.365)
Older age	.041 (1.776)	-.065 (-2.683)***
Male sex	.093 (3.905)***	-.052 (-2.106)*
Higher income	.072 (3.019)***	-.021 (-.870)
Resides in larger town	-.065 (-2.789)***	.107 (4.441)***

The table shows standardized coefficients (betas) and gives t statistics in parentheses.
* $p < .05$, **$p < .02$, ***$p < .01$

Table 4.
Multiple Regression Showing the Influence of Islamic
Orientations on Attitudes toward Democracy in Jordan

	Favorable Attitudes Toward Democracy	Agreement that Democracy Brings Problems
Independent Variables		
Greater Mosque involvement	.039 (.692)	-.084 (-1.477)
Persons holding public office should be religious	.062 (1.684)	-.046 (-1.265)
Religious leaders should not influence how people vote	.016 (.440)	-.045 (-1.242)
Control Variables		
Positive evaluation of government leaders	.102 (2.716)***	-.151 (-4.041)***
Higher education	.073 (1.800)	-.124 (-3.091)***
Older age	-.009 (-.227)	-.007 (-.172)
Male sex	.108 (1.923)	-.092 (-1.635)
Higher income	.057 (1.510)	.085 (2.244)*
Resides in larger town	-.078 (-2.106)*	.042 (1.157)

The table shows standardized coefficients (betas) and gives t statistics in parentheses.
* $p < .05$, ** $p < .02$, *** $p < .01$

Taken together, the findings presented in Tables 3-6 suggest that Islamic orientations and attachments have, at most, a very limited impact on views about democracy. With respect to personal religiosity, at least as measured by involvement in religious activities, there is not a single instance when this variable is related to attitudes toward democracy to a statistically significant degree. Further, there is only one instance when this variable is related to views about whether there are problems associated with democracy. This is the case in Egypt, where individuals with higher levels of involvement in religious activities are more like-

Table 5.
Multiple Regression Showing the Influence of Islamic
Orientations on Attitudes toward Democracy in Morocco

	Favorable Attitudes Toward Democracy	Agreement that Democracy Brings Problems
Independent Variables		
Greater Mosque involvement	.008 (.182)	.018 (.340)
Persons holding public office should be religious	-.042 (-1.017)	.081 (1.641)
Religious leaders should not influence how people vote	.081 (2.040)*	.129 (2.811)***
Control Variables		
Positive evaluation of government leaders	.022 (.541)	-.047 (-1.006)
Higher education	.102 (2.374)**	-.119 (-2.398)**
Older age	.069 (1.672)	-.009 (-.187)
Male sex	.051 (1.164)	-.145 (-2.838)***
Higher income	.027 (.685)	-.150 (-3.249)***
Resides in larger town	.016 (.395)	.080 (1.711)

The table shows standardized coefficients (betas) and gives t statistics in parentheses.
* $p < .05$, ** $p < .02$, *** $p < .01$

ly than others to agree that democracy has drawbacks. The relationship is significant at the .05 level.

As noted earlier, there is very little variance associated with belief in God and self-reported religiosity, and so these questions from the survey instrument have almost no explanatory power. All that can be said is that most people claim to be pious and most also have a favorable opinion of democracy, thus suggesting, in the aggregate, that there is no incompatibility between Islam and democracy. Support for democracy, in other words, is widespread in Arab societies where most citizens have strong Islamic attachments.

Table 6.
Multiple Regression Showing the Influence of Islamic
Orientations on Attitudes toward Democracy in Algeria

	Favorable Attitudes Toward Democracy	Agreement that Democracy Brings Problems
Independent Variables		
Greater Mosque involvement	-.058 (-1.158)	.084 (1.647)
Persons holding public office should be religious	.063 (1.551)	.049 (1.182)
Religious leaders should not influence how people vote	.070 (1.794)	.190 (4.657)***
Control Variables		
Positive evaluation of government leaders	.137 (3.500)***	.037 (.900)
Higher education	.018 (.385)	.055 (1.112)
Older age	.039 (.817)	-.114 (-2.280)*
Male sex	-.003 (-.062)	-.034 (-.712)
Higher income	-.058 (-1.455)	-.004 (-.106)
Resides in larger town	.161 (4.085)***	-.093 (-2.242)*

The table shows standardized coefficients (betas) and gives t statistics in parentheses.
$*p < .05$, $**p < .02$, $***p < .01$

To the extent that the preceding statement shifts the level of analysis, it does not address the central question of the present analysis: do views about democracy vary among men and women in the Arab world as a function of the strength of their Islamic attachments? By contrast, the regressions presented in Tables 3-6 bear directly on this question. Again, they suggest that personal religiosity has little influence of attitudes toward democracy. There is substantial variation with respect to mosque attendance and participation in religious activities in all four countries, and it is notable that those with higher levels of mosque involvement and those with lower levels have similar, and to a substantial extent favorable, views about democracy. Thus, in the on-going debate about the compatibility of democracy and Islam, findings from the World Values Survey suggest, so far as the individual level of analysis is concerned, that strong Islamic attachments do not discourage or otherwise influence support for democracy to any significant degree.

The pattern is only slightly different with respect to attitudes about political Islam. Since there are two measures of attitudes about the role of religious officials in public affairs and two indices measuring views about democracy, four relationships are observable in each of the four Arab countries for which World Values Survey data are available. Of these sixteen relationships, only four are statistically significant, one at the .05 level and three at the .01 level. One of these is in Egypt, none are in Jordan, two are in Morocco, and one is in Algeria. Thus, it is clear that in only a distinct minority of instances do attitudes about the political role of religion and religious leaders have an impact on attitudes toward democracy.

The conclusion that support for political Islam does not lead to unfavorable attitudes toward democracy among ordinary citizens becomes even more evident when the character of the statistically significant relationships is examined. First, only one of the four significant relationships, that in Egypt, involves views about whether persons holding public office should be religious. Moreover, the relationship involves judgments about democracy, not views about associated problems, and it is positive. In other words, those who deem it desirable that persons holding pubic office be religious have a *more* favorable attitude toward democracy than do others.

Second, although the remaining three significant relationships are in the opposite direction, they offer only limited support to those who would argue that Islam discourages pro-democracy attitudes and values. In these instances, those who disagree with the proposition that religious officials should not influence how people vote are less likely to have positive views about democracy. This pattern was observed in only three of the eight instances where relationships are reported, however, and in one of these the relationship is only significant at the .05 level. In addition, statistically significant relationships are found in only two of the four countries, Morocco and Algeria.

The nature of the dependent variables in these relationships is even more important. In two of the cases, the two that are significant at the .01 level, the dependent variable does not involve judgments about the desirability of democracy but rather about whether there are problems associated with democracy. Thus, these respondents do not necessarily have an unfavorable view of democracy or consider other forms of governance to be preferable. They are simply more likely than others to believe that democracy, whether or not desirable or preferable to alternatives, has certain potential drawbacks. In only one instance, then, that of the weak but nonetheless statistically significant relationship observed in Morocco, are persons *more* favorably disposed toward the influence of religion in political affairs *less* favorably disposed toward democratic governance.

Since these findings are much more similar than different across the four countries, it is worth recalling how much of the Arab world's diversity is encompassed by Egypt, Jordan, Morocco, and Algeria. The combined population of these countries is roughly 140 million, perhaps two-thirds of the population of all Arab states. Equally important, as noted earlier, the four countries for which data are available differ with respect to present-day political systems and, in addition, both pre- and post-independence political and ideological trajectories. Accordingly, cross-country comparisons approximate a "most different system" research design, which in turn increases confidence in generalizability when similar findings are observed. So far as the influence of religious orientations on attitudes toward democracy is concerned, this means that the very limited impact of Islamic attachments is a conclusion that in all probability applies to much of the Arab world.

Relationships involving the six control variables are not central to the present study, which is primarily concerned with assessing the degree to which religious orientations influence attitudes toward democracy. Nevertheless, given that research on the initiation, maintenance and consolidation of democratic transitions seeks to identify the broader array of factors that either promote or hinder the emergence of democratic attitudes and values, some brief observations about the explanatory power of these variables may be of interest.

Findings from empirical research in other world areas are somewhat mixed regarding the relationship between demographic characteristics and attitudes toward democracy. On balance, however, there is at least some evidence that support for democracy is positively related to levels of education, socioeconomic status, and male gender. Findings from the present study are for the most part similar. For example, education is positively and significantly related to a more favorable judgment of democracy in at least one instance in three of the Arab countries for which data are available, Algeria being the only exception. Similarly, both male gender and income are positively and significantly related to such attitudes in Egypt and Morocco. However, income is inversely related to one of the dependent variables in Jordan and these variables otherwise do not have explanatory power in either Jordan or Algeria.

Findings about residence are interesting in that the direction of the relationship is different in the two countries where this variable has the greatest influence. Residence is related to both dependent variables to a statistically significant degree in Egypt and Algeria, but in the former country pro-democracy attitudes are associated with residence in *smaller* towns and in the latter country they are associated with residence in *larger* towns and cities. Residence in smaller towns is also positively related to pro-democracy attitudes in Jordan. Finally, the influence of evaluations of the government and its leaders should be noted. Statistically significant relationships involving the evaluation of political leaders are found in at least one instance in every country except Morocco, and in each case a favorable assessment of government leaders is positively correlated with a positive judgment about democracy.

It is beyond the scope of the present inquiry to speculate about the causes and consequences of these cross-national differences. Suffice it to say that the explanatory power of the factors here treated as control variables is not the same in Egypt, Jordan, Morocco, and Algeria. This suggests that future research should strive to shed light on the nature and determinants of cross-national variation in the process by which attitudes relating to democracy and governance are shaped in Arab and other Muslim-majority countries. Such research will be enriched to the extent that additional independent variables are incorporated into the analysis, and perhaps if additional dimensions of the dependent variable are considered as well. The purpose of the present study is more limited, however. It is to assess the role of religious orientations in shaping attitudes toward democracy, and the findings in this connection are clear and straightforward. Islamic attachments, at most, have only a very limited influence on attitudes toward democracy.

While these findings about Islamic attachments do not shed much light on how attitudes *are* formed, they address and offer important conclusions about an issue that is the focus of considerable debate among students of Arab and Muslim societies: do the religious orientations of ordinary citizens retard the emergence of a political culture supportive of democracy and thus help to explain the persistent authoritarianism of the countries in which these men and women live? The answer provided by World Values Survey data, which is consistent with findings based on several less comprehensive data sets (Tessler 2002), is that Islam is not incompatible with democracy and does not discourage the emergence of attitudes favorable to democracy.

In conclusion, there is little evidence, at least at the individual level of analysis, to support the claims of those who assert that Islam and democracy are incompatible. The reasons that democracy has not taken root in the Arab world must therefore lie elsewhere; perhaps in domestic economic structures, perhaps in relations with the international political and economic order, or perhaps in the determination of those in power to resist political change by whatever means are required. But while these and other possible explanations can be debated, what should be clear is that cultural explanations alleging that Islam discourages or even prevents the emergence of support for democracy are misguided, indeed misleading, and thus of little use in efforts to understand the factors shaping attitudes toward democracy in the Arab world.

REFERENCES

ABED, Shukri.
    1995. "Islam and Democracy." In *Democracy, War, and Peace in the Middle East* edited by David Garnham and Mark Tessler. Bloomington: Indiana Univ

Press.

ANDERSON, Lisa.

1999. "Politics in the Middle East: Opportunities and Limits in the Quest for Theory." In *Area Studies and Social Science: Strategies for Understanding Middle East Politics*, edited by Mark Tessler, with Jodi Nachtwey and Anne Banda. Bloomington: Indiana University Press.

ARAB HUMAN DEVELOPMENT REPORT.

2002. New York: United Nations Development Programme. Available online: http://www.undp.org/rbas/ahdr/bychapter.html.

BENNANI-CHRAIBI, Mounia.

1994. *Soumis et rebelles: les jeunes au Maroc.* Paris: CNRS Editions.

BOWEN, Donna Lee.

1993. "Pragmatic Morality, Islam, and Family Planning in Morocco." In *Everyday Life in the Muslim Middle East*, edited by Donna Lee Bowen and Evelyn Early. Bloomington: Indiana University Press.

BRATTON, Michael and Robert Mattes.

2001. "Africans' Surprising Universalism." *Journal of Democracy* 12 (January): 107-121.

BRUMBERG, Daniel.

1995. "Authoritatian Legacies and Reform Strategies in the Arab World." In *Political Liberalization and Democratization in the Arab World: Theoretical Perspectives*, edited by Rex Brynen, Bahgat Korany, and Paul Noble. Boulder: Lunne Rienner Publishers.

CHOUEIRI, Y.

1996. "The Political Discourse of Contemporary Islamist Movements." In *Islamic Fundamentalism*, edited by Abdel Salem Sidahmed and Anoushiravam Ehteshami. Boulder: Westview Press.

CHU, Yun-han, Larry Diamond, and Doh Chull Shin.

2001. "Halting Progress in Korea and Taiwan." *Journal of Democracy* 12 (January):122-136.

CORDESMAN, Anthony.

1999. "Transitions in the Middle East." Address to the Eighth Annual United States Middle East Policymakers Conference. Washington, D.C.

DUCH, Raymond.

1995. "Economic Chaos and the Fragility of Democratic Transition in Former Communist Regimes." *Journal of Politics* 57(February):121-158.

ESPOSITO, John L.

1992. *Islam: The Straight Path.* New York: Oxford University Press.

ESPOSITO, John L. and James P. Piscatori.

1991. "Democratization and Islam." *Middle East Journal* 45:427-440.

AL-FARAWATI, Oula.

1999. "Arab Intellectuals Review Challenges of Globalization." *Jordan Times*, December 9-10.

FLANAGAN, Scott C. and Aie-Rie Lee.

> 2000. "Value Change and Democratic Reform in Japan and Korea." *Comparative Political Studies* 33:626-659.

GIBSON, James L.

> 1995. "The Resilience of Mass Support for Democratic Institutions and Processes in the Nascent Russian and Ukrainian Democracies." In *Political Culture and Civil Society in Russia and the New States of Eurasia*, edited by V. Tismaneanu. New York: M. E. Sharpe.

HALLIDAY, Fred.

> 1995. *Islam and the Myth of Confrontation: Religion and Politics in the Middle East.* London: I. B. Tauris.

HAMDI, Mohamed Elhachmi.

> 1996. "Islam and Democracy: The Limits of the Western Model." *Journal of Democracy* 7(April):81-85.

HARIK, Iliya.

> 1994. "Pluralism in the Arab World." *Journal of Democracy* 5(July):43-56.

HUDSON, Michael.

> 1995. "The Political Culture Approach to Arab Democratization: The Case for Bringing It Back In, Carefully." In *Political Liberalization and Democratization in the Arab World*, edited by Rex Brynen, Bahgat Korany, and Paul Noble. Boulder: Lynn Reinner Publishers.

HUNTINGTON, Samuel.

> 1984. "Will More Countries Become Democratic?" *Political Science Quarterly* 99(Summer):193-218.

HUNTINGTON, Samuel.

> 1993. "Democracy's Third Wave." In *The Global Resurgence of Democracy*, edited by Larry Diamond and Marc Plattner. Baltimore: Johns Hopkins University Press.

HUNTINGTON, Samuel.

> 1991. *The Third Wave.* Norman: University of Oklahoma Press.

INGLEHART, Ronald.

> 2000. "Culture and Democracy." In *Culture Matters: How Values Shape Human Progress*, edited by Lawrence E. Harrison and Samuel Huntinngton. New York: Basic Books.

KARATNYCKY, Adrian.

> 2000. "A Century of Progress." *The Journal of Democracy* 11:187-200.

KEDOURIE, Elie.

> 1994. *Democracy and Arab Political Culture.* London: Frank Cass Publishers.

KHASHAN, Hilal.

> 1998. "History's Legacy." *Middle East Quarterly* V(March):41-48.

KHOURI, Rami G.

> 2000. "A View from the Arab World." *Jordan Times*, July 5.

KORANY, Bahgat.

1994. "Arab Democratization: A Poor Cousin." *PS: Political Science and Politics* 27(September):511-513.

LEWIS, Bernard.
1994. *The Shaping of the Modern Middle East.* New York: Oxford.

MAINWARING, Scott.
1999. "Democratic Survivability in Latin America." In *Democracy and Its Limits: Lessons from Asia, Latin America and the Middle East,* edited by Howard Handelman and Mark Tessler. Notre Dame: University of Notre Dame Press.

MARRADI, Alberto.
1981. "Factor Analysis as an Aid in the Formulation and Refinement of Empirically Useful Concepts." In *Factor Analysis and Measurement in Sociological Research,* edited by Edgar F. Borgatta and David J. Jackson. London: Sage.

MATTES, Robert, and Hermann Thiel.
1998. "Consolidation and Public Opinion in South Africa." *Journal of Democracy* 9(January):95-110.

MERNISSI, Fatima.
1992. *Islam and Democracy: Fear of the Modern World.* Reading, Massachusetts: Addison-Wesley.

MISHLER, William and Richard Rose.
1999. "Five Years After the Fall: Trajectories of Support for Democracy in Post-Communist Europe." In *Critical Citizens: Global Support for Democratic Goverment,* edited by Pippa Norris. Oxford: Oxford University Press.

OTTENMOELLER, Dan.
1998. "Popular Perceptions of Democracy: Elections and Attitudes in Uganda." *Comparative Political Studies* 31:98-124.

ROSE, Richard, William Mishler, and Christian Haerpfer.
1998. *Democracy and its Alternatives: Understanding Post-communist Societies.* Cambridge: Polity Press.

ROSE, Richard.
1997. "Where Are Postcommunist Countries Going?" *Journal of Democracy* 8 (July):92-108.

SCHMITTER, Philippe and Terry Lynn Karl.
1993. "What Democracy Is . . . and Is Not." In *The Global Resurgence of Democracy,* edited by Larry Diamond and Marc Plattner. Baltimore: Johns Hopkins University Press.

SELIGSON, Mitchell and John Booth.
1993. "Political Culture and Regime Type: Evidence from Nigaragua and Costa Rica." *Journal of Politics* 55(August):777-792.

SEN, Amartya.
1999. "Democracy as a Universal Value." *Journal of Democracy* 10:3-17.

SHIN, Doh Chull and Huoyan Shyu.
1997. "Political Ambivalence in South Korea and Taiwan." *Journal of Democracy* 8(July):109-124.

SIVAN, Emmanuel.
2000. "Illusions of Change." *Journal of Democracy* 11:69-83.
SIVAN, Emmanuel.
1997. "Constraints and Opportunities in the Arab World." *Journal of Democracy* 8(April):103-113.
AL-SUWAIDI, Jamal.
1995. "Arab and Western Conceptions of Democracy." In *Democracy, War, and Peace in the Middle East*, edited by David Garnham and Mark Tessler. Bloomington: Indiana University Press.
TALBI, Mohamed.
2000. "A Record of Failure." *Journal of Democracy* 11:58-68.
TESSLER, Mark.
1999. "Arab Politics and Public Opinion." Paper presented at U.S. Government Inter-Agency Conference on "Next Generation Politics in the Muslim World." Washington, D.C.
TESSLER, Mark.
2002. "Islam and Democracy in the Middle East: The Impact of Religious Orientations on Attitudes Toward Democracy in Four Arab Countries." *Comparative Politics* 34(April):337-254.
TESSLER, Mark.
1997. "The Origins of Popular Support for Islamist Movements: A Political Economy Analysis." In *Islam, Democracy, and the State in North Africa*, edited by John Entelis. Bloomington: Indiana University Press.
VOLL, John.
1994. *Islam, Continuity, and Change in the Modern World*. Syracuse: Syracuse University Press.
WALDRON-MOORE, Pamela.
1999. "Eastern Europe at the Crossroads of Democratic Transition." *Comparative Political Studies* 32(February):32-62.
WEI-MING, Tu.
2000. "Multiple Modernities: A Preliminary Inquiry into the Implications of East Asian Modernity." In *Culture Matters: How Values Shape Human Progress*, edited by Lawrence E. Harrison and Samuel Huntinngton. New York: Basic Books.
WELSH, Bridget.
1996. "Attitudes Toward Democracy in Malaysia." *Asian Survey* 36:882-903.
ZAKARIA, Fareed.
1994. "Culture Is Destiny." *Foreign Affairs* 73:109-126.

RELIGIOUS PARTIES AND POLITICS IN PAKISTAN

Farooq Tanwir[*]

ABSTRACT

In October 2002, for the first time in Pakistan's history, a sizeable share of the population voted for religious parties. Some Pakistanis, and most Western analysts, interpret this as signaling the rise of a major fundamentalist religious movement. We suggest, however, that in large part, this phenomenon can be viewed as a protest vote, made as a rebuke to the major political parties, which have failed so far to provide any solutions to Pakistan's poverty and misery. This article examines the viewpoints of various analysts, representing various schools of thought in Pakistan.

An Overview of Major Political Parties

Islam has been a strong social force in the Indo-Pakistan sub-continent since the seventh century, when Arab traders implanted it in South India along the Malabar Coast. It subsequently spread in wide regions through Islamic conquests during the twelfth century, with Muslim rule lasting for many centuries until the British occupation of India. Under British rule, the Muslims of this region struggled to attain an independent state until 1947, when Pakistan was born. Although modernization is taking place, religious faith remains vital, with the Islamic faith being part of peoples' daily lives (Ahmad 1988). Nevertheless, significant numbers of the Pakistani people have never before supported rule by religious leaders, at any time during Pakistan's 54 years of independence. In all the elections conducted previous to 1997, the religious parties only had token representation in the parliament. Only two seats were held by religious parties in the national assembly of 1997.

The founder of Pakistan, Muhammad Ali Jinnah, was a British-educated lawyer. His goal was to create a modern, progressive Islamic state without any element of theocracy. Pakistan was created democratically, and a huge majority voted in favor of an independent Pakistan in 1945, in a referendum before the partition of India. Jinnah argued that only people with an equal awareness of both Western societies and Islamic societies could run the newly created Pakistan properly. He further argued that equal rights for the minorities and for the females, democracy, and tolerance should be the main motives of the new state; and that sectarianism and extremism would not find any place in Pakistan (Wolpert 1989).

Pakistan was achieved through a democratic struggle led by the All India Muslim League, which was created in response to anti-Muslim policies of the Congress Party of India. Jinnah was a member of Congress in the beginning of his political career but later left the party and joined the Muslim league. Educated

* Department of Rural Sociology, University of Agriculture, Faisalabad, Pakistan.

people ran the Muslim League with a little support from the religious leaders or ulema (Munawar 1998).

During the independence movement, some religious leaders opposed the independence movement in general and Mr. Jinnah in particular. One of their arguments was that Jinnah was Western educated and wears Western clothing so he will not be able to run the newly created country within the framework of religion. This argument was in contradiction with basic Islamic values, which emphasize research, the search for knowledge, tolerance for others, and respect for other religions and democracy (Nasr 1996). Furthermore, Jinnah repeatedly rejected rule under "Mulaism" (Qureshi 1972; 1974). But another group of religious leaders like Shabir-ul-Hassan Thanvi, Maulana Ashraf Thanvi, and Allama Shabbir Ahmad Usmani supported Jinnah and the movement for the independence of Pakistan.

Jinnah worked for a separate homeland for Muslims ruled by an educated and enlightened community with western education as well as religious education. He wanted to build Pakistan on modern lines so that it could stand up with the rest of the world shoulder to shoulder. Therefore, whenever Pakistanis exercised their right of vote in general elections, they always voted for parties that had broad political manifestos, which went beyond religion and religious agendas. The rule of the country by religious leaders was totally ruled out in the past (Sahab 1989). The solid proof of these political attitudes is exhibited in the various constitutions introduced in various periods of time. The first constitution in 1956 manifests what Jinnah desired. Similarly, all other constitutions which followed the first one were semi-secular based on the British legal system with required amendments introduced at various times to adjust it to the changing times (Faridi 2002).

Similarly, the system of education is largely the same as the Western education system that was introduced during British colonial rule and the formation of all universities, old or new, were built on the same conventional system. The administrative or bureaucratic system was also the continuation of the old British system with progressive changes according to the changing times (Faridi 2002).

Although Pakistan was created through a democratic struggle, democracy failed to develop strong roots in Pakistan. One reason was the death of Jinnah only a year after the country's creation. Later, in 1951, Prime Minister Liaqat Ali Khan was assassinated. Then a game of musical chairs started in the country's politics. The first general elections in the history of Pakistan were conducted in 1970 when the country was united. These elections resulted in a split mandate in the East and West parts of the country. In the East, the Awami League from Eastern part of the country emerged as the largest party. The delay in the transfer of power to the elected assembly led to civil war in East Pakistan, which ultimately ended in the independence of East Pakistan, as Bangladesh (Sahab 1989).

The Pakistan Peoples Party (PPP) was the largest party in West Pakistan, so it formed its government in the remaining Pakistan under the chairmanship of

Z.A.Bhutto. PPP was a purely secular political party based on an economic approach under the garb of the very vague term "Islamic Socialism." The main slogan of PPP was bread, clothing, and shelter. After Bhutto was hanged in 1979, the chairmanship of PPP was handed over to his daughter Benazir Bhutto who was educated at Oxford and Harvard. PPP has a very solid vote bank and has always done well in the elections (Sahab 1989; Ghani 2002). PPP has a very strong base in the province of Sind. All efforts were made to crush PPP during the Zia regime (1977 to 1988). In doing so, a nationalist group named Mohajar Quami Movement (MQM) was raised in the urban Sind. It brought worse effects, especially for Karachi and Hyderabad. These two cities became a hot spot for many years and the residents witnessed a long wave of lawlessness (Naqvi 2002).

The Muslim League (ML) was the party under which the Muslims in the sub-continent struggled for and achieved Pakistan. In the struggle for Pakistan, ML represented the Muslims of the sub-continent while congress represented the Hindus and a minority of the nationalist Muslims such as Abu-al-Kalam Azad. This was also a broad political party with a solid reservoir of votes. Because of its great role during the independence movement, ML was strongly affected by the thoughts and the ideologies of Jinnah. After independence, ML became a rolling stone. Every ruler and dictator used ML for the accomplishment of a personal political agenda. This led to the division of ML into various groups. In the recent October elections, five splinters from the ML were contesting the elections under different names such as PML (N), PML (Q), PML (J), PML (F), PML (Z) (Saeed 2002). The weakening of ML also resulted in the poor performance of democracy. In the united Pakistan, a large number of middle class people joined the ML from East Pakistan. After the separation of East Pakistan, a series of interruptions in the democracy raised the influence of feudal landlords and big industrialists in the ML (Siddiqui 2002a).

Along with the two major political parties (PPP and PML), the religious political parties constitute another element in Pakistani politics. These parties represent the various religious sects in the society, and they have always tested their luck in the elections but consistently failed to draw people's attention towards them. The percentage of the total votes cast in favor of religious parties in the last three elections which were conducted in 1990, 1993 and 1997 was not very encouraging. It was only 1.76 percent, 6.75 percent, and 1.83 percent, respectively (Warriach 2002).

Rise of Religious Parties

In the 2002 elections, to the great surprise not only of international observers but also to the Pakistani public, the religious parties increased their percentage of the vote from less than 2 percent to over 11 percent and, in the process, won 46 seats in the national assembly. Currently, they are the third largest group in the national assembly after PML (Q) with 77 seats and PPP with 63 seats. The two major parties, the PML and PPP, now find themselves dependent on making a coalition with the religious parties in order to win a majority in the house of 272 and form the government. This is a new trend since the creation of Pakistan in 1947. A numbers of observers are asking: is Pakistan going to be a theocratic state in near future? Is religious fundamentalism rising in Pakistan? This article attempts to analyze the situation and the circumstances that have brought unprecedented political power to the religious parties.

The events of 9/11 not only affected American society but also brought far-reaching consequences for Pakistan. The moment America planned its military operations in Afghanistan, the government of Pakistan was asked not only to provide logistic support to American forces in Afghanistan but also to seal its borders with Afghanistan to enhance the effectiveness of American operations. It is important to mention here that people of Baluchistan and the North West Frontier Province—Pakistani provinces adjacent to the Afghan border—have kin in Afghanistan and belong to the same ethnic group. Pakistani media have reported that American operations caused civilian deaths in Afghanistan. They also reported that the "Northern Alliance" forces that were backed by the Americans killed a huge majority of the Talibans who surrendered to the Americans. And, the media have reported that American agencies like the FBI have made its offices in Pakistan and were directly monitoring its operations in Pakistan. It was also reported that some of the airports had been turned over to American control for a long period of time. These reports created a huge wave of anti-American feelings in Pakistan in general and in the Northwest Frontier Province and Baluchistan in particular.[1]

As mentioned earlier, the religious parties have always tried to get some role in Pakistani politics. Sometimes they formed alliances with other parties like PML and sometimes they tried their fate independently. They had very limited success in all elections except the most recent ones, when the six major religious parties formed an alliance to contest the elections jointly. The two major religious parties in this alliance were Jamat-e-Islami (JI) and Jamiat-ullema-Pakistan (JUP), and they campaigned under the name "Muthida Majlis Amil" (MMA) which could be translated literally as the "Joint Action Organization"; we will refer to them as the Religious Alliance. The Religious Alliance shattered precedent by winning 46 seats in the national assembly and 80 seats in the four provinces. Furthermore, their strength is concentrated in the more impoverished and less populous Northwest Frontier Province and Baluchistan to such an extent that they can independently form the government in the former province, and have emerged as the largest party in Baluchistan. In the current international political scenario, these two provinces are the most sensitive places since they border on Afghanistan. Indeed, they are the base camps of all activities launched by the United States in collaboration with the Pakistani government. Moreover, their populations are ethnically similar to two of the major groups in Afghanistan.

The Religious Alliance was not formed in response to the current Afghan situation. During the last few years, Pakistan has been the torn by religious sectarianism and extremism that resulted in various innocent killings. In response to this situation, some of the major religious parties established a council to eliminate the differences among the various religious groups. The various religious groups have never had a good record of mutual understanding. In fact, most of the time they had been criticizing each other and this may be one of the reasons for their low popularity level in the publics. This council helped reconcile mutual differences. Last year, a meeting of this council was called and the religious parties announced the formation of a common body named the "Afghan Defense Council" (ADC) after 9/11 when America started actions against Afghanistan. After its formation, ADC launched a protest campaign against American actions in Afghanistan. After the Taliban surrender, the ADC was renamed the "Pak-Afghan Defense Council" (PADC). This PADC was later converted to an election alliance for the 2002 elections and was given the name of the Religious Alliance (Warriach 2002). In this sense, the election campaign of the Religious Alliance was a continuation of last year's agitation.

The Religious Alliance launched a nationwide election campaign. Due to the performance of religious parties in the past, the campaign failed to get do well at the national level. But in the Northwest Frontier Province it did very well. The results of the elections were unexpected even for the Religious Alliance leadership. The Religious Alliance won 46 national assembly seats and 80 seats in the provincial assemblies. The important aspect is that out of these 80 seats The Religious Alliance has won 48 seats in The North West Frontier Province (NWFP) which enables them to form their government in NWFP.

Thus, the Religious Alliance has emerged as the third largest group in the national assembly and holds a key position in the power game. In addition to that, the Religious Alliance dominates the provincial assembly of the Northwest Frontier Province and they will easily form the government there. In past, the religious parties only succeeded once to form a government in the Northwest Frontier Province in 1971, but it was a coalition government in alliance with the ANP (Awami National Party), a semi-secular party. The Religious Alliance has emerged as the largest party in the provincial assembly of Baluchistan. It is also likely that they will be able to form the state government there too with the help of some small parties or the independently elected members (Haqani 2002).

Another important implication of the Religious Alliance's victory would be their hold in the upper house of the parliament, the "Senate." All of the four provinces have an equal representation in the senate and due to their huge majority in the Northwest Frontier Province assembly, the Religious Alliance will be able to hold more than one-third of the seats in the senate, providing them with a decisive role in the law making process of the country. For the first time in the history of Pakistan, religious parties have won massive political power.

Analysis of MMA Victory

Since the events of 9/11, the controversial thesis offered by Samuel P. Huntington about the "clash of civilizations" has been among the most widely discussed issues in the intellectual and academic circles of Pakistan. And since the October 2002 elections, the most widely discussed issue in the Pakistan situation has been the victory of the Religious Alliance. All of the national newspapers, and even international media outlets such as *Time Magazine*, *The Economist*, and the *BBC*, have discussed the Religious Alliance victory. These media express the opinion that the most important driving force behind the victory of the Religious Alliance in the provinces of the Northwest Frontier Province and Baluchistan were the anti-American feelings and emotions caused by the American action in Afghanistan in October 2001 and later in the adjacent tribal areas of Pakistan.[2] *Time Magazine*, for example, has reported that president Musharaf's policies about Afghanistan and his alliance with America created the negative reaction that paved the way for the victory of the Religious Alliance. Secondly, Musharaf's negative attitude towards major political parties and leaders (such as Benazir and Nawaz Sharif[3]) created a gap in the national politics that was partially filled by the Religious Alliance. Quite surprisingly, *Time Magazine* has labeled the Religious Alliance an anti-American party. *Time Magazine* has called the 2002 elections the "General's election" but has stated that the Religious Alliance's recent victory was against Musharaf's expectations. *The Economist* has reported that the victory of the Religious Alliance has made both Musharaf and Bush worried about the future situation of the region and the war against Taliban and Al-Qaeda, arguing that the Religious Alliance's victory may affect efforts against the Taliban and Al-Qaeda in Afghanistan and in Pakistan. The magazine has further reported that whether in government or in opposition, the Religious Alliance will be a problem. Zikria (2002) has argued that the American move against Islam may take a dangerous form claiming that Christian fundamentalists such as Jerry Farewell, Pat Robertson, and Franklin Graham have insulted Islamic beliefs. Similarly, *News Link* (2002) reported that the vote cast in the Northwest Frontier Province was an anti-American vote, arguing that American action in Afghanistan has angered the Pashtun ethnic group that dominates the Northwest Frontier Province, and they have displayed their anger: for the first time in the history of Pakistan, the sensitive border province of the Northwest Frontier Province will be ruled purely by religious parties.

Hussain (2002)[4] also described the victory of the Religious Alliance and anti-government parties in the election as a reaction to the American policies in the region, claiming that the Religious Alliance drew its heaviest support in areas that are close to the Afghan border and have had the largest demonstrations against the American action in Afghanistan. He was of the opinion that the main pushing force behind Z.A. Bhutto's popularity was his anti-Indian policy, which continued until the Zia era; but today, the Afghan factor dominates Pakistani politics. Hussain nevertheless has an optimistic view about the Religious Alliance victory in recent elections. He thinks it may eliminate the differences between various religious sects and would also help in reducing the extremist feelings of various religious groups.

Qasmi (2002)[5] was of the opinion that the Religious Alliance has gained the recent victory because of its anti-government and anti-American slogans. According to Qasmi, the main factors of the Religious Alliance victory were: policies of Pakistan government, American's anti-Muslim policies, innocent killings in Afghanistan and the ignorance of Pakistan government on such killings, FBI operations in Pakistan, and investigations from the nuclear scientists. So, in an indirect way, president Musharaf has contributed to the Religious Alliance victory through his policies. Arif (2002)[6] has argued that the Northwest Frontier Province is under heavy influence of Pashtun lords and tribes who are said to be involved in drug and arms business. The Religious Alliance has had a landslide victory (through lower- and middle-class candidates) in that province; therefore, there had to be a very strong force behind their success. According to Arif (2002), the strong force was the heavy anti-American feelings in the Pashtun masses. On top of that, the government crackdowns in tribal areas in search of Al-Qaeda and Talibans and also the actions against the *madrassaas* infuriated people. The secular and anti-religious policies of the Musharaf government have also greatly contributed towards the Religious Alliance success.

Rehman (2002),[7] after winning the elections, has criticized the Musharaf government and has demanded that Musharaf resign from the offices of both the president and the army chief. He has further argued that the removal of American camps from Pakistan soil, and a balanced foreign policy is badly required in the country, enabling us to prepare our own economic policies, independent of the international agencies. He claims that the Religious Alliance will not impose strict policies on the public, like those imposed by the Taliban.

To what extent can the Religious Alliance's emergence as a significant political factor be interpreted as the potential beginning of Pakistan some day becoming dominated by Islamic fundamentalists? Evidence from the World Values Surveys sheds some light on this question. The Pakistani component of the World Values Survey was completed in 2002, constituting a representative national sample of the adult Pakistani public. It enables us to compare the Pakistani public with those of more than 70 other publics, containing more than 80 percent of the world's population.[8]

Religiosity and the Religious Parties

There is no question that the Pakistani public has a strong sense of Islamic identity, and takes religion seriously. One indicator of this is the Pakistani public's response to the question, "Do you agree or disagree with the following statements?—Politicians who do not believe in God are unfit for public office." As Table 1 indicates, the overwhelming majority of the Pakistani public—fully 95 percent of them—believe that politicians who do not believe in God are unac-

Table 1. Must Political Leaders believe in God?
(Percent agreeing that "Politicians who do not believe in God are unfit for Public Office")

Country	%		Country	%
Pakistan	**95**		Croatia	25
Indonesia	**89**		Latvia	22
Egypt	**88**		Russia	22
Morocco	**86**		Slovakia	22
Iran	**83**		*Canada*	*21*
Nigeria	82		Montenegro	21
Jordan	**81**		Lithuania	20
Algeria	**78**		Vietnam	19
Philippines	71		*W Germany*	*18*
Bangladesh	**71**		*Ireland*	*16*
Tanzania	66		Poland	16
Puerto Rico	65		Bosnia	16
Uganda	60		*Italy*	*15*
S Africa	57		*N Ireland*	*15*
Turkey	**57**		*Austria*	*15*
Zimbabwe	53		Estonia	14
Romania	52		*Luxemburg*	*13*
Venezuela	52		*Spain*	*12*
Moldova	44		Hungary	12
Albania	**44**		*Finland*	*12*
India	42		*Slovenia*	*11*
Malta	42		*Britain*	*10*
U.S.	*39*		S Korea	10
Mexico	39		*France*	*9*
Greece	*37*		*Belgium*	*9*
Argentina	35		*Iceland*	*9*
Chile	35		*Japan*	*8*
Macedonia	35		*E Germany*	*8*
Ukraine	34		Czech Rep	6
Serbia	27		*Denmark*	*4*
Belarus	26		*Sweden*	*4*
Bulgaria	25		*Netherlands*	*2*

Note: Countries with an Islamic majority are shown in bold face type; high-income countries (as defined by World Bank in 2000) are in italics.
Source: World Values Surveys.

ceptable. In fact, the Pakistani public ranks highest of the 68 publics to whom this question was asked. The publics of Islamic societies (shown in bold face type in Table 1) are particularly likely to agree with this statement: eight of the ten publics that agree most strongly that politicians must believe in God, are predominantly Islamic, and the two other highest-ranking societies (Nigeria and the Philippines) have sizeable Islamic minorities. But this belief is by no means limited to Islamic societies. A majority of the public agrees with the question in seven non-Islamic societies. Fully 39 percent of the U.S. public also agrees with it, and the American public ranks higher in this respect than the public of any other rich democracy. In this, and many other respects, the United States shows a much more religious out-look than do the publics of most rich democracies.

An overwhelming majority of the Pakistani public believes that political leaders should believe in God. But does this mean that they want to be ruled by religious leaders? Table 2 provides some insight into this question, showing response to the question "Do you agree or disagree with the following state-ment?—Religious leaders should not influence how people vote in elections." As Table 2 indicates, an overwhelming majority of the Pakistani public feels that reli-gious leaders should *not* influence how people vote: politicians should be God-fearing, but they should also be independent. Among the 68 societies for which we have data, in only two—Iran and Algeria—does a majority disagree with this statement, believing that religious leaders should influence how people vote. In the 66 other societies, a majority of the public rejects the idea that religious lead-ers should influence how people vote—and this includes nine Islamic societies, including Pakistan. Interestingly enough, the U.S. public is more likely to accept having religious leaders influence the vote, than are the publics of most Islamic societies (though even in the United States, fully 63 percent of the public reject it). In short, the Pakistani public emphasizes religious values, and believes that their political leaders should believe in God—but does not want religious leaders to dominate political life. It is an important distinction.

It is now 54 years since Pakistan's independence from British colonial rule. In these 54 years, Pakistan has only had 16 years of democracy—the other 38 years being spent under non-elected or military regimes. The first general elec-tions were conducted in 1970 after 23 years of independence. These elections gen-erated a split mandate in both parts of the country and ultimately resulted in the-separation of the country in 1971. From 1977 to 1985 there was martial law and from 1985 to 1999 five general elections were conducted. From 1999 to 2002 there was military rule again. All this reflects that democracy was not permitted and whenever it was permitted it failed to gain strong roots in the country. On the other side, according to the latest estimates, the population of Pakistan is 142.5 million while it was 133 million (in both East and West Pakistan) in 1950 (NIPS 2001). According to a recent FAO report, 35 percent of the total population of Pakistan was living below poverty line. This combination of poverty and political instability has introduced a culture of corruption in the country. According to an

**Table 2. Should Religious Leaders influence Elections?
(Percentage agreeing that "Religious Leaders should
not influence how People vote in Elections")**

Iran	**22**		Bosnia	76
Algeria	**38**		**Albania**	**77**
Egypt	**52**		*Ireland*	*78*
Venezuela	56		*Canada*	*78*
Spain	*62*		Hungary	78
Zimbabwe	62		*Slovenia*	*78*
U.S.	*63*		Romania	78
Mexico	64		*Greece*	*78*
Uganda	64		*Italy*	*79*
Jordan	**64**		**Turkey**	**79**
S Africa	65		*Belgium*	*80*
Netherlands	*66*		Czech Rep	80
Sweden	*67*		Macedonia	80
Finland	*68*		**Morocco**	**80**
India	68		*Iceland*	*81*
Vietnam	68		Belarus	82
S Korea	69		Lithuania	82
Chile	69		Russia	82
Moldova	69		Luxemburg	82
Puerto Rico	70		Ukraine	83
Tanzania	70		Montenegro	83
Britain	*72*		Bulgaria	84
E Germany	*72*		Latvia	84
Nigeria	73		*Denmark*	*85*
Japan	*74*		Poland	85
Argentina	74		*Austria*	*85*
Pakistan	**74**		Estonia	85
Philippines	74		Serbia	85
Bangladesh	**74**		*France*	*86*
Slovakia	74		Croatia	86
Jordan	**74**		**Indonesia**	**87**
W Germany	*76*		Malta	90
N Ireland	*76*			

Note: Countries with an Islamic majority are shown in bold face type; high-income countries (as defined by World Bank in 2000) are in italics.
Source: World Values Survey

estimate made by Transparency International in 1998, Pakistan ranked number two in corruption, lower than only one country, Nigeria.

These issues have been highlighted by some of the analysts analyzing the recent elections. Athar (2002), for example, has argued that Pakistani politics is moving in a vicious circle of foreign debt, poverty, and resources controlled by an elite group. All these factors may have alienated a section of the public from the major politicians and the political parties and they were looking towards other parties of which the Religious Alliance could be a choice. Athar, however, has argued that people may have reservations about the models of Islamization that the various religious parties have with them. Hafiz Idress (2002)[9] has also described the victory of the Religious Alliance in the Northwest Frontier Province and Baluchistan as a reaction to the feudalism, secularism, liberalism, and the corruption of politicians and the political parties in the past. He was of the opinion that these factors have created problems in the grooming of democracy in the country in the past and it has led people to support the Religious Alliance.

Azeem (2002)[10] describes the victory of Religious Alliance as a reaction to the feudal landlords, and to the landed and industrial aristocracy. He was of the opinion that those who have been contesting elections from the inherited family seats are now gradually losing hold on these seats and that Religious Alliance slogans and manifesto is making paths in the publics. He has further described that the head of JI[11] is not just a religious leader but is a Master of Science degree holder and has a very good command over other languages such as English, Pushto, Persian, and Arabic. Nadeem (2002) has described the Religious Alliance vote bank as an anti-establishment vote.

Siddiqui (2002a) points out that in the united Pakistan, the politicians from East Pakistan were predominately from the middle classes, and after the separation of East Pakistan, politics became the game of feudal lords, industrialists, and those with black money. So there was a gap that has now been filled by the middle-class Religious Alliance elected members. He has also argued that the nationalist parties have also been defeated by the Religious Alliance. All this shows that the Religious Alliance's success was not just a reaction to American policies but was also a reaction against the socioeconomic and political deprivations prevailing in the country. He has emphasized the point that the Religious Alliance has to show a balanced behavior now and should not exhibit extremist policies while in power.

Some additional factors have also contributed to the Religious Alliance's accomplishment. Kissana (2002),[12] for example, argues that the Religious Alliance won mainly because the religious parties joined forces, and pooled their votes. Bhai (2002)[13] has stated that in addition to the American factor, there were some other factors. One of them was the reduction in voter age from 21 to 18 years. It led the students of *Madressahas* that are being run by religious parties to come out and cast their votes in favor of Religious Alliance. Naheed (2002)[14] has described that the Religious Alliance's victory was mainly because of reduction in voter age. It led *madressaha* students to vote for the Religious Alliance considering it a religious duty and a contribution to help Afghans. On the other hand, younger people in the cities of Punjab and Sind had low rates of voting, being relatively uninterested in current issues.

Regardless of the reasons for the Religious Alliance's success, it is an established factor now, and it has opened a debate on the possible consequences. President Musharaf, while addressing a public gathering in Peshawar (capital of the Northwest Frontier Province) in April 2002 with regard to his referendum campaign, said that the religious parties and leaders have always deceived the people of Pakistan. He further argued that the people of Pakistan are wise and will never be impressed by the religious parties and their leaders. Musharaf may have his own opinion but a realistic look over the history indicates that the people of Pakistan have never supported the religious parties to come into power and play a political role (*The Daily Nawa-I-Waqat* 2002; *The News* 2002; *The Nation* 2002; *Dawn* 2002).

The success of the Religious Alliance is important because of the sensitive geopolitical situation of the region. The events of 9/11 were strongly condemned by Pakistan, as no religion or moral code allows the killings of civilians. Pakistan not only joined hands with the international alliance to fight against terrorism but also became a front line state, since Pakistan has a long border with Afghanistan. Pakistan provided every possible support and assistance to the allied forces. On the other hand, people in Pakistan were receiving the first hand information and news from Afghanistan about the operation there. The media in Pakistan, too, was focusing heavily on the Afghan situation and bringing reports of innocent killings there. Being a Muslim country, people in Pakistan were also emotionally involved with the Afghan people. All this created a wave of anti-government and anti-American emotions in the people of Pakistan in general and the people of the Northwest Frontier Province and Baluchistan in particular.

In this heated sociopolitical environment, the Religious Alliance launched its election campaign and started criticizing the Afghan situation. This strategy proved its worth and provided the Religious Alliance with a position in the new political scenario. Since this is entirely a new pattern for Pakistani politics, it has brought many questions with it. The issue is so big and important that one has to consider both the negative and the positive aspects to deal with it fairly. Dr. Iqbal (2002)[15] raised the question about the slogan of "Islamization" raised by the religious leaders. He argued that Pakistan is already an Islamic country and people are religious so what else do the *ulema* want? The constitutions of 1956, 1962, and 1973 were very much Islamic in their spirit, so what new things do the *ulema* want to introduce? They have to decide whether they will play a creative or a destructive role in the country. By acting positively, the *ulema* can bring betterment both for people and for the country while their negative role can bring misery for the country.

Discussion and Conclusion

Pakistan is at the crossroads, having already done a lot regarding the war in Afghanistan and is still doing a lot. Although the Taliban government was successful in controlling the warlords, they were not very balanced in their relations with other nations and groups. Forcing the public to perform religious obligations, imposing strict limits on women, and requiring men to have beards did not create a good image of Islam outside the Islamic world. So much so, that a significant segment of the people in Pakistan have many reservations about the Taliban type of Islam. Since it is said that the Taliban were the product of *madrassaas* and many of the Religious Alliance parties are running their own *madrassaas* in Pakistan, people may think that the "Islamization" model of the Religious Alliance would be similar to that of the Taliban. Another free-lancer writer, Tayyaba Zia (2002), based in America has raised similar questions about the Religious Alliance. She has particularly talked about the Pakistani women who are settled in America and are having many doubts after the Religious Alliance's success. She has argued that the Religious Alliance's leadership must not restrict women and should let them contribute productively in the national building process; acting like this will be in line with the true Islamic teachings, which emphasize learning, acting, and being good for others and not just performing religious obligations.

A combination of a reaction against American actions in Afghanistan and people's annoyance with the other political parties seems to have resulted in the Religious Alliance success. The Religious Alliance have to consider that their mandate is not so large and is restricted to a certain area that is under a very sensitive geopolitical situation. This situation can change in the near future and resultantly can again change the political orientation of the people. It would also be important to note that along with the major political parties like PML and PPP, the Religious Alliance has defeated the nationalist parties, which is also an important sign. It can be argued that the current circumstances, at least, have provided a very good platform for the religious parties to act upon and prove what they have been saying from the time when Muslims of the sub-continent started their struggle for Pakistan.

It is also important that the people of Punjab and Sind, the two most populous provinces, have not given a positive response to the Religious Alliance, which won only a few seats in major cities, but that it is generally understood that this victory is mainly because of Religious Alliance adjustment with some other parties like PML (N). This low response may be due to the reservations that people have in their minds about the Religious Alliance. Now is a very good time for the Religious Alliance to present a good model of governance for the people. It should not be a theocratic one. But it should be based on the real Islamic spirit that emphasizes action and not just prayers.

Religious sectarianism and extremism have claimed many lives in Pakistan over the years. It has not only deteriorated the law and order situation of the country but also has decreased the credibility of religious parties in the publics. Now is the time to eliminate this from the society. By doing so, the Religious Alliance can not only make it's vote base strong and wide but can also extend it to the other parts of the country. Acting and behaving otherwise will not only cause problems for the Religious Alliance but also for the whole country. Now we are living in a global village where it would be very hard to ignore the outside world. Pakistan has to live with others. Living in a nutshell can create many problems. The Taliban has experienced it. Having a good level of communication and mutual understanding is important in the global village. Merely criticizing others has proved to be a failed technique.

Another important aspect of the Religious Alliance's success is its victory in Karachi, where the Religious Alliance won five national assembly seats. Karachi is known as mini Pakistan and was a hot spot since the Zia era when military rulers raised MQM[16] against PPP in urban areas of Sind. Now the Religious Alliance can prove it's worth to the people of Karachi. By doing well there they can easily make paths in other urban centers of Pakistan.

Since the recent elections, the outside world is worried about the expected orthodox Islamic rule of religious parties. At this stage, only the implementation of the claimed promises of the Religious Alliance would prove their wisdom. They would have to present a scientifically progressing, economically prospering, and a socially secure, strong Pakistan. None of their policies should exhibit religious extremism. The "un-Islamic" distribution of power in the hands of feudal lords and industrialists should be halted and the rights of the general public should be protected.

The outside world should also realize the fragile circumstances in the region. Use of power everywhere may not bring the same result every time. The chronic regional issues such as Kashmir can spoil the whole region. This is the time to solve such issues on permanent grounds to bring peace and stability for the region in particular and for the rest of the world in general.

Should the success of the Religious Alliance in becoming a significant political factor be interpreted as the first step toward Pakistani political life becoming dominated by religious leaders? We think not. First, the extent of the breakthrough should not be overstated: the Religious Alliance won only 11 percent of the national vote. And evidence from the World Values Surveys indicates that the Pakistani public attaches strong importance to religion and believes that its political leaders should believe in God. But a strong majority (fully 74 percent) reject the idea that religious leaders should influence how people vote in elections. The Pakistanis are Islamic, but they do not want to be ruled by religious leaders.

NOTES

1   Media was closely monitoring the operations in Afghanistan. People in border areas were not only getting information through the media but were also receiving dead bodies and the first hand information from those who were bringing the dead bodies. Families also migrated from Afghanistan and brought with them the stories of what was happening there. For further reference see Arif 2002a; Siddiqui 2002a; Mirza 2002.

2   Arif (2002a and b), *Economist* (2002) Rashak (2002), Qasmi (2002), Haqani (2002), Kissana (2002), Bhai (2002), Siddiqui (2002a and b), Azeem (2002), Nadeem (2002), *Times Magazine* (2002), Mirza (2002), Athar (2002), Mehmood (2002), Sheikh (2002), Ghani (2002), Hussain (2002).

3   Nawaz Sharif was the Prime Minister in October 1999 when the army took over. At that time, Nawaz Sharif was the head of the ruling party named as PML (N). Nawaz Sharif was sent to the jail with certain allegations and later was allowed to go to Saudi Arabia along with other family members under an agreement with the Musharaf administration, which would not let him come back for ten years. Few weeks before the elections, Nawaz appointed his brother Shahbaz as the President of PML (N) but he was also not allowed to come back and contest elections. In the mean while majority of members of the former assembly (1997) formed their own Muslim League and named it as PML (Q) to contest elections. As a result, PML (N) only won 14 seats in the national assembly in the October elections. Nawaz was elected as Prime Minister in 1990 and then in 1997.

   Benazir Bhutto was the leader of opposition in 1997 assembly but went abroad in 1999. In her absence she was prosecuted and find convicted in regard to certain allegations. Currently she is residing in Dubai and her husband is in jail in Pakistan. She was also not in the country at the time of October elections. She was also elected as Prime Minister in 1988 and then in 1993.

4   Mr. Mushahid Hussain was the information minister in the former Nawaz Sharif government, which was sacked by the army in 1999. Mr. Hussain has eye witnessed the various sociopolitical changes and events that have happened in Pakistan over the last few years.

5   Mr. Atta-ul-Haq Qasmi was Pakistan's Ambassador in Norway during the previous Nawaz Sharif government, which was sacked in 1999 by army. By profession, he is a university teacher. He writes frequently for the press.

6   Mr. Irshad Ahmad Arif is a renowned journalist and free-lancer writer. He is famous for his writings on the current national and international issues.

7   Fazal-ur-Rehman is one of the leaders of Religious Alliance. He is head of JUP. He has been nominated by Religious Alliance as the candidate for Prime Minister. His party JUP has a very strong influence in the Northwest Frontier Province and Baluchistan and even in Punjab and Sind as well. JUP is also running many madrassaas in various parts of the country especially in the Northwest Frontier Province and Baluchistan.

8   The World Values Surveys have interviewed representative national samples of societies on all six inhabited continents since 1981. For more details, see the World Values Survey web sites, http://wvs.isr.umich.edu and http://worldvalues survey.com.

9   Hafiz Idress is the provincial president of Religious Alliance in Punjab.

10   Ammer-ul-Azeem is one of the leading figures of Jamat-e-Islami (JI). He is a very senior party member from Punjab. He has been a very active student leader from the plate form of Islami-Jamiate-Tulaba, which is student wing of JI.

11   Jamat-e-Islami (JI) is the largest religious party in Pakistan. This party was formed by the famous scholar Mawdoodi before the formation of Pakistan. The party also has a very strong student wing, which is known as Islami-Jamiat-e-Tulaba. Currently, Qazi Hussain Ahmad is the president of JI. He is a highly educated man. It is said that he was the mastermind behind the formation of Religious Alliance.

12   Israr Ahmad Kissana is a free-lancer writer. He frequently publishes his articles in the national newspapers and journals on the current national and international issues. He is New York based so he provides good comparative analysis.

13   Munno Bhai is a senior leading writer and journalist. He is highly respected in the intellectual circles of Pakistan. He has also written scripts of various dramas that have been presented on television. He has a long list of articles and books in his credit.

14   Kishwar Naheed is a famous writer and poet. She is among the voices that are asking more rights for women in Pakistan. She has reservations about religious parties and their leaders.

15   Dr Javed Iqbal is a famous writer and intellectual. He has the honor of being the son of the great poet Allama Dr. Muha. Religious Allianced Iqbal who is also known as the poet of the East. Allama Muhammed Iqbal was the one who presented for the first time, the idea of Pakistan in 1930. Dr. Javed himself is a retired Chief Justice of Lahore (Punjab) high court. He used to be a member of

the senate.

16   MQM is nationalist party, which got roots during Zia's martial law. It was main-
          ly to restrict PPP, which was considered to be the number one enemy of Zia.
          Since then Karachi has been a hot spot. Violence, firing, strikes, agitation, and
          killings became a routine of life. It was felt that Karachi had been cut off from
          mainstream politics.

REFERENCES

AHMAD, A.S.
    1988. *Discovering Islam: Making Sense of Muslim History and Society.*
    Routledge, London, New York.
ARIF, A.A.
    2002a. "Imtihan," *The Nation*, 14th October, Lahore, Pakistan.
ARIF, A.A.
    2002b. "The Translator," *The Nation*, 18th October, Lahore, Pakistan.
ATHAR, A.
    2002. "Moving in The Circle," *The Nation*, 18th October, Lahore, Pakistan.
AZEEM, A.
    2002. "Religious Alliance and Mubasreen," Editorial, *The Daily Jang*, 16th
    October, Lahore, Pakistan.
BHAI, M.
    2002. "Along The Main Stream," *The Daily Jang*, 19th October, Lahore,
    Pakistan.
DAWN.
    2002. "Musharaf and The Religious Parties" District Reporter, 11th April,
    Karachi, Pakistan.
ECONOMIST.
    2002. "Elections 2002," Reported in *The News*, 21st October, Lahore, Pakistan.
FARIDI, F.U.
    2002. "After 10-10-2002," *The Daily Nawa-I-Waqat*, 12th October, Lahore,
    Pakistan.
GHANI, S.
    2002. "Clothing, Shelter and Food," *The Nation*, 2nd October, Lahore, Pakistan.
HAQANI, I.A.
    2002. "Religious Alliance: Explanations and Challenges," *The News*, 25th
    October, Lahore, Pakistan.
HUSSAIN, M.
    2002. "Pakistan's Election 2002: An Observation," *The Nation*, 15th October,
    Lahore, Pakistan.
IDRESS, H.
    2002. "People and the Politics," *The Awaz*, October, Lahore, Pakistan.

IQBAL, J.

    2002. "Ulema As a Political Power: Destruction or Construction." Ideology of Pakistan Foundation, Lahore, Pakistan. Unpublished manuscript.

KISSANA, I.A.

    2002. "Hikmat-o-Frotni." Editorial, Lahore, Pakistan.

MEHMOOD, S.

    2002. "Religious Alliance and the Foreign Policy," *The Nation*, 20th October, Lahore, Pakistan.

MIRZA, N.

    2002. "Religious Alliance: Musharaf and America," *The Nada-e-Millat*, 14th October, Lahore, Pakistan.

MUNAWAR, Mirza.

    1998. *The Quaid*. Punjab University Press, Lahore, Pakistan.

NADEEM, K.

    2002. "A Trial for the Religious Leaders," *The Daily Jang*, 16th October, Lahore, Pakistan.

NAHEED, K.

    2002. "Fundamentalism and Civilized Muslim Society." Editorial, *The Daily Jang*, 19th October, Lahore, Pakistan.

NAQVI, A.J.

    2002. "Race for Ministry," *The Daily Nawa-i-Waqat*, 16th October, Lahore, Pakistan.

NASR, S.W.R.

    1996. *Mawdudi and the Making of Islamic Revivalism*. Oxford: Oxford University Press.

NEWS LINK.

    2002. "Anti-American Vote in the Northwest Frontier Province," 12th October, Punjab Provincial Bureau Report, Lahore, Pakistan.

NATIONAL INSTITUTE FOR POPULATION STUDIES.

    2001. "Population Growth and Its Implications." Islamabad, Pakistan.

QASMI, A.U.

    2002. "A Defeat For The Anglo Indians," *The Daily Jang*, 12th October, Lahore, Pakistan.

QURESHI, I.H.

    1972. Ulema in Politics, *MA'AREF Limited*, Karachi, Pakistan.

QURESHI, I.H.

    1974. *The Struggle for Pakistan*. Karachi: University of Karachi Press.

RASHAK, A.

    2002. "A Trial of Religious Parties," *The Daily Nawa-i-Waqat*, 19th October, Lahore, Pakistan.

REHMAN, F.U.

    2002. "Musharaf: President or the Army Chief," *The Online Bureau*, 19th October, Lahore, Pakistan.

SAEED, F.K.
   2002. "Beautiful Dreams," *The Daily Nawa-i-Waqat*, 20th October, Lahore, Pakistan.

SHUHAB, Qudrat.U.
   1989. *Shuhab Nama*. Sang-e-Mail Publications, Lahore, Pakistan.

SHEIKH, A.A.
   2002. "Religious Alliance: A Ray of Hope," *The Nation*, 20th October, Lahore, Pakistan.

SIDDIQUI, I.
   2002a. "Koza Gari," *The Daily Nawa-I-Waqat*, 14th October, Lahore, Pakistan.

SIDDIQUI, I.
   2002b. "Doubts," *The Daily Nawa-I-Waqat*, 20th October, Lahore, Pakistan.

THE DAILY NAWA-I-WAQAT.
   2002. "Musharaf Addresses the Public." Editor's note, 11th April, Lahore, Pakistan.

THE NATION.
   2002. "Musharaf Speaks." Peshawar correspondent report, 11th April, Lahore, Pakistan.

THE NEWS.
   2002. "Future of Pakistan." Staff Reporter, 11th April, Lahore, Pakistan.

TIMES MAGAZINE.
   2002. "General's Election." Reported in *The Nation*, 10th October, Lahore, Pakistan.

WARRIACH, S.
   2002. "Election 2002, Facts and Figures," *The Daily Jang*, 10th October, Lahore, Pakistan.

WOLPERT, S.
   1989. *Jinnah of Pakistan*. Oxford: Oxford University Press.

ZIA, T.
   2002. "A Request to Religious Alliance," *The Daily Nawa-i-Waqat*, 19th October, Lahore, Pakistan.

ZIKRIA, F.
   2002. Forthcoming Issue of *Newsweek*. Reported in *The Nation*, 15th October, Lahore, Pakistan.

MUSLIMS AND DEMOCRACY
AN EMPIRICAL CRITIQUE OF FUKUYAMA'S CULTURALIST APPROACH

Fares al-Braizat[*]

ABSTRACT

This paper intends to demonstrate three objectives: (1) Fukuyama's theory of the triumph of liberal democracy is cross culturally plausible at the attitudinal level; (2) Fukuyama's claim that Islam is resistant to modernity (characterized by liberal democracy and capitalism) does not hold up to empirical testing. That is, using Islam as an explanatory variable of democracy/authoritarianism is largely uncorroborated; and (3) Explore alternative explanations for the absence of democracy in most of Middle Eastern countries. The paper concludes by emphasizing the importance of Human Development and Political Opportunity Structure for the explanation of democracy/authoritarianism. The main conclusion of the paper is that Islam is largely irrelevant as an explanatory variable for authoritarianism/democracy.

Introduction

Since the nineteenth century the question of Islam and modernity has been at the heart of intellectual debates in both the "Muslim" world and the "West." Throughout this time-span three distinct but somewhat analogous strands of debates have emerged. One believes that the religion of Islam is incompatible with modern thinking and scientific rationality. The second posits the opposite view (i.e., a compatibility thesis). A third view posits that there are some elements that can be incorporated, adapted, and adopted by the Islamic world but simultaneously rejects other elements of modernity or deem them as alien. These three views have advocates both within and outside of the "Muslim" world. Their rationale to adopt a particular view may differ; Muslim advocates of the incompatibility thesis would advance their view in the name of cultural "authenticity," while Western counterparts would advance their view in the name of, for example, ethnocentricity or secularism.

Recently, Francis Fukuyama claimed that, in his view, Islam and modernity are incompatible. He argued, "there does seem to be something about Islam, or at least the fundamentalist versions of Islam that have been dominant in recent years, that makes Muslim societies particularly resistant to modernity" (Fukuyama October 11, 2001). For Fukuyama, it is institutions such as liberal democracy and capitalism that characterize modernity. The prevalence of these

* Department of Politics and International Relations, Rutherford College, University of Kent at Canterbury, Kent, CT2 7NX. U.K. The author is also an affiliated researcher to the Centre for Strategic Studies at the University of Jordan, Amman, Jordan.

two institutional systems in a given society qualifies that society as "modern" or, according to Fukuyama, as having "reached the end of history" (Fukuyama October 11, 2001). Fukuyama remains at the macro level of analysis. Accordingly, his claim will be tested at the appropriate level. Due to limitations of space, I will restrict the analysis to democracy.

Fukuyama uses Islam as a "yardstick" that offers an easy cultural essentialist explanation for the absence of democracy from most Muslim countries. In this he converges with other culturalists blaming Islam for whatever goes wrong in a Muslim country. This cultural essentialism, when empirically tested, does not seem to offer much explanation. Is there a better model that can explain the undemocratic nature of political systems in most Muslim countries, especially in the Middle East? In order to find out, we must test Fukuyama's theory in a Muslim context.

The analysis will be carried out at the macro level and will focus on democracy as one dimension of modernity. It is beyond the scope of this paper to examine other manifestations. Even democracy will be examined at the abstract level, for instance, measuring support for democracy as an ideal form government as opposed to other forms of government. The data available from the World Values Survey (WVS) and European Values Survey EVS allow for comparative analysis covering 80 percent of the world population. At the macro level, two statistical techniques are implemented. First, a correlation analysis is used to establish the strength of the relationship between the dependent variables (support for democracy, years of uninterrupted democracy) and the independent variable (religiosity with a focus on Islam). Then, regression analysis is implemented to evaluate the impact of religiosity (Fukuyama's single explanatory variable is religion), Human Development, and Political Opportunity Structures (POS) upon support for democracy. The latter is meant to measure the over-stretched state structure in the Muslim Middle East.

I argue that support for democratic ideals is universal, although the institutional state of democracy may not reach the ideal, or falls far short of it, in some societies (particularly Muslim societies). Many prominent scholars (Fukuyama 2001; Huntington 1996) have attributed this state of affairs to cultural factors. It is the aim of this paper to evaluate these claims. The data set, which consists of representative samples of each population, covers Islamic countries as varied as Arab-Islamic societies such as Jordan, Egypt, and Morocco and None-Arab Islamic societies such as Iran, Bangladesh, Indonesia, Pakistan, and Turkey. Additionally, it covers countries of Latin America, North America, South East Asia, South Asia, Western Europe, Eastern Europe, Africa, and Australia. These societies represent different cultural traditions, religions, languages, and ethnicities.

Cultural Essentialism

Reflecting on the debate that followed the tragic terrorist attacks on the United States on September 11, 2001, Fukuyama remains convinced there is "nothing else towards which we could expect to evolve but liberal democracy and capitalism" (Fukuyama October 11, 2001). This seems to be a plausible assumption. However, Fukuyama's line of argument was diluted by rival claims and counter claims, especially after September 11, such as the "Clash of Civilizations" thesis in which Huntington argues, "rather than progressing toward a single global system, the world remained mired in a 'clash of civilizations' in which six or seven major cultural groups would co-exist without converging and constitute the new fracture lines of global conflict" (Fukuyama October 11, 2001). It seems that both theories are partly right. We anticipate that the empirical evidence will show universal and overwhelming support for democracy and, at the same time, show the persistence of diverse cultural heritages and traditions in Huntington's cultural zones. But does this mean that conflicts would be driven by cultural differences? Are some cultures (in particular Islamic) resistant to democracy and its ideals, while other cultures are receptive of these ideals (Christian)?

     The danger of involvement in a conflict may come about as a result of the absence of democracy in a given society but quite certainly not of cultural differences.[1] The atrocities of September 11 committed by Muslim ultra-extremists promoted the idea of the clash of civilizations and many have taken it for granted; identifying the Islamic cultural zone in contrast with the West symbolized by the United States. Even Fukuyama himself, who advocated a single model of evolution to "modernity," has accepted a version of Muslim exceptionalism in which Islam or some versions of Islam are incompatible with modernity. By exempting Muslim societies, Fukuyama undermines the universality of his own thesis. Because liberal democracy and capitalism have universal appeal, Muslim societies should be attracted to them as any other society in the world. It is understood that if religion, in general, constitutes a hindrance to democracy, it should hold true for all religions with no exceptions. Some religions may be less restrictive than others depending on whether they have been through a major reform in modern times (e.g., Protestantism).

     But can we really reduce the whole issue to religion as the only factor? As the literature suggests, the answer is no (Rueschemeyer et al. 1992; Vanhanen 1997; Dahl 1998; Inglehart 1997). There are more factors to look at such as modernization, industrialization, urbanization, literacy, colonial legacy, international trade, international political economy (weapons and oil), interpersonal trust, well-being, secularization, social class, globalization, openness of the market, distribution of economic and intellectual resources, regional and international conflicts, nationalism, state structure, elite orientation, and state legitimacy. All of these factors play some role in determining the shape of the political system a society may have or prefer to have. The concern here is to test the impact of religiosity on support for democracy.

We can anticipate that high levels of support for democracy are to be found in societies where it has functioned properly and successfully for well over a century, for instance, Western Europe and North America. In other underdeveloped societies, democracy may have even higher levels of support because it represents the hope of the people for development, since almost all societies that embraced these democratic institutions are well-to-do societies.

Fukuyama (2001) argues,

> modernity has a cultural basis. Liberal democracy and free markets do not work everywhere. They work best in societies with certain values whose origins may not be entirely rational. It is not an accident that modern liberal democracy emerged first in the Christian west, since the universalism of democratic rights can be seen as a secular form of Christian universalism. (Fukuyama October 11, 2001).

Modernity may have cultural bases but what are they? Is it religious cultural heritage that makes democracy attainable in one society and unattainable in another? Fukuyama seems to implicitly acquiesce that the religion of Islam cannot accommodate modernity. Clearly, this cultural essentialism requires examination. Because cultural values are epiphenomena, a more comprehensive test is required. For example, high religiosity is more likely to be found in less developed societies, while more aesthetic values are more likely to be found in rich and developed societies (Inglehart 1990, 1997). Therefore, levels of development largely condition both sets of values. In addition to the impact of socioeconomic modernization, the institutional structures of states contribute to understanding how a given country could have 90 percent of its population supporting the ideals of democracy and yet not be a democracy.

Equating universalism of democratic rights to Christian universalism seems to be an oversimplification. For all democratic states today are more or less secular. Moreover, the introduction of Christianity to Africa did not bring about Liberal democracies. Further, if one equates the universalism of democratic rights to Christian universalism, why did Central and Eastern Europe, Russia and Latin America not develop liberal democracies and capitalist free-market economy simultaneously with Western Europe? Instead they developed systems of an opposite nature: political authoritarianism and economic communism as opposed to democracy and free markets. Fukuyama's cultural yardstick of "Christian universalism" does not account for Japan's (Confucian) democracy and free market. Catholic Christian societies are different from the protestant Christian societies. They have different patterns of development and have experienced similar circumstances to some Islamic, Buddhist, Orthodox Christian, and Confucian societies. The fortunes of democracy in many of these societies explicitly indicate that there is more to the story than religion and cultural tradition.

Fukuyama (1992) posits,

> there have been pressures for greater democracy in various Middle Eastern coun-
> tries like Egypt and Jordan, following the Eastern European revolutions of 1989.
> But in this part of the world [the Middle East], *Islam has stood as a major bar-
> rier to democratization.* As demonstrated by the Algerian municipal elections of
> 1990, or by Iran a decade earlier, greater democracy may not lead to greater lib-
> eralization because it brings to power Islamic fundamentalists hoping to establish
> some form of popular theocracy. (P. 347; emphasis added)

Clearly, Fukuyama adopts and promotes a cultural essentialist argument.
By emphasizing Islam as *the* obstacle, he underestimates, if not ignores, the
dynamics of political processes within which "political Islam"[2] functions. Also,
the same process can explain support for liberal democracy.

As Katerina Dalacoura (1998) forcefully argues,

> if liberalism and Islamic Liberalism are bound together in Middle Eastern soci-
> eties, the implication is that secularism is not an essential requirement for liber-
> alism. The input of Islamic liberalism in political culture would not be authori-
> tarian, although it would undoubtedly be conservative, as in the case of Christian
> Democratic parties in the European experience. (P. 192)

Using Islam as a yardstick to justify (by rulers of the region) and explain
(by theorists in the West) the absence of democratic political practice at the macro
level in the Middle East is undoubtedly not without misconception and serious
oversimplification. Political actors, whether individuals, political parties, elites,
mass social movements, or governments, constitute essential instruments in the
understanding of why democracy has not yet fully developed in the Muslim
Middle East.

Given the weakness of cultural explanations in general, and Fukuyama's
in particular, I think there are two other theories that better explain the absence of
democracy in the Muslim Middle East: the structures of political opportunities
available to political actors within and without the "modern nation states" and the
levels of socioeconomic development. In the following section, I expound some
of the factors that contribute to the continuity of authoritarian regimes in the Arab
Middle East and further explore the extent to which the religion of Islam has been
employed to justify completely opposite political ends.

Strategic Rent as an Obstacle to Democratization

At the international level some political regimes in the Muslim Arab Middle East
have greatly benefited from strategic rent-seeking throughout the cold war peri-

od. After the end of the cold war, democratization swept the then undemocratic countries and it was thought that the stagnant authoritarian regimes of the Middle East would follow suit. Alas, stagnation continued to be the dominant feature of politics and oppression went on. The international political environment, which made the transitions of East European countries possible, stopped at the environs of the Muslim world. Not surprisingly, the capitalist liberal democracy of the United States, while encouraging democracy in Eastern Europe, supported and legitimated dictatorial regimes like Saudi Arabia, Egypt, the Gulf states, Jordan and Iran under the Shah, to secure its interests.[3] Such regimes have felt relatively secure and thus did not seem to have to change their political outlook. Therefore, these regimes have implemented severe political oppression over many decades resulting in the creation of two generations of a frightened public that cannot even think about political participation without thinking about the severe consequences that such action ultimately entails under authoritarian regimes. Measures like passport confiscation, job dismissal, and imprisonment without trial (let alone a fair one) proved very effective to prevent citizens from political involvement.

Furthermore, in the name of Islam, the Saudi political regime has been suppressing the political aspirations of its people.[4] The pretext of "Islam" also played into the hands of some of the American administrations advisors until today. In contrast to the Saudis, Iran, under an "Islamic" regime, has experienced political participation and the Iranian transition to reform the system under president Khatami is paving the way to a more democratic Iran.[5] Time and again, in Egypt "the [regime] has sought to promote itself as the guardian of true legitimacy, the correct alternative to excess Islamist zeal" (Ghazaleh December 27, 2001). These regimes embraced the events of September 11 as a new pretext for rent-seeking and the continuation of authoritarianism. A year later, Condoleezza Rice, speaking on behalf of the American administration, made it clear that the United States is serious about democratizing the regimes in the Muslim world.[6] These events changed the American administration commitment to support authoritarian regimes in the Middle East. The Egyptian Foreign Minister, Ahmad Maher responded to Rice's comments by saying "the Arab and Islamic World knows its way ahead and we do not need lessons from anybody" (*Al-Ahram* September 25, 2002). Maher is not an elected official to speak on behalf of the "Arab and Islamic World." Such comments reflect the threats which these authoritarian regimes may encounter in the near future. Because of these threats, they will defy all calls for democracy by invoking "cultural particularity" and "national sovereignty."[7]

Ironically, following the introduction of Military Courts in the United States to try terrorists, President Hosni Mubarak, in an interview with the state-run daily *Al Gumhurriya*, referred to new anti-terror measures in Britain and America as proof that military trials and other emergency measures in place in Egypt for the past 20 years were always the "right" policy.[8] Regimes like in Saudi Arabia and Egypt are pointing to the alternative, stating that if they were not in power, Islamic extremists would be the alternative. Thus, such regimes have found

new ways to seek political rent and increase their grip on power under the security justification. Similarly, the French/American backed Algerian army stepped in
on January 12, 1992, disregarding the majority of voters, and prevented the *Front
Islamique du Salut* (FIS) from enjoying its electoral victory.[9] As a result of the
"extreme measures"(Kenioua 2002) taken by the military, a civil war erupted and
claimed thousands of lives[10] and democracy was swept away. Thus the political
opportunities available to would-be political actors, whether Islamists or otherwise, were very minimal. Such closed political systems to opposition constitute a
major barrier to democracy. In this process, Islam is exploited to either legitimize
a regime (Saudi Arabia) or justify the existence of a regime as the guardian of the
"modern state" against the Islamists (Egypt and Algeria).

To illustrate this point further, Fareed Zakaria (2001) states

> it is always the same splendid setting—and the same sad story. A senior
> American diplomat enters one the grand presidential palaces . . . from which
> president Hosni Mubarak rules over Egypt . . . Then the American gently raises
> the issue of human rights and suggests that Egypt's government might ease up on
> political dissent, allow more press freedoms and stop jailing intellectuals.
> Mubarak tenses up and snaps, 'If I were to do what you ask, the fundamentalists
> will take over Egypt. Is that what you want?' The diplomat demurs and the con-
> versation moves back to the last twist in the peace process. (Pp. 24-29)

Egypt is not the only country in the Middle East that uses such discourse. The
Palestinian authority uses this discourse too.

Again Zakaria (2001) notes:

> When President Bill Clinton urged Yasir Arafat to sign on the Camp David peace
> plan[11] in July 2001, Arafat is reported to have responded with words to the effect,
> 'If I do what you want, Hamas will be in power tomorrow.' The Saudi monarchy's
> most articulate spokesman, Prince Bandar bin Sultan, often reminds American
> officials that if they press his government too hard, the likely alternative to the
> regime in not Jeffersonian democracy but Islamic theocracy. (Pp. 24-29; footnote
> added)

In Tunisia, too, Bin Ali has exploited the "Islamist threat" to justify his authoritarian rule (Sadiki 2002:68). In Jordan, on August 15, 2002, the king postponed
the elections until spring 2003 citing "regional circumstances" as an obstacle.[12]
Ironically, on August 20 (5 days later) the PM of Jordan said, "difficult regional
circumstances must not hamper Kingdom's reforms."[13] The PM's words are
understood as including political reform (*Jordan Times* 2002). [14]

Therefore, the deformed state structure in the Middle East, and current
political regimes' fear of radical and moderate political Islam, make the introduction of democratic politics a risky game for these regimes. In Egypt, democratic

parliamentary elections are, to a great extent, manipulated by the regime.[15] Moderate Islamic activists who wanted to be part of the political process and participate in decision-making were not allowed to freely run for seats in the last elections of 2000.[16] The security forces detained many of them. The moderate Islamic parties in Jordan and Morocco have participated in elections and gained parliamentary seats. For example, the Islamic brotherhood movement in Jordan participated in the cabinet by holding five ministerial offices in 1990 to 1991. They won 22 out of 80 seats in the 1989 parliamentary elections and 16 out of 80 in the 1993 elections. In 1997 they boycotted the general elections because they thought the government was trying to undermine them by introducing a new electoral system, which was designed (according to the Islamic Action Front Party, IAFP) to reduce their chances of acquiring more seats in the parliament. In January 2002, the IAFP conference was held in an atmosphere where the moderate members' opinion prevailed by electing a moderate leadership that is expected to lead the party to participate in the upcoming general elections scheduled for spring of 2003.[17]

The apparent pattern of behavior of the regimes in many Arab Middle Eastern countries is that they use a democratic discourse to justify undemocratic practices. For example, when they talk about Islamic radicalism as the likely alternative to themselves, one would understand that they have a good sense of what their people want. If this is the case, why do these regimes need to torture and imprison many of their political opponents? They do everything possible in order to stay in power. "These men fear a public that they barely know," as one commentator has stated (Zakaria 2001:29). The practices of these regimes are the main reason why democratic aspirations in the peoples of the Middle East are not transformed to democratic institutions. One may ask why the peoples of the Middle East do not take action to force the regimes to democratize? There are many important reasons. One important reason is the well-spread fear of authorities. To be sure, 79 percent of the Jordanian population reported that they couldn't criticize the government verbally without fearing economic security and governmental punishment. Moreover, three quarters could not take part in peaceful political activities (i.e., authorized demonstrations) for the same reasons (Center for Strategic Studies 2002). This evidence suggests that there is more to the story than just culture/religion. In order to evaluate the role of culture, we will examine Fukuyama's argument in the following analysis.

Testing Fukuyama's Theory

Methodology: Variables and Descriptive Analysis

1. The dependent variables for comparative analysis

    Indicator 1: preference for a democratic political system[18]

    I'm going to describe various types of political systems and ask what you think about each as a way of governing this country. For each one, would you say it is a very good, fairly good, fairly bad, or very bad way of governing this country? *Having a democratic political system.*

For this variable I am using the percentage of people in each country that reported "very good."

Indicator 2: democracy is better than any other form of government

I'm going to read off some things that people sometimes say about a democratic political system. Could you please tell me if you agree strongly, agree, disagree or disagree strongly, after I read each of them? *Democracy may have some problems but it's better than any other form of government.*

For this variable I am using the percentage of people in each country who agreed or strongly agreed.

The third indicator (below) spells out support for authoritarian political system characterized by support for undemocratic strong head of government.

Indicator 3: preference for a strong head of government who does not have to bother with parliament and elections

I'm going to describe various types of political systems and ask what you think about each as a way of governing this country. For each one, would you say it is a very good, fairly good, fairly bad, or very bad way of governing this country? *Having a strong head of government who does not have to bother with parliament and elections.*

For this variable I am using the percentage of people in each country who reported very good or good.

2. The independent variable for comparative analysis

Religiosity

Independently of whether you go to religious services or not, would you say you are...

1. A religious person

2. Not a religious person

3. A convinced atheist

For this variable I am using the percentage of people in each country that described themselves as religious people.

Comparative Analysis

Democracy has several cultural qualities that enable a democratic political system to work once it kicks off. Interpersonal trust is one such qualities (see, for example, Warren 1999; Fukuyama 1995; Putnam 1993). Fukuyama argues that a cultural heritage of low trust positions a society at a competitive disadvantage in global markets because it is less able to develop large and complex social institutions (Fukuyama 1995). Have societies with low levels of interpersonal trust been less able to develop such institutions? Is there a religious/cultural context that determines low or high levels of interpersonal trust, which defines the ability of a given nation to build modern institutions? It is imperative to examine Fukuyama's claim in different religious contexts to determine whether Islam, in particular, is *the obstacle* to modernity and its institutions.

The empirical data available suggest that Islamic societies are *unexceptional* to other societies as far as interpersonal trust is concerned. They do show relatively low levels of interpersonal trust. For example, on interpersonal trust, Turkey scores 19 percent, Bangladesh 23.3 percent, Morocco 21.7 percent, Jordan 27 percent, Egypt 37.5 percent, and Iran 55.4 percent. Denmark, Sweden, and Norway are the only countries (for which data are available) that have higher values on interpersonal trust than Iran. Yet, Turkey and Pakistan score higher than the Catholic Brazil, Argentina, Peru, Philippines, Zimbabwe, Poland, Colombia, Venezuela, Georgia, and Romania. Moreover, Islamic Jordan scores almost as high as the predominantly Protestant U.K. (30 percent) and higher than the Roman Catholic France, Poland, Hungary, Chile, Romania, and Orthodox Russia. The point is that interpersonal trust as a necessary value for capitalist development and free market economy theoretically holds a similar value for democratic development, because democratic development is linked to capitalist development (Rueschemeyer et al. 1992). Thus, the relationship between democracy, interpersonal trust, and capitalist development is reciprocal (Inglehart 1997). Nonetheless, interpersonal trust is contextual, for instance, it is influenced by societal context and particularly by the level of socioeconomic development in a given society (Inglehart 1999). The aforementioned examples suggest that it is misleading to attribute capitalist and democratic development exclusively (as Fukuyama seems to do) to levels of interpersonal trust.

However, support for democracy (democracy is better than any other form of government) is very high in Islamic societies: Bangladesh (98 percent), Jordan (89 percent), Turkey (88 percent), compared to the U.K. (78 percent), (United States 87 percent), and Canada (87 percent). Furthermore, it seems that only predominantly protestant societies (W. Germany, Denmark, Finland, Norway, Netherlands, and Sweden) and Confucian societies (Japan) score highest on trust and support for democracy. Predominantly Islamic, Catholic, Orthodox, and ex-communist societies show similar levels of interpersonal trust and are very supportive of democracy although not as high as Protestant and Confucian societies.

Thus, Fukuyama's essentialist cultural sweeping generalization about Islamic societies as resistant to modernity is largely unfounded as far as support for democracy and interpersonal trust (a democratic quality) are concerned.

Approached from a different angle, support for authoritarian leadership correlates negatively and significantly with interpersonal trust ($r = -.331$). Support for "a rule by strong leader who does not have to bother with parliament and elections" tends to correlate with low levels of interpersonal trust. Low levels of interpersonal trust tend to correlate with authoritarian orientations, while societies that demonstrate high levels of interpersonal trust tend to be significantly less supportive of authoritarian leadership. For example, Brazil has a value of 3 percent on trust and 61 percent on authoritarianism, Macedonia has 8 percent and 62 percent, Philippines: 9 percent and 63 percent; Romania: 19 percent and 67 percent; Pakistan: 19 percent and 62 percent; India: 39 percent and 59 percent; Turkey: 19 percent and 72 percent, respectively. However, there is a huge gap between Islamic countries on authoritarianism: with Turkey topping the list with a value of 72 percent, Pakistan: 62 percent; Jordan: 41 percent; Iran: 39 percent; Indonesia: 19 percent; Morocco: 18 percent; Bangladesh: 12 percent; Egypt and Azerbaijan: 7 percent each. This signifies the meager relevance of cultural tradition, including interpersonal trust as a cultural trait, as a single explanatory variable in attempting to understand authoritarian orientations. The evidence suggests that authoritarianism is an irreducibly complex phenomenon that cannot be explained by reference to a religio-cultural tradition. If religious tradition explains authoritarian orientations, the Islamic countries included in the sample would have scored identical values and this should hold true for other religious traditions as well. Since this is not the case, we can make a strong point against cultural explanations and suggest alternative ways of understanding authoritarianism (For more examples, see Table 1).

The empirical data sketched above suggest that support for authoritarianism is not necessarily tied to a particular religion or culture whether Islamic, Christian, or Confucian. Remarkably, all societies that score high on authoritarianism and low on trust are not ranked as highly developed societies according to the UNDP's Human Development Index (HDI), 2000. Whereas, with the exception of Bangladesh (low HDI) and Azerbaijan and Egypt (Medium HDI), almost all societies with high values on trust and low on authoritarian orientations are developed societies and yet they *do not* share a similar historical or cultural background. Looking at societies with above 50 percent value on interpersonal trust, we observe that they are (in descending order) predominantly Protestant Christian (Norway, Sweden, Denmark), Islamic (Iran), again Protestant (Netherlands), and then predominantly Confucian (China). Moreover, five Islamic countries are among the highest 25 countries on authoritarianism and five Islamic countries are among the lowest 25 countries on authoritarianism. Hence, is China more culturally fertile for democratization than Islamic Iran or Egypt? If Egypt and India have similar values on trust, why is India a democracy while Egypt is not, although both countries are ranked at a medium human development? The answer, perhaps, lies in examining the political process and regime strategies among a host of other factors. Table 1 shows that low values of support for authoritarianism are to be found cross-culturally, with Islamic Azerbaijan and Egypt scoring the second lowest values after Tanzania. The evidence largely supports the conclusion that neither interpersonal trust nor authoritarianism are culture-specific phenomena. By and large, high levels of interpersonal trust seem to be associated with high levels of human development, while authoritarianism is determined by other factors such as the political context, whether nationally or internationally. So far, I have not examined the direct link, if any, between religion (Islam in particular) and support for democracy as such. To this we must now turn.

Table 1. Authoritarianism and Interpersonal Trust

Authoritarian Leadership is very good or good %						Most people can be trusted %	
Vietnam	99	Jordan	41	Sweden	21	Norway	65
Turkey	72	Taiwan	41	New Zealand	20	Sweden	64
Romania	67	Belarus	41	Slovakia	20	Denmark	58
Philippines	63	Iran	39	Hungary	20	Iran	55
Pakistan	62	Peru	39	Serbia	19	Netherlands	54
Macedonia	62	S. Africa	37	Indonesia	19	China	53
Georgia	61	Fracne	35	N. Ireland	19	New Zealand	49
Brazil	61	Puerto Rico	33	Spain	19	Finland	49
India	59	Belgium	32	Estonia	19	Ireland	47
El Selvador	59	Uganda	31	China	19	Indonesia	46
Ukraine	59	USA	30	Morocco	18	Iceland	44
Latvia	58	Switzerland	29	Czech Republic	17	N. Ireland	44
Moldova	57	S.Korea	28	Italy	16	W. Germany	42
Lithuania	54	Japan	28	Austria	16	Taiwan	42
Mexico	54	Dominican R.	28	Montenegro	15	Basque Country	41
Bosnia	53	Netherlands	27	Norway	14	Australia	40
Armenia	53	Ireland	27	Denmark	14	Japan	40
Colombia	53	Zimbabwe	27	W. Germany	13	India	39
Russia	49	UK	26	Bangladesh	12	Vietnam	39
Venezuela	48	Finland	25	Iceland	11	Egypt	38
Bulgaria	45	Australia	25	Croatia	11	Switzerland	37
Chile	43	Slovenia	24	Greece	9	Canada	37
Albania	43	Canada	24	Egypt	7	USA	36
Nigeria	43	E. Germany	23	Azerbaijan	7	Belgium	34
Argentina	42	Poland	22	Tanzania	3	Montenegro	33

Religiosity and Support for Democracy as an Ideal Form of Government

1) Democratic political system (DPS) is a "very good" way of governing this "country"

This indicator differs from the next one and therefore has been independently analyzed. It differs in the sense that only people who reported that a democratic political system is a very good way of governing their country were included. This gives us slightly polarized attitudes, that is, only people who firmly believe that DPS is a very good way of governing their country. For example, Russia has a value of 8 percent on this indicator. If we add it up to the percent of Russians who reported good, the percent will be 62 percent. Nigeria is an interesting case in this context; on the next indicator (democracy better than any other form of government) the sum of very good and good was the lowest among all societies included, while on the DPS indicator the percent of Nigerians that reported DPS is a very good way of governing Nigeria is among the highest. This suggests that for 45 percent of Nigerians, democracy is not the best form of government, but nonetheless for 73 percent of them, DPS is a very good way of governing Nigeria.[19]

The correlation between support for DPS as a very good way of governance and religiosity is insignificant although slightly positive. Predominantly Islamic societies show very high levels of support for DPS as a very good way of governing their countries, while simultaneously showing high levels of religiosity. Although Egypt is the most religious Islamic society (98 percent of Egyptians identify themselves as religious people), it scores 40 percent higher than the most religious predominantly Catholic society (Poland) on support for DPS as a very good way of governance. None of the Islamic societies fall beneath 40 percent, while the majority of societies under 40 percent are Christian: Catholic, Roman Catholic, and Orthodox but not Protestant. Furthermore, the highest scoring country is Morocco (84 percent). Some Islamic countries score as high as the United States, France, and the Netherlands. Among the 16 countries that have percentage scores between 49 and 52, Turkey scores at 49 percent, Jordan at 51 percent, and Iran at 52 percent sharing similar percentage values with Netherlands at 49 percent, the United States at 51 percent, India at 52 percent, and Canada, Australia, and France at 52 percent each. Albania, a country where 65 to 70 percent of its population is Muslim and 20 to 30 percent Christian Orthodox and Catholic, shows a very high value on this indicator (Annual Report on International Religious Freedom 2001). However, a cluster of four ex-communist countries (Russia, Estonia, Latvia, and Ukraine) can be spotted as the least scoring on support for DPS as a very good way of governance. Moreover, Muslim countries like Bangladesh, Egypt, and Morocco share a similar value with Christian countries like Iceland, Norway, and Sweden. Thus, people in Islamic societies tend to have a propensity towards democracy but what makes it less possible for them to achieve democratic political governance is the nature of the over stated, over blown and over stretched[20] state structure and the heavy-handed authoritarian regimes (in most cases) in power at present. Therefore, current political regimes in most of the Muslim world are lagging behind popular expectation not only, as we have seen, on the political front but also on the economic front. Yet again, Fukuyama's claim about Islam as resistant to democracy, to put it mildly, is seriously challenged.

Figure 1.
Correlation between Support for Democratic Political System and Religiosity

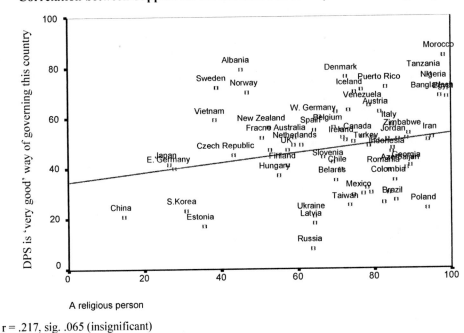

r = .217, sig. .065 (insignificant)

2) Democracy better than any other form of government (percent agreed)

The overall trend in the relationship between religiosity and support for democracy is negative and insignificant. By and large, Islamic societies (Bangladesh, Turkey, Morocco, Egypt, and Jordan) are not unique in showing high levels of support for democracy simultaneously with high levels of religiosity. These Islamic societies share these attitudes with Catholic, Protestant, and Orthodox societies like Poland, Venezuela, Italy, the United States, Georgia, Lithuania, Hindu/Muslim India, and Confucian Japan. Societies like Japan, East Germany, and Sweden are the least religious and among the most supportive of democracy. However, support for democracy tends to marginally and insignificantly decrease simultaneously with increases in religiosity. This relationship does not apply to all countries; there are exceptional cases deviating from the norm due to a unique set of factors pertinent to them. For example, the United States has a value of 83 percent on religiosity and 87 percent on support for democracy, Nigeria 97 percent and 45 percent, respectively. Generally, as we found that high support for democracy is a cross-cultural phenomenon, lower levels of support for democracy are also cross-cultural and were found in Orthodox and Catholic Christian societies like Russia, Moldova, Armenia, Macedonia, and Romania; and Islamic countries like Iran and Indonesia. Nonetheless, with the exception of Nigeria none of the 74 countries in the sample analyzed has recorded below 62 percent (Russia) on support for democracy. This evidence overwhelmingly endorse Fukuyama's thesis of universal support for democracy. However, his other claim is unfounded. That is, had Fukuyama been right about Islam as a hindrance to democracy, the Islamic societies would have been grouped near the right corner at the bottom of figure 2 (below) indicating that because they are Islamic and have high religiosity, Islam is, therefore, very unsupportive of democracy. A glance at the scatterplot leaves us with the observation that Islamic societies are roughly clustered at the top right corner (Egypt, Morocco, Bangladesh, Azerbaijan, Jordan, Turkey) meaning they are very religious and simultaneously very supportive of democracy. Yet again the evidence do not support Fukuyama's claim.

Figure 2.
Correlation between Support for Democracy and Religiosity

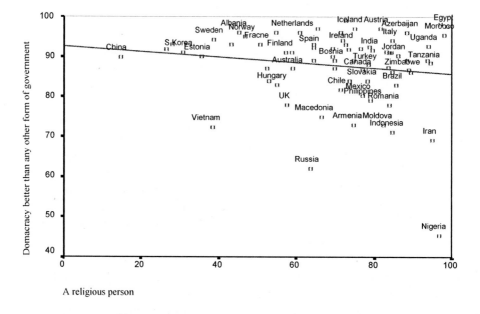

A religious person

r= -.146 sig. .220 (insignificant)

3) Religiosity and support for authoritarianism; support a strong leader who does not have to bother with parliament and elections (very good + good) way of governing this "country" (see Figure 3 below).

The previous two indicators directly address support for democracy. In order to validate these indicators and establish whether support for democracy is qualified by rejection of its alternatives, we need to examine the relationship between religiosity and authoritarianism. By and large, religiosity is positively correlated (r =

.040) with authoritarianism, though insignificantly. However, it has a lot to say about the relationship between Islam and authoritarianism. Two major Islamic countries (Egypt and Turkey) represent extreme cases; Turkey with a value of 72 percent is the second highest and Egypt, along with Azerbaijan, are the second lowest on authoritarianism with a value of 7 percent. Moreover, other Islamic countries (Morocco, Bangladesh, and Indonesia) show very low levels of support of authoritarianism along with Denmark, Norway, Tanzania, Austria, Iceland, Sweden, and West Germany. The cases of Egypt and Turkey, perhaps, could be partly explained by the experiences that these two countries went through. The Turkish "want another Kemal Atatürk" according to a Turkish political scientist.[21] The Egyptians, perhaps, do not want another Naser, Sadat, or Mubarak. All of them were strong authoritarian leaders, but the Egyptian leaders have failed to deliver the modernization, though unpretentious, that Ataturk managed to deliver to Turkey. The predominantly Hindu India,[22] the largest democracy in the world, is quite high in support for authoritarian leadership. Bangladesh[23] and Azerbaijan[24] are also very low on authoritarianism with a value of 12 percent and 7 percent, respectively. The Jordanian case with a value of 42 percent on authoritarianism is not very surprising. The image of the late King Hussein (died 1999) as a strong leader who managed to survive all the political turbulence of the Middle East for 47 years of rule, undoubtedly has a huge impact on two generations of the Jordanian public that were brought up under his rule. Islamic Iran with a value of 39 percent on authoritarianism is no exception to the Christian Catholic Peru (39 percent), Christian mixed South Africa (37 percent), predominantly Roman Catholic France (35 percent), Orthodox/Catholic Belarus (41 percent), or Confucian Taiwan (41 percent). However, the dispersion of Islamic societies on authoritarianism indisputably defies the cultural essentialist proposition that Islam, as a belief system, makes its followers prone to authoritarian values.

Taken as a whole, authoritarianism correlates positively though insignificantly with religiosity. These data suggest that with high levels of religiosity, it is more likely that we will find stronger support for authoritarian orientations. At the aggregate level Protestant and Confucian societies seem to have relatively low values on authoritarian orientations. But they are unexceptional; they share similar values with developed and developing countries from Catholic, Orthodox, and Islamic traditions. Table 2 below lists all societies that have reported more than 50 percent of support for authoritarian leadership; it shows that these societies differ sharply in their cultural heritage, political history, and socioeconomic development.

Nevertheless, with the exception of Pakistan and Lithuania (in bold), which have low and high human development respectively, all other societies fall in the category of medium human development. Only two Muslim societies appear on the list of societies with high and relatively high support for authoritarianism compared to thirteen Christian countries. This neither suggests that Christianity and Islam have a propensity towards authoritarianism, nor does it endorse the claim that a particular religion is the reason to blame for the absence of democracy or presence of authoritarian rule in a given society. It does, however, suggest that there is more to explore than just a religious tradition to understand authoritarian orientations. One can safely conclude, even by the criteria of authoritarianism, that there is enough empirical evidence to suggest that Fukuyama's claims about Islam as resistant to democracy, and by implication Islam as being prone to authoritarianism, are largely unfounded. It is evident that cultural generalizations, unless seriously examined and thoroughly operationalized, do not offer much to the understanding of socio-political phenomenon like democracy or authoritarianism. Fukuyama, like many other orientalists, has rightly used evidence from the Middle East today (no Islamic country can be counted as a democracy but Turkey) to support his sweeping generalization about the culture of Islam as being anti-democratic. He, like many others, has failed to address the serious issues involved in such a state of affairs in the Islamic Middle East (mainly capitalist interests in oil and weapons trade). The evidence is conspicuous to those with minimum interest in world affairs as they are to the "experts" on the Middle East. The United States' unqualified support to oppressive regimes like Saudi Arabia and Egypt is an unambiguous substantiation.

Table 2. Authoritarian Leadership and Human Development

Country[1]	% of people who are pro authoritarian leadership	Human development index HDI ranking Out of 162 countries included*
Vietnam	99	101
Turkey	72	82
Romania	67	58
Philippines	63	70
Macedonia	62	60
Pakistan	62	127
Brazil	61	69
Georgia	61	76
India	59	115
El Salvador	59	95
Ukraine	59	74
Latvia	58	50
Moldova	57	98
Lithuania	54	47
Mexico	54	51
Armenia	53	72
Colombia	53	62

*High HDI = 1 - 48, Medium HDI = 49 - 126, Low HDI =127 - 162.
[1] Turkey: 99% Muslim; Philippines: 85% Roman Catholic, other Christian denominations constitute about 8.7%, and 4.6% are Muslims; India: 82.4% Hindu and 12% Muslim; Romania: 86.8% Romanian Orthodox Church; Pakistan: 95% Muslim; Macedonia: nominally about 66% of the population are Macedonian Orthodox, about 30% are Muslim, about 1% are Roman Catholic, and about 3% are of other faiths (largely various Protestant denominations); Brazil: 75% Roman Catholic, roughly 20% Protestants; Georgia: 75% Georgian Orthodox Church, 5% Muslim, 1% Jewish, and the remaining belong to other Christian Churches; Ukraine: predominantly Christian 99% and a small but insignificant population are Muslim and Jewish. El Salvador: 90% Catholic; Latvia: well above 90% Christian; Moldova: over 90% Orthodox Christian; Mexico: over 90% Catholic; Lithuania: over 90% Christian; Armenia: over 90% Christian; Colombia: approximately 90% Catholic Christian; see http://www.uscirf.gov/dos01Pages/irf_colombia.php3.

Figure 3. Correlation Between Religiosity And Authoritarianism

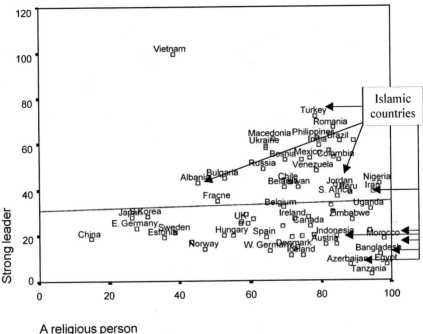

r= .040 sig. 0.741 (insignificant)

Alternative Explanations

As religiosity has been shown to be an insignificant variable in explaining author-itarianism, we must explore other variables that could better explain a propensity for authoritarianism. Religiosity may contribute to the formation of authoritarian ideologies, but its role is insignificant. Human development seems to give a much better explanation. The bivariate correlation between the Human Development Index and support for a strong leader reveals a negative correlation (-.220). The pattern observed in the correlation analysis below points to two main themes per-tinent to the relationship between human development and authoritarianism. First, high human development represents a sharp contrast with authoritarianism. Second, authoritarianism tends to present some association with low and medium human development. The first pattern is best demonstrated by a cloud of countries concentrated at the bottom right corner of Figure 4 (below) representing highly developed societies with *overall* low levels of support for authoritarianism. In other words, none of the highly developed societies demonstrate medium or high support for authoritarianism. In relative contrast to this, we found that societies with low (India and Pakistan) and medium human development (Turkey, Romania, Philippines, Georgia, Ukraine, Moldova, Latvia, and Macedonia) tend to possess a propensity towards authoritarianism. However, there are exceptions to this. Muslim societies like Egypt, Azerbaijan, and Bangladesh, are among the least supportive of authoritarianism. In sum, high levels of development play an important role in determining the political values of a given society. Religiosity, although correlates positively and insignificantly with authoritarianism does not account for a substantial amount of variation in authoritarianism.

Figure 4. Correlation between Strong Leadership and HDI

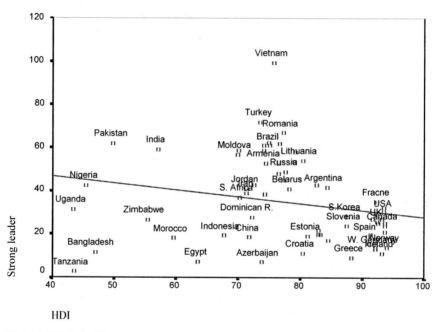

r= 0.220 sig. 0.072 (insignificant)

Multivariate Analysis

In order to determine the impact of the independent variables on support for democracy, I will introduce two analytical regression models:

> **Model 1**: The *dependent variable* is support for democracy (democracy better than any other form of government). The *independent variables* are: (1) years of uninterrupted democracy; (2) human development index (HDI); (3) religiosity; (4) Islamic countries (dummy variable).
>
> **Model 2**: The *dependent variable* is years of uninterrupted democracy. The *independent variables* are: (1) HDI; (2) religiosity; (3) Islamic countries (dummy variable).

Model 1 aims at explaining what is the most important factor that determines support for democracy as an ideal form of government among the explanatory variables utilized. Model 2 aims at explaining the continuity of democracy, for instance, what is the most important factor in sustaining democracy amongst the variables employed in the model.

It is important to make clear that there are many other variables that should be used to explain the durability of democracy, but what I am concerned with now is the impact of development, religion, and political opportunity structures.

Hypothesis 1: Human development is more important than any other factor in explaining support for and durability of democracy.

Hypothesis 2: If a country is Islamic, the likelihood of support for democracy among its citizens is very high, but the political system of that country does not allow this support to manifest in democratic political order. High public support and closed political systems do live together because the political opportunities available within the political system are very minimal; to the extent that they cannot be exploited to change the existing system or democratize it.

Before testing the hypotheses, I must introduce a correlation matrix to show the strength of the relationship between these variables. The correlations in Table 3 reveals that the dependent variable (years of uninterrupted democracy) correlates best and highest with the HDI and correlates negatively with religiosity; in both the correlations are significant. Moreover, years of uninterrupted democracy correlates positively but weakly with Islamic countries. Support for democracy is more likely to be associated with increasing levels of human development. Democracy is more likely to be institutionalized as levels of development increase. Religiosity is likely to hinder democracy and a country being Muslim does not seem to hinder support for democracy, but it surely correlates negatively and significantly with years of uninterrupted democracy. Obviously, given that none of the Islamic countries have had a continuous democratic experience, we should expect a significantly negative correlation between the variables: "Islamic countries" and "years of uninterrupted/continuous democracy." What is remarkable, however, is the strong negative correlation between religiosity and human development. It reinforces one of the basic premises of modernization theory: religiosity is basic to traditional societies. Religiosity correlates positively and insignificantly with support for authoritarianism. If we look at the relationship between support for authoritarianism and all other variables in the correlation matrix above, we observe that support for authoritarianism does not coincide with

Table 3.
Pearson Correlation (pair wise exclusion of missing values)

	HDI	Democracy better than any other form of government	A religious person	Islamic countries	Years of continuous democracy 1920-2000	Strong leader (Authoritarianism)
HDI	1	.295*	-.519**	-.400**	.708**	-.220
N=	81	67	68	81	74	68
Democracy better than any other form of government	.295*	1	-.146	.055	.302*	-.485**
N=	67	74	72	74	68	73
A religious person	-.519**	-.146	1	.316**	-.269*	.040
N=	68	72	81	81	69	72
Islamic countries	-.400**	.055	.316**	1	-.321**	-.121
N=	81	74	81	97	79	75
Years of continuous democracy 1920-2000	.708**	.302*	-.269*	-.321**	1	-.376**
N=	.000	.012	.026	.004	.	.001
Strong leader (Authoritarianism)	-.220	-.485**	.040	-.121	-.376**	1
N=	68	73	72	75	69	75

* Correlation is significant at the 0.05 level (2-tailed).
* Correlation is significant at the 0.01 level (2-tailed).

support for democracy; it is the second strongest significant negative correlation in the matrix. This validates further the reliability of the variables used to measure support for democracy. Religiosity is more likely to hinder support for democracy although the correlation between authoritarianism and religiosity is weak, it is still positive. However, we are quite sure that religiosity is very likely to coincide with human underdevelopment; the strongest negative and significant correlation in the matrix above is between HDI and religiosity. A plausible argument is to recite the classical modernization theory assumption that religiosity is more likely to be found in less developed societies. This is relevant because democracy constitutes part of human development/modernization (Welzel, Inglehart, and Klingemann 2001). Democratic tradition is more likely to be found in developed societies and developed and democratic societies are more likely to be less religious and largely less supportive of authoritarianism.

Testing the Regression Models

Model 1: R=46.4; R square=21.5

The regression analysis in Table 4 reveals that the most important variable in Model 1 is HDI with a standardized coefficient Beta of .437 and t-value of 2.125, while religiosity is an irrelevant variable in explaining support for democracy.

The second important variable in explaining support for democracy is if a country is predominantly Muslim with a standardized coefficient Beta of .371 and t-value of 2.583. However, what is noticeable in this model is the irrelevance of the impact of years of uninterrupted democracy on support for democracy. It was expected that democratic tradition would be important in that respect. Although support for democracy is strong in Islamic societies, they have not experienced open political systems whereby opposition groups can take part in the political process. This analysis points to the weakness of the cultural essentialist argument, which mainly blames the culture of the religion of Islam for whatever goes wrong in the Middle East and attributes the unrealized fortunes of democracy in the Middle East to Islamic mentality, political culture, belief system, and teachings. These components of Islam as cultural variables may help explain (to a very small

Table 4, Model 1.
Coefficients
Dependent Variable: Democracy Better than any other form of Government
(Strongly Agree + Agree)

Model		Unstandardized Coefficients		Standardized Coefficients	t	Sig.
1		B	Std. Error	Beta		
	(Constant)	60.256	14.511		4.152	.000
	Islamic countries	9.585	3.711	.371	2.583	.012
	HDI	.341	.161	.437	2.125	.038
	% of religious persons	-3.198E-02	.068	-.064	-.469	.641
	Years of Continuous Democracy 1920-2000	3.129E-02	.052	.105	.606	.547

degree if at all) the absence of democracy in most Muslim countries, but they do not constitute solid factors, that is, they do not offer a reliable explanation. They do, however, offer a very superficial and "easy way out" of the complexity of the problem that democracy faces in the Middle East.

Model 2: R=73.9; R Square= 54.7

The dependent variable in Table 5, Model 2 is "years of uninterrupted democracy." The model explains 54.7 of the variance in the dependent variable; most of it is attributed to HDI, which has a standardized coefficient Beta .777 and a t-value of 6.182. The three other variables are irrelevant, including support for democracy. What does this mean? It is obvious that the cultural variable religion has no leverage as far as durability of democracy is concerned. Human development is the only variable that can effectively influence the development of democracy. As

Table 5, Model 2
Coefficients
Dependent Variable: Years of continuous democracy 1920-2000

		Unstandardized Coefficients		Standardized Coefficients	t	Sig.
Model 2		B	Std. Error	Beta		
	(Constant)	-166.445	36.156		-4.603	.000
	Islamic countries	3.836	10.017	.044	.383	.703
	HDI	2.042	.330	.777	6.182	.000
	% of religious persons	.149	.174	.089	.859	.394
	Democracy better than any other form of government	.205	.338	.061	.606	.547

far as Muslim countries are concerned, the absence of democracy is not attributable to the religion of Islam or its cultural traits. Had the argument about Islam being the obstacle to democracy been concrete, we would have seen less support for democracy in Muslim countries in comparison with others. As our model shows, human development is the most important factor in facilitating and maintaining democracy. Religion (whether Islam, Christianity, or any other religion) does *not* account for the presence or absence of democracy.

Conclusion

Although Fukuyama's argument regarding the prevalence of democracy holds up against empirical examination, his claim pertaining to Islam as "resistant to modernity" does not. Unfortunately, his assertion belongs to an antiquated set of ideas elucidated by Said's Orientalism. The cultural essentialist argument as applied by Fukuyama is epistemologically dogmatic. It is dogmatic in the sense that it makes him envisage isolated examples as complete truths that *totally* explain complex phenomena, although they are partial truths that can only *assist* in explaining socio-political phenomena. This point is made most clear through Fukuyama's own examples: He posits that "Islam . . . is the only cultural system that seems regularly to produce people . . . who reject modernity lock, stock and barrel" (Fukuyama October 11, 2001). Essentializing Islam as an independent variable, to explain very complex socio-political phenomena in the Middle East or elsewhere, does not seem to be a good strategy for analysis and research; other factors at play are also innately indispensable to a comprehensive understanding of Muslim societies. For example, the role of the postcolonial "modern" state in the Middle East in distributing economic resources is vital to the understanding of the durability of authoritarian, patriarchal, and patrimonial political regimes in the region.

Generally, religiosity in general does not seem to be conducive to high support for democratic ideals. The indicators of democracy that we have analyzed in relation to religiosity show a negative correlation of various degrees. Surprisingly, religiosity does show a significant and relatively high negative correlation with interpersonal trust. Therefore, it is not at all unanticipated to find a negative correlation between support for democracy and religiosity. However, Protestant societies do slightly differ from the pattern outlined above. These societies are among the most supportive of democracy and show higher levels of interpersonal trust than Catholic, Orthodox, and Muslim societies. Thus, historically Protestant societies seem to be the only societies that show a stable trend of support for democracy. While other societies, especially Catholic and Islamic, seem to fluctuate considerably from one indicator to another. This can be clearly seen in levels of support for a strong leader who does not have to bother with parliament and elections (authoritarianism); some Islamic societies are on the extremes with Turkey as the second highest society (after Vietnam) that support authoritarianism, and Egypt and Azerbaijan are the second lowest (after Tanzania) on authoritarianism. By and large, Protestant societies stand out as a group that shows low levels of support for authoritarianism but this support is better explained by HDI rather than "Protestant culture."

The fluctuation of societies of diverse religious heritages that we have seen throughout the aforementioned analysis does point to some general trends on the relationship between religiosity and democracy. Meanwhile, this fluctuation indicates that there are some other variables that we should take into account in order to better understand the factors underlying support for democracy and authoritarianism. The examination of the levels of human development in the societies we have looked at could give us a better understanding of support for democracy and its perceived alternatives. Concentrating on religion as the sole independent variable or a yardstick (as Fukuyama uses it) could be seriously misleading and spurious. Finally, since Islam neither explains democracy nor authoritarianism, one can confirm Nazih Ayubi's theory that Islam is not a political religion (Ayubi 1991).

NOTES

1   For example, Fawaz A Gerges (1999) argues that the United States does not have a comprehensive, coherent policy regarding the role of Islam in the political process (pp. 1-19). He writes that there are major inconsistencies between what American officials say and what they do regarding the role of Islam in the political process (pp. 59-86). However, he also argues that strategic and security considerations, rather than conflicts of culture, ideology or history, have the greater influence on U.S. thinking and on the official U.S. foreign policy discourse on the Islamist revival. For example, Gerges argues that Clinton's own pronouncements

on Islam display enlightened sensitivity, realism and tact, and thus standin stark contrast to some of the material found in the U.S. media (pp. 86-115).

2   By political Islam I mean organised groups and parties presenting a political agenda from an Islamic worldview.

3   There are other factors pertaining to the political processes within these countries, which facilitated dictatorial governance. For example, the patron-client way in which these regimes distribute economic resources in exchange for political loyalties effectively meant a continuation of oppression. Politically, people's acceptance of these norms is a rational response to authoritarian rule.

4   In an interview with the Kuwaiti daily, Al-Siyasa King Fahad of Saudi Arabia said " The democratic system prevalent in the world is not appropriate for us in this region . . . our peoples in their makeup and characteristics differ from that . . . world. The elections system has no place in the Islamic creed, which calls for a government of advice and consultation and for the shepherd's openness to his flock, and holds the ruler fully responsible before his people" (quoted in Sisk 1992:50).

5   In a conference convened with the help of Bill Clinton (one of the sponsors) at New York university, Houchang Chehabi, a Professor of international relations at Boston University said that there are two norms of morality in the Islamic world—one for the public life and one for the private life. "In the public realm, the norms of the Islamic morality must be maintained. Take the case of Iran, the country of which I am a citizen. There's no doubt in my mind that Iran currently enjoys more political freedom than it ever did under the Shah. And yet, since it has a state that tells half the population—women—how to dress, it is perceived as being less modern and more repressive than under the Shah" (see Krastev 2002).

6   Speaking in an interview with the *Financial Times* (September 23, 2002), Condoleezza Rice, U.S. National Security Adviser said the United States will be "completely devoted" to the reconstruction of Iraq as a unified, democratic state in the event of a military strike that topples Saddam Hussein. Reinforcing the Bush administration's message that the values of freedom, democracy, and free enterprise do not "stop at the edge of Islam," Ms Rice underlined U.S. interest in the "democratisation or the march of freedom in the Muslim world." She said of reform in places such as Bahrain, Qatar and—" to a certain extent"—Jordan: "There are a lot of reformist elements. We want to be supportive of those."

7   I expect that the near future, if the Americans press for democracy we will see a flow of literature about "Islamic Values" with an aim to delay calls for democra-

cy. Fred Halliday (2000) argues that the arguments of cultural particularity regarding human rights have been developed under pressure from the authoritarian regimes. These regimes, he argues, support some authors to enhance this argument. I agree with this assessment.

8   Mubarak was reported to have told the paper, "the introduction of military trials in America and a new law that allows detention without trial in Britain proves that we were right from the beginning in using all means . . . [in response to] these great crimes that threaten the security of society." However, Mubarak denied that the military courts or the emergency laws that created them had been used against civilians. "We took some criticism because we used emergency law, but we did not use it except in confronting terrorism, and we did not and we will not use it against opinion or thought." He added, "There is no doubt that the events of September 11 imposed a new concept of democracy that differs from the concept that Western states defended before these events, especially in regard to the freedom of the individual." Hafez Abu Seada, the Secretary-General of the Egyptian Organization of Human Rights (EOHR), told the Middle East Times that the government had been using the courts to stamp out opposition and freedom of expression. For example, Saad Eddin Ibrahim, a lecturer at the American University of Cairo and a human rights activist, has been the most prominent non-violent campaigner to face the "special courts" in recent years. In May 2001, he was sentenced by a state security court to seven years in prison for "receiving funds f rom abroad without government permission, embezzling funds and spreading misinformation and rumors abroad" (see Khan 2002).

9   For a detailed account and a chronological order of the events in the Algerian case see Esposito and Voll (1996:150-172).

10   Gerges (1999) comments that the Bush administration's response to the Algerian crisis was notable largely for its passivity, in contrast to its outspoken record in advocating political pluralism elsewhere (pp. 75-80). A commitment to democracy and to political pluralism would seem to entail support for the FIS. Yet the Bush administration gave no such support.

11   Palestinian officials deny that there was a genuine peace deal on offer at Camp David; the Palestinian Minister, Nabil Shaath said in an interview with the *Time Magazine*: "the Israelis did not offer Palestine on a silver platter. There was no sovereignty over the air, over the sea, over the borders. Nothing for the Palestinian refuges. It was a bum deal" *Time Magazine*, April 15, 2002, p. 63).

12   Many observers of Jordanian politics (myself included) interpret the decision to postpone the election and leave the country without an elected parliament for the period between June 2001 and spring 2003 is attributed to the regime's fear of the

opposition (Islamic, Pan-Arab, and Left parties) wining a majority because of the Palestinian and Iraqi crises. I think this fear is largely unfounded. The latest data available from Jordan strongly support this claim. Only 17 percent will vote for "Islamic Trend" and only 6.7 percent reported that The Islamic Action Front Party represents their aspirations. The latter figure is down from 70.5 percent in 1996, 66 percent in 1997, 59.5 percent in 1998, 60.6 percent in 1999, 52.4 percent in 2000, 18.5 percent in 2001, and 7 percent in September 2002 (Centre for Strategic Studies 2002:25-27). Inclusion of Islamists would turn them from mystical figures to practical politicians.

13   Given the fact that he was brought up and live most of his life in the U.K. and United States, the king was perceived to be a democratic ruler, but his endorsement of his government recommendation to postpone the elections twice evaporated the hopes of most of those (my self included) who had hoped that he will enhance democracy in Jordan.

14   Since the dissolution of parliament in June 2001, the government introduced more than 100 provisional legislations restricting public freedoms, increasing prices, doubling compulsory insurance on cars among host of other issues. No elected body approved these legislations.

15   The elections of November 1995 were extensively denounced as fraudulent by many independent observers. For example, see the Egyptian Organisation of Human Rights (EOHR) (1995), "Democracy Jeopardised: Nobody 'Passed' the Elections: The EOHR Account of the Egyptian Parliamentary Elections." Moreover, In a censored article entitled "Egypt Marks 15 years of Mubarak" in the *Middle East Times* (see Negus 1996) the writer says: "The great political liberalizations of the Mubarak regime occurred in the first half of his administration. They peaked around 1987, with the election of a parliament dominated by the opposition. But the last few years, particularly 1995, saw the erosion of those democratic gains. The year-long law campaign by the press humiliated the opposition parties, and while it left them with their freedoms essentially intact, it showed them that those freedoms were a matter of presidential whim. The People's Assembly elections told the parties that, though their participation in elections was welcomed cosmetically, they could never expect a real share in power." Among the reasons for censorship the *Middle East Times* lists: "Discuss modern, unorthodox interpretations of Islam." It seems that the Egyptian political regime defends an interpretation of Islam that justifies the despotic nature of the regime. A challenge to the established religious authority, "Al-Azhar" would mean a challenge to its guardian (the current political regime).

16   During the election campaign the authorities arrested a large number of Islamists in an attempt to thwart them from standing for the elections.

17   During the last week of January 2002, the IAFP internal polls for a new Shura
      Council—the policy making body of the party—reflected a landslide victory for
      the moderates. They won 80 percent of the 120 seats council, while the "hawks"
      won 14 seats only. The moderates secured all but one seat in the executive com-
      mittee (*Jordan Times* 2002).

18   The latest data available for each country from the WVS are used.

19   This case requires a detailed analysis to uncover the uniquely deviant case of
      Nigeria. Some explanations may be found in the political process, development,
      religious divide, and elite behaviour.

20   Drawing on Nazih Ayubi's (1995) *Over-stating the Arab State: Politics and Soc-
                  iety in the Middle East*, Katerina Dalacoura (1998:196-198) has ade-
quately illus-   trated how "types" of states contribute to the rise of a particular type of
opposi-   tion and ideology including Islamists.

21   This was the answer given to me by Prof. Yilmaz Esmer from the department of
      political science at Bogazici University in Istanbul during the World Values Sur-
      vey Conference in Stellenbosch University—South Africa, November 17-20,
      2001.

22   In India, 82.4 percent of the population are Hindu, Muslims: 12.7 percent,
      Christians: 2.4 percent, Sikhs: 2.0 percent, Buddhists: .7 percent, Jains: .4 per-
      cent, and others, including Parsis (Zoroastrians), Jews, and Baha make up .4 per-
      cent (see http://www.uscirf.gov/dos01Pages/irf_india.php3).

23   Sunni Muslims constitute 88 percent of the population. About 10 percent of the
      population are Hindu (see U.S. Department of State 2001).

24   Azerbaijan population consists of 90 percent Muslim, 3 percent Christian and
      approximately 1 percent Jewish (see U.S. Department of State 2001).

REFERENCES

AYUBI, Nazih.
       1995. *Over-stating the Arab State: Politics and Society in the Middle East.*
       London: I.B. Tauris.
AYUBI, Nazih.
       [1991] 1998. *Political Islam: Religion and Politics in the Arab World.* London:
       Routledge.
CENTRE FOR STRATEGIC STUDIES, UNIVERSITY OF JORDAN.

2002. *Democracy in Jordan Survey*. Amman: CSS.
DALACOURA, Katerina.
1998. *Islam, Liberalism and Human Rights*. London: I.B. Tauris.
ESPOSITO, John and John Voll.
1996. *Islam and Democracy*. Oxford: Oxford University Press.
EGYPTIAN ORGANISATION OF HUMAN RIGHTS (EOHR).
1995. "Democracy Jeopardised: Nobody 'Passed' the Elections: The EOHR Account of the Egyptian Parliamentary Elections." Cairo: EOHR.
FINANCIAL TIMES.
2002. Interview with Condoleezza Rice By James Harding and Richard Wolffe in Washington and James Blitz, in London. Retrieved September 23, 2002 (http://www.ft.com).
FREE SAADEDDIN IBRAHIM CAMPAIGN.
2002. "ME Times: Mubarak says Military Trials were always 'Right' Policy." Retrieved January 1, 2001 (http://groups.yahoo.com/group/free_saadeddin_ibrahim/message/143).
FUKUYAMA, Francis.
2001. "The West Has Won: Radical Islam Can't Beat Democracy and Capitalism." *The Guardian*, October 11.
FUKUYAMA, Francis.
1995. *Trust, The Social Virtues and Creation of Prosperity*. New York: Free Press.
FUKUYAMA, Frances.
1992. *The End of History and the Last Man*. London: Hamish Hamilton.
GERGES, Fawaz.
1999. *America and Political Islam: Clash of Cultures or Clash of Interests?* Cambridge: Cambridge University Press.
GHAZALEH, Pascale.
2001. "Sex, Lies and Censorship." *Al Ahram Weekly*, December 27. Retrived May 3, 2002 (http://democracy-egypt.org/files/Press/12-27-01AlAhramWeekly.htm).
HALLIDAY, Fred.
2000. *Nation and Religion in the Middle East*. London: Saqi Books.
HUNTINGTON, Samuel.
1996. *The Clash of Civilizations and the Remaking of the World Order*. New York: Simon & Schuster.
INGLEHART, Ronald.
1990. *Culture Shift in Advanced Industrial Society*. Princeton, N.J.: Princeton University Press.
INGLEHART, Ronald.
1999. "Trust, Well-being and Democracy." Pp. 88-120 in *Democracy and Trust*, edited by Mark Warren. Cambridge: Cambridge University Press.
INGLEHART, Ronald.
1997. *Modernization and Postmodernization: Cultural, Economic and Political Change in 43 Societies*. NJ: Princeton University Press.

JORDAN TIMES.
2002. "PM: Difficult Regional Circumstances must not Hamper Kingdom's Reforms." *Jordan Times*, August 20. Retrived August 20, 2002 (http://www.jordantimes.com).

KHAN, Amil.
2002. "Mubarak says military trials were always 'right' policy." *ME Times*, January 1. Retrived May 3, 2002 (http://democracy-egypt.org/files/Press/2002press/01-01-02MiddleEastTimes.htm).

KENIOUA, Ahmed.
2002. "Algeria on the Eve of the Elections." Lecture delivered at Center for Strategic Studies, February 13, 2002, Amman, Jordan. Available at (http://www.css-jordan.org/activities/lectures/01_02/2002/kenioua.htm).

KRASTEV, Nikola.
2002. "Misperceptions between Muslims and Americans not likely to Improve." *Radio Free Europe—Radio Liberty (RFE/RL)*, January 29. Retrieved January 29, 2002 (http://www.middleeastwire.com/islam/stories/20020129_meno.shtml).

PUTNAM, Robert.
1993. *Making Democracy Work: Civic Traditions in Modern Italy.* Princeton, N.J: Princeton University Press.

RUESCHEMEYER Dietrich, Evelyne H. Steohens, and John D. Stephens.
1992. *Capitalist Development and Democracy.* Cambridge: Polity Press.

SADIKI, Larbi.
2002. "Bin Ali's Tunisia: Democrcay by Non-Democratic Means." *British Journal of Middle Eastern Studies* 29(1):57-78.

SISK, Timothy D.
1992. *Islam and Democracy: Religion, Politics, and Power in the Middle East.* Washington: United States Institute of Peace.

NEGUS, Steve.
1996. "Egypt marks 15 years of Mubarak." *Middle East Times.* Retrieved December 5, 2002 (http://metimes.com/cens/c2.htm).

TIME MAGAZINE.
2002. Interview with Nabil Shaath by Scott Macleod. April 15, p 63.

UNITED STATES COMMISSION ON INTERNATIONAL RELIGIOUS FREEDOM.
2001. "Annual Report on International Religious Freedom." Released by the Bureau of Democracy, Human Rights, and Labor, U.S. Department of State. Retrieved October 26, 2001 (http://www.uscirf.gov/dos01Pages/irf_albania.php3).

WARREN, Mark E., ed.
1999. *Democracy and Trust.* Cambridge: Cambridge University Press.

WELZEL, Chris, Ronald Inglehart, and Hans-Dieter Klingemann.
2001. "Human Development as a Theory of Social Change: A Cross Cultural Perspective." Presented at the World Values Survey Conference, November 17-21, University of Stellenbosch, Stellenbosch, South Africa.

ZAKARIA, Fareed.
　　2001. "How to save the Arab World." *Newsweek* CXXXVIIIM(26): December 24, pp. 24-29.
U.S. DEPARTMENT OF STATE.
　　2001. "Annual Report on International Religious Freedom." Released by the Bureau of Democracy, Human Rights, and Labor, United States Commission on International Religious Freedom. Retrieved October 26, 2001 (http://www.uscirf.gov/dos01Pages/irf_albania.php3).

TRENDS IN POLITICAL ACTION:
THE DEVELOPMENTAL TREND AND THE
POST-HONEYMOON DECLINE

Ronald Inglehart and Gabriela Catterberg[*]

ABSTRACT

More than two decades ago, the authors of Political Action (Barnes et al. 1979) predicted that what was then called "unconventional political participation" would become more widespread throughout advanced industrial societies, because it was part of a deep-rooted intergenerational change. Time series data from the 1974 Political Action survey, together with data from four waves of the World Values Surveys demonstrates that this change has indeed taken place—to such an extent that petitions, boycotts, and other forms of direct action are no longer unconventional but have become more or less normal actions for a large part of the citizenry of post-industrial societies.

This type of elite-challenging actions also played an important part in the Third Wave of democratization—but after the transition to democracy, most of the new democracies subsequently experienced a post-honeymoon phase of disillusionment with democracy, in which direct political action declined. This paper analyzes data from more than 70 countries containing more than 80 percent of the world's population, interpreting the long-term dynamics of elite-challenging political participation in both established democracies and new democracies. Our interpretation implies that the current decline in direct political action in the new democracies is a "post-honeymoon" period effect; in the long run, we expect that elite-challenging activity will move on an upward trajectory in most of the new democracies, as has been the case in virtually all established democracies.

The Rise of "Unconventional Political Participation"

More than 25 years ago, Inglehart (1977:5, 317-321) predicted declining rates of elite-directed political mobilization and rising rates of elite-challenging political behavior among Western publics. One source of change was the intergenerational shift from Materialist to Postmaterialist values: Materialists tend to be preoccupied with satisfying immediate physiological needs, while Postmaterialists feel relatively secure about these needs and have a greater amount of psychic energy to invest in more remote concerns. Noting that, throughout advanced industrial societies, the younger birth cohorts also have higher levels of political skills than older cohorts, he concluded that the processes of value change and cognitive mobilization tend to go together: the publics of these societies are coming to place increasing value on self-expression, and their rising levels of

[*]   Institute for Social Research, University of Michigan, 3067 ISR, Ann Arbor, Michigan, 48106-1248, USA.

skills enable them to participate in politics at a higher level, increasingly shaping specific decisions rather than simply entrusting them to more skilled minorities. Subsequently, analyzing data on elite-challenging political action, Inglehart (1990) found:

> Postmaterialists are more likely to engage in unconventional political protest than are Materialists. Moreover, one's values interact with cognitive mobilization in such a way that at high levels of cognitive mobilization, the differences between value types are magnified considerably . . . Among those with Materialist values and low levels of cognitive mobilization, only 12 per cent have taken part, or are willing to take part in a boycott or more difficult activity. Among Postmaterialists with high levels of cognitive mobilization, 74 per cent have done so or are ready to do. The process of cognitive mobilization seems to be increasing the potential for elite-directing political action among Western publics. Pp. 361-362

This prediction may seem surprising because, as everyone knows, voter turnout has been declining throughout advanced industrial societies. But partisan loyalties and party organizations were the main reason for the high electoral turnout of earlier years. Hence, we find two divergent trends: on one hand, the bureaucratized and elite-directed forms of participation such as voting and party membership have declined; while the individually-motivated and elite-challenging forms of participation have risen.

Similarly, Barnes, Kaase et al. (1979) predicted the spread of what was then called "Unconventional Political Participation." They developed a set of scales to measure both "conventional" political action, such as voting and writing one's representative in parliament; and "unconventional" forms of political action, such as demonstrations, boycotts and occupation of buildings. Finding that the latter forms of behavior were strongly correlated with Postmaterialist values, and were much more prevalent among younger birth cohorts than among the old, they predicted that "unconventional" political action would become more widespread. "*We interpret this increase in potential for protest to be a lasting characteristic of democratic mass publics and not just a sudden surge in political involvement bound to fade away as time goes by*" (Barnes, Kaase et al. 1979: 524, italics in original text).

More than two decades later, it seems clear that they were right—despite widespread assumptions since the 1970s about the decline of civic and political activism in post-industrial societies (Pharr and Putnam 2000; Crozier et al. 1975; Habermas 1973). Crisis of democracy theories have consistently predicted the weakening of representative democracies, and ultimately of the role of citizens, in Western nations. Most recently, Putnam and Goss (see Putman 2002) have argued that:

> Ironically—just at the moment of liberal democracy's greatest triumph there is also unhappiness about the performance of major social institutions, including the institutions of representative government, among the established democracies

of Western Europe, North America, and East Asia. At least in the United States, there is reason to suspect that some fundamental social and cultural preconditions for effective democracy may have been eroded in resent decades, the result of a gradual but widespread process of civic disengagement. P. 4

Despite these predictions, time series data from the Political Action surveys, together with data from the four waves of the World Values Surveys/European Values Surveys, demonstrates that a significant increase in elite-challenging political participation has taken place—to such an extent that petitions, demonstrations, boycotts, and other forms of elite-challenging activities are no longer unconventional, but have become more or less normal actions for a substantial part of the citizenry of post-industrial nations. We do not find a widespread pattern of civic disengagement—either in the United States or elsewhere. What we find is more complex.

Our findings contradict claims that the publics of postindustrial societies are disengaging themselves from civic life in general. We believe that these claims are only partly right. We emphatically agree that Putnam (2000) was right in claiming that people are deserting such organizations as the Elks, the Moose, and the Rotary. Elite-directed hierarchical organizations such as labor unions and churches are losing members. Membership in political parties is falling sharply (Dalton and Wattenberg 2001). Big city political machines have lost control of once-realiable blocs of voters, so voter turnout is stagnant or declining (Wattenberg 1996). There is declining trust in government and rising political cynicism among the publics of most rich democracies (see Norris 1999; Nye, King, and Zelikow 1997). The publics of advanced industrial societies *are* becoming more critical of authority in general, and political authority in particular, and less and less likely to become members of bureaucratized organizations. Since this is the type of organization that keeps membership lists, the written record shows a predominantly downward trend. But this is only part of the story. These same publics are becoming *increasingly* likely to engage in types of political action that do not leave written membership lists, because they are elite-challenging activities that are loosely coordinated by ad hoc groups that come into existence suddenly and disappear just as suddenly. The public is not withdrawing from civic action in this broader sense. Quite the contrary, it is clear that the shift toward rising levels of elite-challenging participation that was predicted more than 25 years ago, has taken place in virtually all advanced industrial societies.

Although passive and elite-directed forms of public participation, such as voting and church attendance, have stagnated or declined, time series data show that these newer forms of participation have become increasingly widespread. For the most part, these ad hoc groups do not keep permanent membership lists, so the written record does not provide an accurate measure of how many people took part in such activities. Their participation rates go unrecorded unless someone carries out surveys that take the initiative to ask, and record, who did what.

Fortunately, the Political Action surveys, together with the World Values Surveys, have done just this, and the results are unequivocal—and they flatly contradict the image of an increasingly disengaged public. It turns out that the publics of the United States and other advanced industrial societies are becoming less likely to passively attend the meetings of oligarchically-controlled organizations, but much more likely to engage in activities that challenge elite decisions in which they take a personal interest.

A major change is taking place. It is not a trend toward civic inertness, but an intergenerational shift from elite-directed participation toward increasing rates of elite-challenging participation. Intergenerational value change has important implications concerning the changes we can expect over the coming decades. As younger, better-educated, and more Postmaterialist cohorts replace older ones in the adult population, intergenerational population replacement will tend to bring a shift toward increasingly participant publics.

But political change is not simplistically driven by cultural change alone. Cultural change interacts with economic, social, and political developments in the given society. As Inglehart (1997) demonstrated, the shift toward Postmaterialist values from 1970 to 1997 displayed both a long-term intergenerational shift, and short-term period effects. Recessions brought a movement toward increased Materialism among all cohorts, but with the return of prosperity, the respective cohorts were as Postmaterialist as ever.

Similarly, we expect underlying cultural changes to gradually increase mass participation in elite-challenging actions, but people do not protest in a vacuum: they respond to current problems, such as war or peace, prosperity or economic collapse, the ideologies of specific political parties, and the personalities of given leaders.

Consequently, we would expect to find (1) long-term trends, based on intergenerational population replacement, and (2) short-term period effects. Intergenerational population replacement is a long-term force that tends to work in a consistent and foreseeable direction over many decades—but its impact is magnified or reduced by short-term changes in the economy or political system.

We will test these expectations using the data from the World Values Surveys carried out from 1981 to 2001. Since this period included the collapse of communism and the Third Wave of democratization that peaked in 1989-1991, it is clear that we are dealing with a period in which we can expect some dramatic period effects. Transitions to democracy took place in dozens of countries. These transitions to democracy evoked (and were facilitated by) mass mobilizations of elite-challenging activity. "People Power" helped bring democratic regimes to power in numerous countries from East Asia to Latin America and was particularly apparent in the collapse of the communist regimes. But in the aftermath of the transition we would expect to find a "Post-honeymoon" effect. As the immediate need for participation recedes and the euphoria of democratization wears off, we would expect to find declining levels of mass participation—particularly in cases where democratization brings severe disillusionment.

There are elements peculiar to the dynamics of democratic transitions that usually stimulate people's expectations about the effectiveness of new administrations, ultimately leading to skepticism. During the third wave of democratization, the original belief among the public— often reinforced by elite discourse—that democracy not only provides civil liberties but also improves economic well-being was a crucial factor in motivating these high expectations (Linz 1996).[1] If the economy subsequently performed poorly, disillusionment with democracy was likely. Moreover, the experience of living under an authoritarian regime engendered unrealistic expectations about democracy and democratic politics: "Expectations among activists were perhaps unrealistic, incorporating a too idealistic belief in real influence from below . . . [Yet] politics as it is being carried out does not, in the eyes of many, work for people" (Ruschemeyer 1998:101-102).

These high expectations caused rising frustration among those interested in being active or who actually were politically involved; a frustration with their inability to exert significant influence. As Mishler and Rose (1998:575) claim, fear of the old authoritarian systems and hope for an improving economy in the foreseeable future have strongly affected support for new regimes: "If the present regime falters, nostalgia for the past could occur. If perceptions of the current economy and expectations for the future begin to erode, economic hope could turn to despair."[2] An increasing discrepancy between expectations and reality led to democratic disillusionment, especially where the new regimes seemed incompetent. If this was true, it would dramatically lower expectations about the efficacy of democratic participation, and withdrawal from the abnormally high period of elite-challenging participation linked with the transition to democracy.

Thus, we would expect to find rising rates of elite-challenging political participation in rich democracies, reflecting a long-term developmental trend; but declining rates of elite-challenging action linked with a post-honeymoon period effect in new democracies in general, but especially in those where the transition to democracy had produced disillusioning results. In contrast with these predictions, if the crisis of democracy school is correct in finding signs of a pervasive Civic Disengagement that extends to all types of participation and not just the decline of bureaucratic, elite-directed participation, then we should find declining rates of elite-challenging political action in all or most established democracies (this school makes no explicit predictions about what may be happening in the new democracies).

In testing these predictions, we are fortunate to have a relatively long time series of survey data available for analysis, utilizing the data from the 1974 Political Action surveys and four waves of the World Values Surveys. Let us start by examining changes in response to five measures of elite-challenging action that were developed in the Political Action survey, and replicated in the values surveys.

Table 1 shows the percentage of the public saying that they have actually engaged in various forms of unconventional political action in each of the eight Western democracies surveyed in the 1974 Political Action study—and how this behavior changed during the next quarter of a century. The first section of this table (Table 1a) shows the percentage reporting that they have signed a petition.[3] Outside the United States, this was still a relatively unusual activity in 1974: across the eight countries, an average of only 32 percent said they had done it (with the figures ranging from a low of 17 percent in Italy to a high of 60 percent in the United States). During the next 25 years, the percentage saying they had signed a petition increased in every one of the eight societies and the increase was dramatic. Overall, the percentage almost doubled from 32 percent in 1974 to 63 percent in 2000. By the latter year, this had become a normal activity, something that a majority of the public in almost every country said they had done.

A similar pattern applies to the other forms of political action for which Table 1 provides evidence. In every one of the eight countries for which we have

**Table 1. The Rise of "Unconventional" Participation,
1974 - 2000**

Table 1 a. Percentage who have signed a petition

Country:	1974	1981	1990	1995	2000	Net Shift:
Britain	23	63	75		81	+58
W. Germany	31	47	57	66	47	+16
Italy	17	42	48		55	+38
Netherlands	22	35	51		61	+39
U.S.	60	64	72	71	81	+21
Finland	20	30	41	39	51	+31
Switzerland	46		63	68		+22
Austria	39		48		56	+17
Mean:	32	42	57	58	63	+30

Note: In case a cell is empty, the mean for each column is calculated by inputting the figure for the last available year for that country.

Table 1 b. Percentage who have taken part in a demonstration

Country:	1974	1981	1990	1995	2000	Net Shift:
Britain	6	10	14		13	+ 7
W. Germany	9	15	21	26	22	+13
Italy	19	27	36		35	+16
Netherlands	7	13	25		32	+25
U.S.	12	13	16	16	21	+ 9
Finland	6	14	14	13	15	+ 9
Switzerland	8		16	17		+ 9
Austria	7		10	16		+ 9
Mean:	9	13	19	20	21	+12

Note: In case a cell is empty, the mean for each column is calculated by inputting the figure for the last available year for that country.

long-term data, the percentage reporting that they have participated in a demonstration rose from 1974 to 2000. As Table 1b demonstrates, the overall percentage saying they had taken part in a demonstration more than doubled, from 9 percent in 1974 to 21 percent in 2000. The percentage saying they had taken part in a consumer boycott also increased in every one of these eight countries. Overall, this figure also more than doubled, rising from 6 percent in 1974 to 15 percent in 2000.

Sections 1d and 1e show the percentages saying, respectively, that they have taken part in an unofficial strike and those saying they have occupied buildings. These were still unconventional activities, even in 2000, and the numbers engaging in them were small. But from 1974 to 2000 the percentage saying they had participated in an unofficial strike rose in seven of the eight societies (Finland being the sole exception). The percentage saying they had occupied a building increased in five of the eight societies (the other three showed no net change). We have data on five activities across eight societies. Among these 40 tests, we find the predicted increase in 36 cases, no change in 3 cases, and a decrease in one case. The net trend is overwhelmingly toward rising rates of elite-challenging political action.

But the pattern is not universal. Our theory holds that rising rates of elite-challenging political action are a component of a cultural shift from survival values toward self-expression values. This shift is not universal—it is linked with high levels of existential security, so it is much more likely to be found in rich countries than in poor ones. All eight of the societies for which we have data from 1974 are high-income countries (as was typical of survey research in that era). The WVS/EVS surveys provide data from a much wider range of countries (though for a shorter time span) and they help complete the picture. Table 2 shows the changes in the percentages saying they have signed a petition, across all 50 of the societies for which we have data from more than one time point. This form of political action rose in 30 of these societies and declined in 19 of them (one country, Nigeria, showed no change).

The pattern is far from random. As Figure 1 indicates,[4] in rich democracies the percentage saying they had signed a petition rose substantially—from an overall mean of 43 percent in 1981, to an overall mean of 62 percent in 2000. But the figures *fell* significantly in the ex-communist countries and in the non-communist developing countries. We do not have 1981 data from an adequate number of these societies, so our time comparisons extend only from 1990 to 2000. This was a distinctive historical period—the decade immediately after the major wave of democratization that occurred in 1989-1991. We suspect that the significant decline in political action observed in both the ex-communist world and the developing countries, reflects a post-honeymoon period of disillusionment, reflecting a period effect rather than a persisting value shift. We do not have data from the years before 1990, but we suspect that the dramatic transitions to democracy in 1989-91 led to exceptionally high rates of political activism, which could not be

Table 1 c. Percentage who have taken part in a consumer boycott

Country:	1974	1981	1990	1995	2000	Net Shift:
Britain	6	7	14		17	+11
W. Germany	5	8	10	18	10	+ 5
Italy	2	6	11		10	+ 2
Netherlands	6	7	9		22	+16
U.S.	16	15	18	19	25	+ 9
Finland	1	9	14	12	15	+14
Switzerland	5			11		+ 6
Austria	3		5		10	+ 7
Mean:	6	8	11	12	15	+ 9

Note: In case a cell is empty, the mean for each column is calculated by inputting the figure for the last available year for that country.

Table 1 d. Percentage who have taken part in an unofficial strike

Country:	1974	1981	1990	1995	2000	Net Shift:
Britain	5	7	10		9	+4
W. Germany	1	2	2	4	2	+1
Italy	1	3	6		5	+4
Netherlands	2	2	3		5	+3
U.S.	2	3	5	4	6	+4
Finland	5	6	8	5	3	-2
Switzerland	1		2	2		+1
Austria	1		1		2	+1
Mean:	2	3	5	4	4	+2

Note: In case a cell is empty, the mean for each column is calculated by inputting the figure for the last available year for that country.

Table 1 e. Percentage who have occupied buildings

Country:	1974	1981	1990	1995	2000	Net Shift:
Britain	1	3	2		2	+1
W. Germany	1	2	1	2	1	0
Italy	5	6	8		8	+3
Netherlands	2	2	3		6	+4
U.S.	2	2	2	2	4	+2
Finland	0	1	2	1	1	+1
Switzerland	1			1		0
Austria	1		1		1	0
Mean:	2	2	3	3	3	+1

Note: In case a cell is empty, the mean for each column is calculated by inputting the figure for the last available year for that country.

Source: "1974" figures are from the Political Action surveys (actual field-work was carried out in 1973-1976); the figures for 1981-2000 are from the World Values Surveys/European Values Surveys. The "1990" surveys were carried out in 1990 and 1991; the "1995" surveys in 1995 and 1996; and the "2000" surveys in 1999-2000.

sustained subsequently. For it is clear that political action *did* decline during this period in both the ex-communist countries and in the developing countries, even while it was rising substantially in the rich democracies. In this respect, the world does not seem to be converging toward a common model. Quite the contrary, the differences between rich and poor countries seem to be increasing. The comforting assumption that we are moving toward a global village in which everyone thinks and acts in similar ways, seems mistaken.

Table 2. Rising Elite-Challenging Participation 50 Societies, 1981-2000
(Percentage who have Signed a Petition)

COUNTRY	1981	1990	1995	2000	Shift Ratio*	COUNTRY	1981	1990	1995	2000	Shift Ratio*
Belgium	24	47		71	2.96	Slovenia		28	19	31	1.11
Czech			26	56	2.15	Spain	24	21	22	26	1.08
Ireland	29	42		59	2.03	Switzerland		63	68		1.08
Mexico	10	35	30	19	1.90	Turkey		14	20	15	1.07
Netherlands	35	51		61	1.74	Nigeria		7	7	7	1.0
N Ireland	35	60		57	1.63	Brazil		50	47		.94
Slovakia			35	57	1.63	Portugal		28		26	.93
Sweden	54	72	72	87	1.61	Ukraine			13	12	.92
Finland	30	41	39	48	1.60	Philippines			12	11	.92
Serbia			19	29	1.53	E Germany		69	57	60	.87
Poland		14	20	21	1.50	Croatia	43		43	36	.84
France	45	54		67	1.49	Hungary		18	25	15	.83
Iceland	37	47		52	1.41	Chile		23	17	19	.83
S Africa	20	34	19	27	1.35	Argentina	34	22	31	23	.68
Japan	48	62	55	63	1.31	Puerto Rico			28	19	.68
USA	64	72	71	81	1.27	Venezuela			23	15	.65
Britain	63	75		79	1.25	Bangladesh			25	14	.56
Denmark	44	51		55	1.25	Romania			17	9	.53
Italy	42	48		52	1.24	Estonia		39	14	19	.49
S Korea		42	40	52	1.24	Bulgaria		22	7	10	.45
W Germany	47	57		56	1.19	Lithuania		58	31	25	.43
Canada	62	77		74	1.19	Russia		30	11	11	.37
Norway	56	61	65		1.16	Belarus		27	18	8	.30
India		25	27	29	1.16	Latvia		65	31	18	.28
Austria		48		55	1.15						

* For countries showing an increase, the Shift Ratio is in bold face type.
Source: 1981-2000 World Values Surveys.

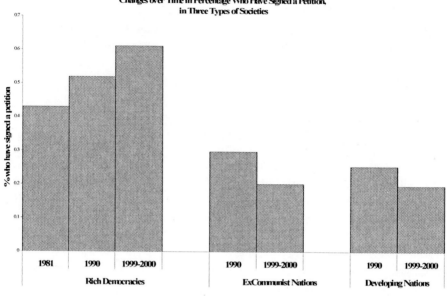

Figure 1
Changes over Time in Percentage Who Have Signed a Petition,
in Three Types of Societies

source: 1981-2001 World Values Surveys

The trends found with signing petitions, apply to elite-challenging politi-cal action more broadly. Figures 2.1-2.2 show the changes from the two earlier surveys, to the two latest surveys, in the percentage that had engaged in at least one of the five elite-challenging actions, presenting evidence from all 17 rich

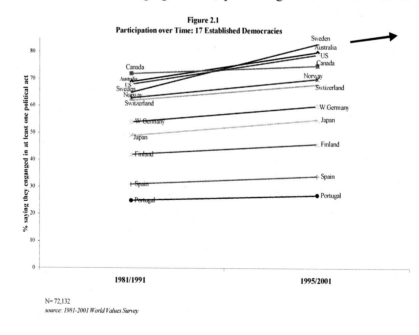

Figure 2.1
Participation over Time: 17 Established Democracies

N= 72,132
source: 1981-2001 World Values Survey

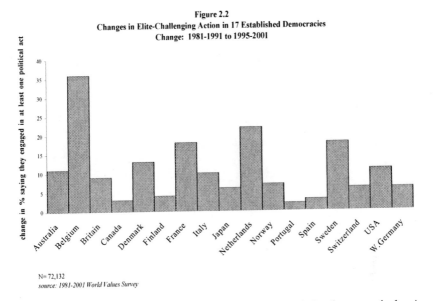

Figure 2.2
Changes in Elite-Challenging Action in 17 Established Democracies
Change: 1981-1991 to 1995-2001

N= 72,132
source: 1981-2001 World Values Survey

democracies that were surveyed in both the earlier and the later periods. Again, the evidence is unequivocal: we find increases in 17 out of 17 cases.

The new democracies show a contrasting pattern (Figures 3.1-3.2). Here, we examine the changes that took place from the period *before or during* regime change, to a period *after* regime change occurred, in order to examine the impact

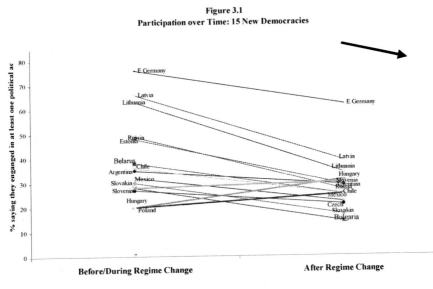

Figure 3.1
Participation over Time: 15 New Democracies

N= 59,654
source: 1981-2001 World Values Surveys

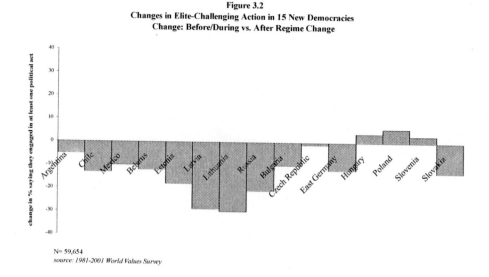

Figure 3.2
Changes in Elite-Challenging Action in 15 New Democracies
Change: Before/During vs. After Regime Change

N= 59,654
source: 1981-2001 World Values Survey

of regime change. This means that the times of the "before or during" and "after" necessarily vary from country to country, but we have before and after data for a total of 15 new democracies.[5] In twelve of the fifteen cases, we find declines in elite-challenging political action. The three exceptions are Hungary, Poland, and Slovenia—three societies that coped with the transition from communism far better than most ex-communist countries.

This points to a broader contrast: the post-communist transition has been far more traumatic in the Soviet successor states than in the non-Soviet societies of Eastern Europe. While Hungary, Poland, Slovenia, the Czech Republic, and former East Germany are now enjoying relative prosperity and are candidates for membership in the European Union (or already part of it, in the East German case), in most of the ex-Soviet societies, living standards are far lower than they were under communism. In Russia, life expectancy itself has fallen sharply below its former level. As Figures 4 and 5 demonstrate, the "post-honeymoon" decline in elite-challenging political action has been much more severe in the former Soviet republics than in the East European ex-communist states or in Latin America.

Figure 6 illustrates that, even after all the changes associated with the transition to democracy and the subsequent post-honeymoon decline, there is a strong relationship between a society's level of economic development and its level of elite-challenging political action. The vertical dimension of this figure shows the percentage saying they engaged in at least one political act, and the horizontal dimensions shows GNP per capita. Even a cursory glance makes it evident that elite-challenging action was substantially higher in nations with higher economic development, or post-industrial societies. In those nations with per capita

Figure 4
Participation over Time: New & Established Democracies

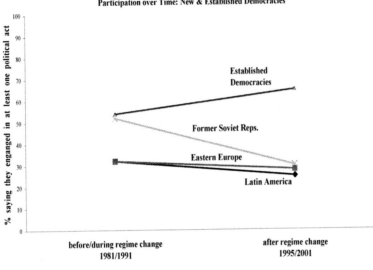

N= 131,786
source: 1981-2001 World Values Survey

Figure 5
Change in Elite-Challenging Action: New vs. Established Demcracies
Change: Before/During vs. After Regime Change, 1981-1991/1995-2001

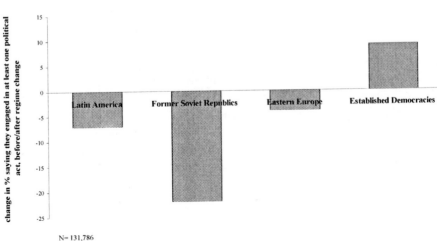

N= 131,786
source: 1981-2001 World Values Survey

GNP higher than $20,000, more than 50 percent of the public engaged in elite-challenging action. In nations with GNP below $15,000, less than 30 percent were involved in such activities. Moreover, the relationship between economic development and political action became stronger in the new democracies after regime change than it was before.

Figure 6
Elite-Challenging Action, by Level of Economic Development
In 1995-2001

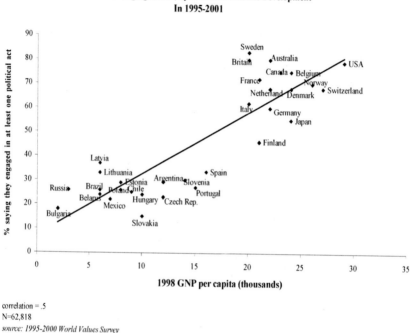

correlation = .5
N=62,818
source: 1995-2000 World Values Survey

Interestingly, participation in elite-challenging political action remains at significantly lower levels in Spain and Portugal than in other established democracies. One might argue that this reflects the fact that they democratized considerably later than the other "established democracies." But Spain and Portugal experienced regime change at least a decade earlier than most Latin American and Eastern and Central European nations, and do not show significantly higher levels of elite-challenging action than these new democracies. The pattern in Figure 5 seems to reflect different levels of economic development, above all.

Conclusion

Despite a growing body of literature concerning a decline in political activism in post-industrial societies, our findings indicate that the upward tendency of protest politics predicted by the Political Action's scholars more than thirty years ago has materialized, producing a sustained and systematic increase in elite-challenging activities during the last quarter of the twentieth century. While less than half of the eight publics engaged in at least one activity in 1981, more than two-thirds were involved in 2000. As the public becomes increasingly critical of elite decision-making, and increasingly ready to intervene actively in order to influence specific decisions, the nature of citizen politics in advanced democracies has changed.

In most new democracies, on the other hand, there has been a sharp contraction of political action during the years immediately following regime change. Post-transitional problems—especially the combination of rising aspirations of economic well-being and persisting inequality—led to an erosion of democratic support and declining participation rates.

Mass involvement in elite-challenging activities was particularly influential during the process of regime change in Latin America and Eastern and Central Europe. Systematic mobilizations against authoritarian regimes took place across the regions. Even in nations with relatively weak participatory traditions, such as Latvia, Lithuania, and Estonia, more than half of the publics were involved in elite-challenging politics. The evidence shows that the struggle for democracy motivated the organization of ordinary men and women into a variety of groups— sometimes illicit, even illegal—which collectively had the effect of "aiding the assaults on the seats of power" (Haynes 1997).

Pro-democracy movements had a major impact because they allowed individuals by uniting, to overcome fear, and revealed the authoritarian systems' failure to dissolve group identities and inhibit collective action, reintroducing political space for civil society. Moreover, they forced governments to make concessions. Once democracy was reestablished, however, demonstrations and other forms of mass political behavior became relatively sporadic. As Rueschemeyer et al. (1998) sum it up, "the enthusiasm of the transition period gave way to a predominance of passive behavior" (p.267).

In established democracies, on the other hand, elite-challenging action systematically increased during the last three decades. We suspect that the current decline of elite-challenging political action in the new democracies is a temporary period effect, which we term a "post-honeymoon" decline. Assuming that these societies reestablish economic growth, we anticipate that in the long run they will experience the gradually rising levels of elite-challenging political action linked with economic development—as have virtually all of the established democracies. In these societies, publics are becoming less likely to passively attend the meetings of oligarchically-controlled organizations, but increasingly likely to engage in elite-challenging participation.

NOTES

1   As Raúl Alfonsín famously said during his 1983 presidential campaign, "Con la democracia se come, ...y se educa."

2   Their analysis primarily focuses on post-communists nations.

3   Putnam (2000) find exactly the opposite trend in petition-signing in the United States, but the data he uses from the Roper Archive seem to be less reliable than those from the WVS, which show a clear increase in signing petitions—not only in the United States but in all Western democracies for which we have data.

4   This figure compares three groups of societies, based on data from the following: "Rich democracies" (surveyed in 1981, 1990, and 2000): United States, Canada, Japan, South Korea, Britain, Ireland, N. Ireland, France, Germany (West), Italy, Belgium, Netherlands, Denmark, Sweden, Finland, Iceland, and Spain; "Ex-communist" (surveyed in 1990 and 2000): Belarus, Bulgaria, China, Czech Republic, Estonia, Hungary, Latvia, Lithuania, Poland, Romania, Russia, Slovakia, and Slovenia; "Developing Countries" (surveyed in 1990 and 2000): Argentina, Chile, India, Mexico, Nigeria, South Africa, and Turkey.

5   In the case of Argentina, "before or during" refers to the 1981 wave, while "after" includes the 1990, 1995, and 2000 surveys. In Chile, "before or during" indicates data from 1990, while "after" refers to the third and four waves. In the Mexican case, "before or during" corresponds to the 1981 and 1990 data, while "after" indicates the 1995 and 2000 surveys. Finally, in former communist nations, "before or during" includes the 1989-1991 surveys; referring "after" to the 1995 and 2000 waves.

REFERENCES

BARNES, Samuel and Max Kaase et al., eds.
    1979. *Political Action: Mass Participation in Five Western Societies*. California: Sage.

CROZIER, Michael.
    1975. *The Crisis of Democracy: Report on the Governability of Democracies to the Trilateral Commission*. NY: New York University Press.

DALTON, Russell J. and Martin Wattenberg, eds.
    2001. *Parties without Partisans*. New York: Oxford University Press.

HABERMAS, Jurgen.
    1973. *Theory and Practice*. Boston: Beacon Press.

HAYNES, Jeff.
    1997. *Democracy and Civil Society in the Third World: Politics and New Political Movements*. Cambridge: Polity.

INGLEHART, Ronald.
    1977. *The Silent Revolution: Changing Values and Political Styles among Western Publics*. Princeton: Princeton University Press.

INGLEHART, Ronald.

1990. *Culture Shift in Advanced Industrial Society*. Princeton: Princeton University Press.

INGLEHART, Ronald.

1997. *Modernization and Post-Modernization*. Princeton: Princeton University Press.

NORRIS, Pippa, ed.

1999. *Critical Citizens: Support for Democratic Government*. New York: Oxford University Press.

NYE, Joseph S., Philip D. Zelikow, and David C. King, eds.

1997. *Why People Don't Trust Government*. Cambridge, MA: Harvard University Press.

PHARR, Susan and Robert Putnam, eds.

2000. *Dissaffected Democracies: What's Troubling the Trialateral Countries?* Princeton: Princeton University Press.

PUTNAM, Robert.

2000. *Bowling Alone: The Collapse and Revival of American Community*. New York: Simon and Schuster.

PUTNAM, Robert, ed.

2002. *Democracies in Flux: The Evolution of Social Capital in Contemporary Society*. Oxford: Oxford University Press.

ROSE, Richard and William Mishler.

1998. *Democracy and its Alternatives: Understanding Post-Communist Societies*. Cambridge: Polity Press.

RUESCHEMEYER, Dietrich, Marilyn Rueschemeyer, and Bjorn Wittrock.

1998. *Participation and Democracy, East and West: Comparisons and Interpretations*. Armonk: M.E.Sharpe.

WATTENBERG, Martin.

1996. *The Decline of American Political Parties: 1952-1994*. Cambridge: Harvard University Press.

EFFECTIVE DEMOCRACY, MASS CULTURE, AND THE QUALITY OF ELITES: THE HUMAN DEVELOPMENT PERSPECTIVE

Christian Welzel*

ABSTRACT

This article demonstrates that low corruption and high female representation are two characteristics of elite quality that go closely together and help make "formal" democracy increasingly "effective." However, the quality of elites is not an inherently independent phenomenon but is shaped by a pervasive mass factor: rising self-expression values that shift cultural norms toward greater emphasis on responsive and inclusive elites. Self-expression values, in turn, tend to be strengthened by growing human resources among the masses. Considered in a comprehensive perspective, these various components are linked through the emancipative logic of Human Development: (1) human resources, (2) self-expression values, (3) elite quality, and (4) effective democracy all contribute to widen the scope of human autonomy and choice in several aspects of people's lives, including their means and skills, their norms and values, as well as their institutions and rights.

Introduction

The spread of democracy that took place in recent decades by the Third Wave of democratization (Huntington 1991) attracted extraordinary academic attention (see, for instance, O'Donell and Schmitter 1986; Higley and Gunther 1992; Casper and Taylor 1996; Linz and Stepan 1996). At the beginning of the Third Wave, some political scientists saw in the emergence of new democracies the advent of a glorious democratic era (Fukuyama 1989; Pye 1990). After a while, however, a more realistic view became dominant, reflecting the insight that democratic regimes do not work everywhere with similar effectiveness. Observers noticed that many of the newly emerging democracies show severe deficiencies, especially in their human rights performance. O'Donnell (1993) and Finer (1999), among others, warned against confusing "façade democracies" with "effective democracies." According to these authors (see also, Linz and Stepan 1996; Rose 2001), the difference between façade democracies and effective democracies rests in the "rule of law" and its most fundamental manifestation: people's freedom rights.

The adoption of a constitution that grants freedom rights—such as having free speech and information, religious freedom, freedom of professional and artis-

*   International University Bremen (IUB), School of Humanities and Social Sciences, P.O. Box 750 561, D – 22725 Bremen, Germany.

tic activities, freedom of private and public self-expression, as well as freedom of choice in elections and referenda—is a necessary condition for democracy. Without these rights, there can be no democracy. But legal guarantees do not suffice to make freedom rights effective. As outlined in earlier work (see, for example, Almond and Verba 1963) and re-emphasized in recent work (see, among others, Heller 2000), beneath a surface of legal guarantees, there can be informal social mechanisms that hinder people in practicing their rights effectively. Among the mechanisms that reduce the effectiveness of given rights, elite corruption and elite closure are the most detrimental ones, since both work against core principles of democracy. Elite corruption, on one hand, violates the rule of law; elite closure, on the other hand, undermines the equality of rights. Whether there is democracy in at least a formal sense, depends on people's constitutional entitlement to freedom rights. But whether democracy is effective or not does not automatically follow from the institutionalization of rights. It depends on the features of a society's elites: their sensitivity to people's rights and their openness to underprivileged groups, among which women are the potentially largest one, accounting for at least half of the population in any society.

From a human development perspective that focuses on human autonomy and choice (see Welzel 2002; Welzel, Inglehart, and Klingemann 2003), freedom rights are essential because they give people a legal space to exert autonomous choices in their private and public activities. Hence, the freedom rights performance is a prime indicator of a democracy's intrinsic quality. This insight is shared by both human rights theorists (Donnelly 1993; Haas 1996) and proponents of sustainable development (Anand and Sen 2000; Sen 2001).

The increased attention to freedom rights meets two other lines of research that have been strengthened in recent times: one is concerned with the role of elite corruption as a mechanism that undermines rule of law (Lipset and Lenz 2000; Olson, Swarma, and Sany 2000; Rose 2001), and the other is concerned with elite closure against women as a phenomenon that reflects violations of the equality of rights (Inglehart and Norris 2003; Paxton 2000).

Low corruption among elites and openness of elites to potentially underprivileged groups, such as women, are essential to the effectiveness of given freedom rights. The presence of legal guarantees for freedom does not mean that these rights work in practice. A formal democracy, such as India, is not necessarily equal to an effective democracy in which people face no social barriers that prevent them from exerting their rights (Heller 2000). One of the conditions needed to make given freedom rights effective is that a society's decision makers respect and follow these rights in their activities. Wide spread corruption among decision makers, by contrast, indicates that elites make their service to the people dependent on bribes instead of rights—which violates the rule of law. Without rule of law, given freedom rights are worthless no matter what their status is in a constitution. Hence, low elite corruption, or what I call "elite integrity," is an indispensable factor in making freedom rights effective (Lipset and Lenz 2000; Rose 2001).

Another indicator of effective democracy is elite openness to potentially underprivileged groups, such as women (Paxton 2000; Inglehart and Norris 2003). A nation's constitution may grant equal freedom rights to both women and men, but to the degree that women are excluded from the elites, these rights are ineffective for half of the population (and even a majority in most countries). Heavy under-representation of women among a nation's decision makers indicates that there are discriminating social sanctions at work, preventing women from exerting their rights as effectively as their male compatriots. Hence, female representation is a crucial factor in making given freedom rights fully inclusive and effective. The ideal of democracy prescribes an equal use of freedom rights for both sexes. It is therefore legitimate to measure a society's democratic performance against this ideal. Thus, the degree of female representation among elites, or "elite openness," is another core indicator of effective democracy.[1]

Recent research has emphasized the role of corruption and female representation among elites, and few scholars will doubt that low corruption and high female representation among elites help to make democracy more effective. However, corruption and female representation have been examined in complete isolation from each other, as if these two factors had little in common. This is implausible because both corruption and female representation are basic characteristics of the quality of elites. These characteristics indicate the elites' responsiveness to ordinary people's rights and their openness to women as the largest underprivileged group in any society. In the following, I conceptualize low elite corruption as "elite integrity" and high female representation as "elite openness." Moreover, I present evidence that elite integrity and elite openness go closely together, converging in a common dimension that I interpret as an "elite quality factor." As I will show, elite quality operates as an efficacy factor that determines how effective given freedom rights are in practice. Depending on the scope of freedom rights that are legally guaranteed, there may be high or low levels of formal democracy. But it depends on the quality of elites as to how effective these rights are in practice.

On the other hand, elite quality is not an inherently independent phenomenon. Quite the contrary, the quality of elites reflects a pervasive mass-factor: a cultural shift towards rising emphasis on self-expression in which mass demands for accountable and inclusive elites are strengthened at the same time.

At this point I refer to work by Inglehart (1997) as well as Inglehart and Baker (2000). These authors have identified a broad dimension of survival vs. self-expression values that tends to unfold with growing human resources among the masses. But I go one step further. Following Welzel (2002), as well as Welzel, Inglehart, and Klingemann (2003), I argue that there is an even broader dimension of Human Development that integrates (1) human resources, (2) self-expression values, (3) the quality of elites, and (4) effective democracy into one theme, in which each part widens the scope of choice in particular aspects of people's lives:

their means and resources, their beliefs and values, as well as their rights and institutions. Growing human choice on a mass-scale is the common denominator of all the components involved here.

In the first part, I describe the measures and data sources. The second part proceeds with quantitative analyses on the cross-national level, presenting evidence for the relationships described above. The third part ends with a theoretical conclusion, unfolding my theory of Human Development.

Data and Measurement

ELITE INTEGRITY (i.e., low elite corruption): To measure elite integrity, I use the corruption perception scores from Transparency International.[2] These scores are expert ratings. They judge how corrupt the political, bureaucratic, and economic office holders of a country are, that is, in how far decision makers sell their services as "favors" for the price of a bribe. One indication of the validity of these estimates is that they strongly correlate with aggregate measures of the citizens' perception of elite corruption in representative surveys (Rose 2001). The Transparency scores range from 1 to 100, with 100 indicating the greatest amount of corruption. Reversing these scores, one obtains a measure of law-abiding elite behavior or elite integrity. I use the most recent scores referring to the end 1990s.

ELITE OPENNESS (i.e., high female representation): To measure female representation, or elite openness, I use the "gender empowerment index" provided by the United Nations. This standardized index is based on the percentages of women that are represented in a country's legislatures, in high ranking administrative offices, and in business management positions (see Human Development Report 2001 for description of data sources and scaling procedures). Female representation in high offices is a valuable measure of elite openness because women are the largest potentially discriminated group in any society, accounting almost everywhere for at least half of the population. The opportunities of women to shape their living conditions and to practice their rights effectively are diminished to the degree that women are excluded from the elites. Unequal opportunities and rights violate core principles of democracy. Hence, openness of elites to the female population is a core factor in making formal democracy effective. The gender empowerment index provided by the United Nations measures the degree of female representation on a scale from 0 to 1. I take measures referring to the end 1990s and use them as an indicator of elite openness.

SELF-EXPRESSION VALUES: I will show that core characteristics of the quality of elites, namely elite integrity and elite openness, reflect emancipative orientations among the masses. I operationalize emancipative orientations as self-expression values. In order to measure self-expression values I use the largest available database, the European/World Values Surveys, which cover 73 countries representing 80 percent of the world's population.[3] I measure self-expression values using a scale of factor scores summarizing several attitudes that Inglehart and Baker (2000) have identified as indicators of self-expression values. I use data

Table 1. The Dimension of Self-Expression Values

Variables:	Levels of Analysis:		
	Individual level within nations (mean loadings)	Individual level across nations (pooled loadings)	Aggregate cross-national level
Strong self-expression values imply:			
- Tolerance of human diversity [a]	.47	.68	.82
- Inclination to civic protest [b]	.45	.65	.87
- Liberty aspirations [c]	.54	.59	.82
- Trust in people [d]	.34	.47	.64
- Self-satisfaction [e]	.13	.44	.76
Weak self-expression values imply the opposite.			
Explained variance	23%	29%	54%
Number of cases	137 national surveys	158,803 individuals	137 nation per wave units

Notes: Entries are factor loadings. Explorative principal components analysis (extraction of factors with 'Eigenvalues' above 1 adviced), no rotation. *Source*: European/World Values Surveys I-IV.
[a] "Not mentioned" for "disliked neighbors" coded "1" and dichotomized against 0; scores added for neighbors with AIDS (V58) and homosexual neighbors (V60). Aggregate data are national averages on this 0-2 scale.
[b] "Already done" for "signing petitions (V118) coded "1" and dichotomized against "0." Aggregate data are national percentages already done.
[c] Respondents' first and second priorities for "giving people more say in important government decisions" and "protecting freedom of speech" (V106-107) added to a four-point index, assigning 3 points for both items on first and second rank, 2 points for one of these items on first rank, 1 point for one of these items or second rank and 0 for none of these items on first or second rank. Aggregate data are national averages on this 0-3 scale.
[d] Respondents believing "most people can be trusted" (V27) dichotomized as "1" against "0." Aggregate data are national percentages of people trusting.
[e] 10-point rating scale for life satisfaction (V65). Aggregate data are national averages on this 1-10 scale.
Source: Welzel, Inglehart, and Klingemann (2003).

based on a replication of their analyses published in Welzel, Inglehart, and Klingemann (2003). Table 1 is taken from this source.

The emancipative logic of self-expression values points to what Putnam (2000) and Dahl (2000) termed "enlightened understanding" or what Rawls (1993) calls a "rational sense of reciprocity." People who have self-respect and emphasize their liberty tend to show great respect of the liberty of their fellow citizens. In a way, it is natural when people who emphasize their own liberty respect other people's liberty as well. Self-expression values, in this sense, reflect the logic and the experience of mutual human exchange, which rests on giving and taking: people tend to treat their peers like they have been, and want to be treated, by them (Axelrod 1983). Thus, self-expression values do not only include an "ego-emphasizing" attitude, reflected in liberty aspirations[4] and an inclination to protest activities (such as signing petitions),[5] but also an attitude of openness towards "alter-ego," as reflected in tolerance of human diversity and interpersonal trust (see the footnotes in Table 1 for the operationalization of these variables).

Moreover, self-expression values are linked with greater life satisfaction, implying that striving for self-expression is embedded in human motivation in that it creates stronger feelings of fulfillment. Maslow has already emphasized this (1988:100). Additional support for this insight is given by recent results in experimental psychology, showing that people whose activities are targeted at "promotion" feel happier than people whose activities are directed towards "prevention" (Förster, Higgins, and Idson 1998).

As Table 1 shows, factor loadings increase systematically from the individual level within nations to the pooled individual level to the aggregate level across nations. The reasons for this phenomenon have been explained in Welzel, Inglehart, and Klingemann (2003) and are only briefly mentioned here. First, there are pronounced mass tendencies within nations that bound individuals' value orientations into a relatively small range. Individual-level variations within this range are to a large degree random. Thus, the linkage between individual-level attitudes is not so clearly structured within nations: hence, the smallest factor loadings at the individual-level within nations. Second, variations in mass tendencies between national populations are more pronounced and less random than individual-level variations within nations. Therefore, taking cross-national variation into account by pooling individual-level data brings the linkage between individual-level attitudes more clearly to the fore: compared to the individual-level within nations, the factor loadings are larger at the pooled individual-level. Third, but still there are measurement errors at the individual level. Aggregating the data to the national level eliminates this measurement error (random deviations from a mean cancel each other out), making the linkage between mass attitudes even more evident: hence, the strongest factor loadings occur at the aggregate-level.

The Elite Quality Factor

Figure 1 shows the relationship between contemporaneous measures of elite integrity and elite openness (see Appendix, Table A1 for an overview of all measurements). The graph shows a strikingly strong relationship, reflecting that rising levels of elite integrity go hand in hand with rising levels of elite openness.

The close relationship shown in Figure 1 supports the argument that elite integrity and elite openness are twin elements, representing the same underlying dimension: the overall quality of elites. Clearly, this justifies summarizing elite integrity and elite openness into one factor scale, with little loss of information. Indeed, both variables correlate with a common underlying factor by $r=.98$. Hence, I calculated a factor scale adding z-standardized scales of elite integrity and elite openness, transforming the resulting index into a range from 0 to 1. In the following, this factor scale is labeled as the "elite quality factor":[6]

Elite Quality Factor = Elite Integrity + Elite Openness

The combination of elite integrity and elite openness reflects the "quality" of elites with respect to a particular feature of democracy: the effectiveness of

Figure 1. Elite Openness and Elite Integrity

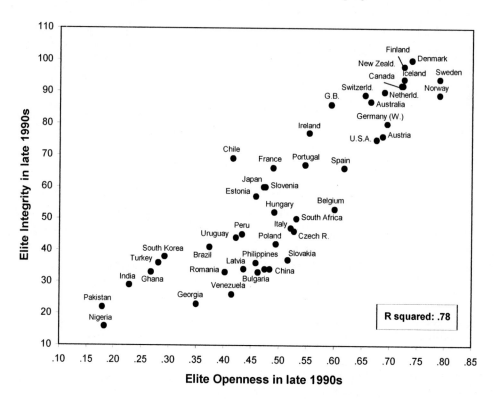

given freedom rights. And, this is true for both components of the elite quality measure. Elite integrity, on the one hand, indicates how far the elites abstain from corruption, thus, basing their service to the community on rights instead of bribes. Elite openness, on the other hand, reflects how far the elites are open to the female population—which is a prime criterion for gender-equality in the practice of given opportunities and rights.

Unlike other authors (see, for instance, O'Donnell and Schmitter 1986; Higley and Gunther 1992), I do not consider elite characteristics as something inherently independent. Instead, I believe that features of a nation's mass culture have a strong imprint on elite characteristics. In particular, I hypothesize that emancipative orientations among the population are a powerful social force in shaping the quality of elites. Rising self-expression values make the public sensitive to such moral questions as equal civic rights, gender discrimination, and corruption—putting elites under the pressure of mass expectations that are targeted at equal and effective freedom rights. Evidence from the World Values Surveys, indeed, shows that publics that place strong emphasis on self-expression have large proportions of people who refuse the statement "men make better political leaders than women" and who are sensitive of "how much respect there is for human rights in their country."

The latter findings nourish the expectation that the strength of self-expression values among the public fuel elite integrity and elite openness. The evidence supports this assumption. Cross-national variations in the strength of self-expression values among the public explain 71 percent of the cross-national differences in elite integrity and 73 percent in elite openness (not documented here). And, since elite integrity and elite openness represent a common factor of elite quality, it is logical that self-expression values must have a similarly strong impact on precisely that factor. As Figure 2 demonstrates, this is actually the case: cross-national differences in self-expression values explain 77 percent of the cross-national differences in the quality of elites.

Figure 2. The Impact of Emancipative Values on the Quality of Elites

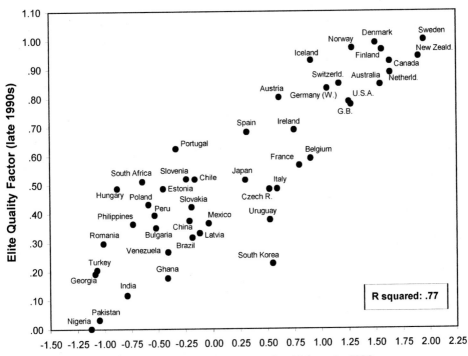

Reflecting on the causality in the relationship between self-expression values and elite quality, one must recognize the temporal order of the variables in Figure 2. The self-expression values in this figure refer to the year 1990, while the measures of elite quality refer to the end 1990s, which is almost ten years later. Since effects cannot precede their causes, the quality of elites at the end 1990s cannot have produced self-expression values among mass publics in 1990. But let me elaborate a bit more on the question of causality.

Elite Behavior and Mass Culture

The linkage between elite quality and self-expression values depicts the relationship between elite behavior and mass culture. The causality of this relationship may be rather complex, such that there is not a one-directional effect of mass culture on elite behavior but a reciprocal relationship. For instance, the elites may not avoid corruption and open their ranks for women because they are pushed to do so by mass expectations deriving from self-expression values. Instead, the elites themselves may have internalized emancipative orientations that channel their behavior towards less corruption and less exclusion of women. But even if so, the question remains whether the elites' own value orientations either shape or reflect those of the masses.

Almost all research on elite attitudes indicates that elites have distinctive orientations that differ considerably from non-elites (see, for instance, Brint 1984; Dalton 1985; Iversen 1994). In particular, elites tend to be more liberal, more progressive, and more postmaterialistic than the average population. However, most of this research has been done within Western societies, with limited evidence on the cross-national variation between elite orientations. Hence, we have little knowledge which attitudinal differences are larger: the differences between elites across nations or the within-nation differences between elites and non-elites. Considering this question, the World Values Surveys provide a reasonable testing ground because the cross-national variance of this global sample can hardly be larger.

Although the World Values Surveys are not elite surveys, one can use a crucial insight of elite research in order to take advantage of these data: elites in any society are disproportionately recruited from the most highly educated layers of the population. Hence, people with university education form the primary pool of elite recruitment. Given that this is true, one can use the orientations of people with university education as a proxy for the orientations that prevail among the elites. Based on this premise, Figure 3 plots for each nation the strength of self-expression values among people with university education against the strength of self-expression values found among the rest of the population.[7]

The "isoline" in this figure marks all locations of national publics that are possible on the condition that the educated elite and ordinary citizens place identical emphasis on self-expression values. Accordingly, deviations from the "iso-

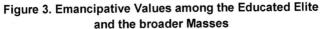

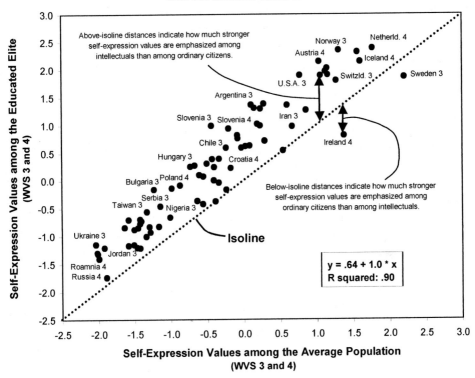

Figure 3. Emancipative Values among the Educated Elite
and the broader Masses

line" measure the margin by which the educated elite's emphasis on self-expression surpasses or falls below that of the ordinary citizens. Upward-deviations from the "isoline" indicate how much more emphasis the educated elite places on self-expression. Downward-deviations indicate how much less emphasis the educated elite places on self-expression. As one can see, almost all national publics are located above the "isoline." This implies that a nation's educated elite usually places stronger emphasis on self-expression values than the average population. One may interpret this finding as a universal emancipative effect of education: university education tends to promote emancipative orientations.

However, the margins by which the educated deviate from the population (consider the distances from the "isoline") are rather small and almost constant (varying slightly around a .64 standard unit). Indeed, the distances from the "isoline" are much smaller than the distances between the different national publics. Accordingly, differences in emancipative orientations are much more pronounced between nations than between the educated and non-educated within nations. In fact, cross-national differences between the emancipative orientations of the educated are to 90 percent explained by corresponding differences between the masses. Hence, although there is a universal effect of education making the educated more emancipative than the broader public, the margin of this effect is bound within the broader public's central tendency.

The broader public's central tendency has a much stronger impact on the emancipative orientations of the educated than has their education. This is a clear indication that the educated do not and cannot freely choose the level of emancipative values that they might consider as appropriate for the rest of the population to follow. Otherwise, much larger differences between the values of the educated and those of the masses would have to be observed: showing that the educated could run ahead at any level of emancipative values, leaving the masses behind with a considerable catch up time-lag, resulting in much larger differences than the ones observed in this cross-section. What we see, however, is that the emancipative orientations of the educated rest closely on those of the masses, being only slightly enhanced by higher education.

Provided that elites are primarily recruited from the educated stratum of the population, these findings suggest that even if the elites are guided by their own values to avoid corruption and female exclusion, these values will rest on corresponding values among the masses. In other words, self-expression values among the masses channel elite values and behavior towards greater integrity and openness. Thus, the quality of elites is derivative of mass cultural features, such as those reflected in self-expression values.

To be sure, this does not exclude the presence of reciprocal effects—such that high elite quality, once it is in place, unfolds a positive reversal effect in strengthening already existing self-expression values. But even if so, this does not rule out a prior effect of self-expression values on elite quality—which is my core argument.

Yet, I cannot rule out the possibility that the effect of self-expression values on elite quality simply reflects an artifact of other social forces. There are at least three broader social forces that might be responsible for this effect: religious traditions, past democratic experience, and economic development.

Alternative Explanations

RELIGIOUS TRADITION: Following Max Weber (1958 [1904]), sociologists pronounced that religious traditions have a lasting impact on a society's overall make-up. More specifically, Protestant societies have been described as being more attuned to individual liberty, freedom rights, rule of law, and gender equality. For instance, Protestant societies have been among the first to introduce female suffrage. More recently, Huntington (1996) outlined that liberal traditions once primarily typical of Protestant societies are nowadays shared by many Catholic societies as well. There is a much sharper division between "Western Christianity" (i.e., Protestantism and Catholicism) and "Oriental" societies (non-Western religions of Eurasia, including Orthodox Christianity), the latter being historically linked to the tradition of "Asian Despotism."

Provided that both elite integrity and elite openness are positively influenced by liberal traditions and negatively by despotic traditions, one would assume that the liberal tradition of the "West" is reflected in comparatively high levels of elite quality among Protestant and Catholic societies; while the despotic tradition of the "Orient" is reflected in a low elite quality among societies with a non-Western religious tradition.

The religious tradition of a society can be measured by the religious composition of its population. In historically Protestant societies, Protestants are still the largest religious group and in historically Islamic societies, Muslims are the largest religious group and so on; while societies that were influenced by different religious traditions show a mixed religious composition. I gathered data on the proportions of a society's religious groups[8] (Protestants, Catholics, Orthodox Christians, Muslims, "other believers"[9]) and tested if the size of these religious groups is linked with elite quality. Actually, this turned out to be the case: the proportion of people of a Western religion (Catholics and Protestants) has a significantly positive impact, and the proportion of people of a non-Western belief has a significantly negative effect on the quality of elites. To be more specific, among Western beliefs, Protestantism has a stronger positive effect than Catholicism; while, among non-Western beliefs, Islam has a stronger negative effect than other non-Western beliefs.

To capture the full explanatory power of the religious composition, I added the proportions of all major religious groups—after having them multiplied by "impact factors," that is, weights[10] whose signs indicate the direction and whose magnitudes indicate the strength of their influence on elite quality. This "impact weighted" religious composition captures a Western versus non-Western religion dimension, with Muslims and Protestants as the most extreme opposites at its two poles:

$$\text{Impact Weighted Religious Composition} =$$
$$.65*\%\text{Protestants} + .03*\%\text{Catholics} - .23*\%\text{Orthodox} - .45*\%\text{Muslims}$$
$$- .31*\%\text{Other Believers}$$

DEMOCRATIC EXPERIENCE: Political scientists have claimed that a country's past regime experience is important for many of its current features (Linz and Stepan 1996). As these authors maintain, this is most evident for the length of a country's experience with democracy. There are obvious reasons that the length of the democratic experience should have an influence on both components of the elite quality factor.

In the long run, the existence of democratic institutions should produce higher rates of elite integrity because democracy institutionalizes sanctions against corrupt elites—sanctions that do not exist in autocracies (Dahl 2000). For instance, democracies entitle people to deselect a ruling party if its leaders proved to be corrupt. Moreover, democracies establish press freedom and informational pluralism, which enables the media to monitor and delegitimize corrupt elite behavior. Likewise, democratic institutions provide the female population access to more channels of public activity and better judicial protection against discrimination than do other regimes. Hence, other conditions being equal, elite integrity as well as elite openness should be positively linked with democracy.

Provided that democratic institutions indeed have these effects, they should be the stronger, the longer the time democracy has had to unfold these effects. Hence, the length of a society's democratic experience should increase both components of the elite quality.

I measure the democratic experience by the number of years a country spent under democratic institutions. Since this experience should be temporally prior to the dependent variable, elite quality, I measure the number of years under democracy until 1990.[11]

ECONOMIC DEVELOPMENT: There are obvious reasons why economic development, too, should increase both components of the elite quality factor. Economic development is linked with rising mass prosperity, rising levels of formal education, and growing access to information. This process increases the monetary, technological, intellectual, and informational resources of the public, equipping people with greater means and skills to exert popular pressure on parasitic elites, which should tend to increase elite integrity.

In addition, economic development should tend to increase elite openness to women. Economic development puts a premium on professional activities that involve cognitive rather than manual work. Since physiological sex differences are irrelevant for cognitive work, professional activities in modern societies are far less dependent on sexual differences. This is reflected in a growing female participation in both the labor market and higher education. Moreover, leadership roles in developed societies are based on formal education. Since larger proportions of women tend to acquire high levels of formal education, their chances to enter the elites are growing. Hence, other things being equal, elite openness to women should improve with economic development.

I measure economic development by the human resources available to the masses, using an index of human resources provided by Vanhanen (1997). This index measures the accumulation and distribution of material, monetary, and intellectual resources and combines them multiplicatively to produce an overall index of human resources.[12] I prefer this composite measure to single indicators, such as per capita GDP, in order to operate with a more complete measure of human resources.[13]

It should be noted that aggregate measures of human resources reflect a long-term factor. Societal stocks of human resources are not only present once they are measured but have accumulated over long periods of time. Consequently, a society that shows contemporary high levels of human resources had already been on high resource-levels for quite a while. Hence, although the measure of human resources I am using refers to the late 1980s, this measure is indicative of resource-levels in earlier years as well.

Controlling Alternative Explanations

How do religious tradition, democratic experience, and available human resources perform in predicting the quality of elites compared to self-expression values? Is the effect of self-expression values shown in Figure 2 simply an artifact of these factors? I guess "no." For even if these three factors have independent effects on the quality of elites, it is implausible that these effects do completely bypass the impact of prevailing mass values. In my view, the social force that pushes elites

Table 2. Explaining the Quality of Elites: Regression Analyses

Dependent Variable: **Elite Quality Factor** in late 1990s (elite integrity plus elite openness)

	Model 1	Model 2	Model 3	Model 4
Predictors:	B (T-value)	B (T-value)	B (T-value)	B (T-value)
Self-Expression Values [a]	.26*** (12.05)	.21*** (7.56)	.24*** (7.06)	.21** (4.31)
Religious Tradition [b]		.003** (3.19)		
Democratic Experience [c]			.0003 (.82)	
Human Resources [d]				.003 (1.37)
Constant	.48*** (22.76)	.45*** (22.59)	.45*** (13.45)	.37*** (10.11)
Adjusted R^2	.76	.80	.76	.77
N	46	46	46	46

a) Factor scale, scores aggregated at the national level (see Table 1, right column).
b) Impact weighted religious composition during 1980s (factor scale).
c) Years under democracy until 1990.
d) Vanhanen-index of Human Resources, late 1980s.

Significance Levels: * $p<.100$ ** $p<.010$ *** $p<.001$

for more integrity and openness is the public and its demands, rather than anonymous social factors, such as religious tradition, democratic experience, and human resources. For the reasons just mentioned, these factors probably also have an effect, but one that is less direct and at least in part mediated through their impact on mass values. Hence, religious tradition, democratic experience, and human resources may well add to the effect that self-expression values have on elite integrity and elite openness. But it does not seem likely that these factors simply rule out the impact of self-expression values.

Regression analyses in Table 2 demonstrate that the impact of self-expression values on the quality of elites is not just an artifact of other social factors: not only does this effect remain robust against controls for religious composition, regime experience and human resources; self-expression values also show the most significant single effect on the quality of elites.

Controlling for self-expression values, only the religious tradition has a significant effect on the quality of elites, adding 4 percent of explained variance to the sole impact of self-expression values (compare models 1 and 2). By contrast, neither the past democratic experience nor human resource levels add a significant effect to that of self-expression values on elite quality. The democratic experience, in particular, is literally irrelevant. With human resources, the case is different insofar as their effect comes closer to the significance-hurdle and reduces to some degree the T-value of self-expression values. As I will show in the next section, this reflects that human resources absorb part of the effect of self-expression values because self-expression values themselves are shaped to a considerable degree by human resources.

What Shapes Self-Expression Values?

Self-expression values are the strongest single force in shaping the quality of elites. But what, in turn, shapes the rise of self-expression values? Regression analyses in Table 3 provide some insights. A society's past democratic experience, its religious tradition,[14] and its accumulated human resources all have a significant effect on self-expression values. In fact, self-expression values tend to be the

Table 3. Explaining the Strength of Self-Expression Values among Populations: Regression Analyses

	Model 1	Model 2	Model 3	Model 4
	— Dependent Variable: **Self-Expression Values** about 1990 (factor scores)			
Predictors:	B (T-value)	B (T-value)	B (T-value)	B (T-value)
Religious Tradition [a]	.02*** (4.94)	.01*** (4.14)		.02*** (4.12)
Democratic Experience [b]	.01*** (7.31)		.004* (2.12)	.003* (1.77)
Human Resources [c]		.04*** (12.71)	.04*** (8.48)	.03*** (7.52)
Constant	-.51*** (-6.23)	-.99*** (-12.71)	-1.05*** (12.42)	-.94*** (-11.52)
Adjusted R^2	.68	.82	.79	.83
N	71	73	71	71

a) Impact weighted religious composition during 1980s (factor scale).
b) Years under democracy until 1990.
c) Vanhanen-Index of Human Resources, late 1980s.

Significance Levels: * $p<.100$ ** $p<.010$ *** $p<.001$

stronger, (1) the longer a society's past experience with democracy, (2) the stronger the presence of Western religious traditions and the absence of non-Western religious traditions, and (3) the greater its accumulated human resources. These three effects account for 83 percent of the cross-national differences in self-expression values.

Yet, the relative strength and significance of these effects differ greatly. To reach this conclusion, compare models 1 to 3 with the full model (model 4). Removing the democratic experience from the full model (see model 2) reduces the explained variance in self-expression values by only 1 percent; and removing religious tradition (see model 3) reduces the explained variance by 4 percent; but removing human resources (see model 1) reduces it by 15 percent. Accordingly, a society's accumulated human resources have, by far, the strongest impact on its emphasis on self-expression values; while the democratic experience, once again, turns out to have an almost negligible effect.

To illustrate this finding, Figures 4A and 4B depict the partial effects of human resources and the democratic experience on self-expression values, under mutual controls. Isolating the effect of human resources on self-expression values from the effect of the democratic experience (Figure 4A), human resources still explain 51 percent of the variance in self-expression values. By contrast, isolating the effect of the democratic experience from that of human resources (Figure 4B), explains only 6 percent in the variance of self-expression values. These figures illustrate clearly that self-expression values reflect primarily the presence of human resources—irrespective of the democratic experience. Thus, the emergence of an emancipative culture is hardly derivative of pre-existing democratic institutions. This finding strongly supports Putnam (1992) and Inglehart (1997) against the claims of Muller and Seligson (1994) and Jackman and Miller (1998) who have argued that a democratic culture is endogenous to democratic institutions.

Comparing these findings with those of Table 2 points to the following conclusions. First, controlling for self-expression values, past democratic experience has no direct effect on the quality of elites; at best, the democratic experience has a negligible indirect effect that operates through its minor impact on self-expression values—the factor with the strongest direct effect on elite quality. Second, controlling for self-expression values, the religious tradition has a weak direct effect on the quality of elites and a similarly weak indirect effect operating through its small effect on self-expression values. Third, controlling for self-expression values, human resources have no direct effect on the quality of elites but a strong indirect effect that operates through their pronounced impact on self-expression values.

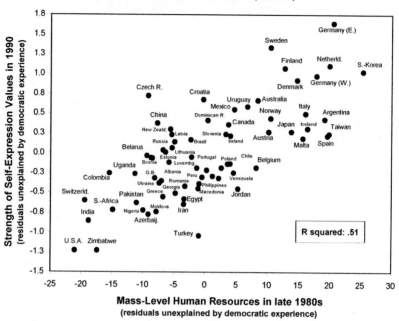

Figure 4A. The Impact of Human Resources on Emancipative Values
(Effect isolated from Democratic Experience)

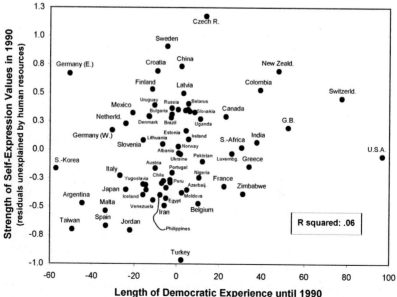

Figure 4B. The Impact of Democratic Experience on Emancipative Values
(Effect isolated from Human Resources)

These findings can be summarized into two major effects: a society's self-expression values are most strongly influenced by its accumulated human resources; but even controlling for human resources as their strongest predictor, self-expression values still have the most powerful direct effect on the quality of elites.

Formal Democracy, Effective Democracy, and Façade Democracy

I argued that elite integrity and elite openness converge in an overall factor of elite quality. The quality of elites, I argued further, indicates how effective given freedom rights work in a society's practice. The quality of elites, in other words, operates as an efficacy factor. But the quality of elites is by no means indicative of the *scope* of rights that is made effective. The quality of the elites may be so high that it makes a given scope of freedom rights fully effective, but precisely the scope of these rights may be very narrow. This situation is unlikely but logically possible. It would correspond to an authoritarian regime whose elites are almost uncorrupt and very open to women. In this case, citizens would not be deprived of their rights by elite corruption and women would not be hindered more than men to exert their rights, but still these rights could be small. Given rights would be fully effective but the scope of these rights would be narrow. Certainly no one would characterize such a situation as an effective democracy.

These reflections clarify that the quality of elites—although it makes given rights more effective—*cannot* compensate for deficiencies in the scope of rights. Hence, in order to obtain a meaningful measure of effective democracy, one must operationalize the interaction between the scope of freedom rights[15] and the quality of elites as the factor that makes these rights more or less effective.

Doing this in a way that does not allow the elite quality factor to compensate for deficiencies in the scope of rights requires a weighting procedure: I weight a given scope of freedom rights by the elite quality factor, measured in fractions from 0 to 1. In this case, the elite quality factor cannot do more than reproduce a given scope of freedom rights. Even if we have a maximum elite quality of 1.0 (no elite corruption and fully proportional representation of women), this factor cannot multiply a narrow scope of freedom rights. The elite quality factor can only make effective the scope of rights that is given: autocracy remains autocracy, whatever the quality of the elites. On the other hand, low elite quality can heavily devalue a wide scope of freedom rights, creating large variances in the degree of "effective" democracy among "formal" democracies.

A wide scope of freedom rights, or formal democracy, still is a necessary condition to reach a high score in effective democracy, but it is not enough. The elite quality factor must be also on a high level, which is realistic. Imagine a country whose constitution includes a full range of freedom rights and imagine this country is governed by highly corrupt elites that exclude women almost completely from their ranks. Wouldn't it be justified to conclude in such a case that people, and women in particular, are deprived of their constitutional rights, leaving these rights largely ineffective? My answer is "yes" and so I measure effective democracy as follows:

$$\text{Effective Democracy} = \text{Formal Democracy} * \text{Elite Quality Factor}$$
$$\text{(Percentages)} \qquad \text{(Fractions from 0 to 1)}$$

where Formal Democracy measures the scope of institutionalized freedom rights, and where the Elite Quality Factor summarizes measures of elite integrity and openness.

How are formal democracy and the elite quality factor related to effective democracy? Figures 5A and 5B display an interesting result. Obviously, the elite quality factor and formal democracy have a very different relationship to effective democracy, although this result is in no way pre-determined by the way I combine these components to create the measure of effective democracy. While the elite quality factor shows a strongly linear relationship to effective democracy, formal democracy deviates largely from effective democracy: huge differences in the lower four fifths of formal democracy do not create corresponding differences in effective democracy; whereas strong homogeneity in the upper fifth of formal democracy allows for large variations in effective democracy.

According to this result, there are nations, such as India and China, that differ greatly in their levels of formal democracy, but high elite corruption and strong elite closure against women devalue these differences considerably: whether a constitution contains many or few freedom rights does not make much of a difference, if these rights are ineffective. On the other hand, many nations that share similar high levels of formal democracy show huge differences in elite corruption and elite closure, producing large differences in effective democracy. In summary, large differences in formal democracy can result in little differences in effective democracy and low differences in formal democracy can translate into large differences of effective democracy.

The finding that degrees of formal democracy deviate strikingly from effective democracy, while the elite quality factor is strongly in line with effective democracy, is crucial. It demonstrates that the quality of elites operates as a force that rectifies formal democracy's aberrations from effective democracy. And, since the elite quality factor is itself strongly influenced by self-expression values, this factor shapes democracy in a way that brings it in line with emancipative mass values. Thus, while variations in *formal* democracy are to some degree random to self-expression values, variations in *effective* democracy correspond systematically with these values.

To be sure, where self-expression values are strong, there is almost always a high degree of formal democracy: in each society in which the public's emphasis on self-expression is stronger than in Croatia, the level of formal democracy reaches at least 70 percent of the possible maximum. Self-expression values are

Figure 5A. Formal Democracy and Effective Democracy

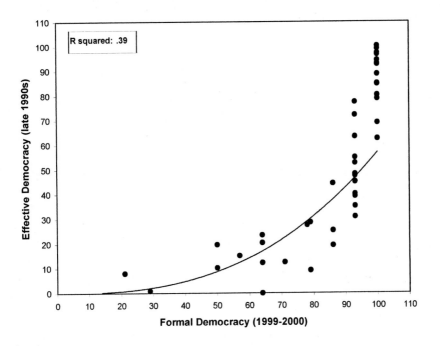

Figure 5B. The Quality of Elites and Effective Democracy

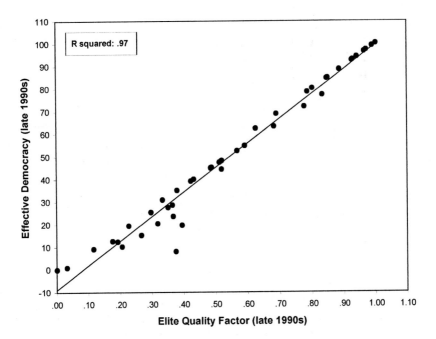

therefore a sufficient condition to create high levels of formal democracy. But high levels of formal democracy can also exist in societies whose citizens place little emphasis on self-expression values: societies who place the same or weaker emphasis on self-expression than the Croats can be on almost any level of formal democracy. Hence, self-expression values are a sufficient but not a necessary condition to create formal democracy.

Formal democracy is random to emancipative cultures in the sense that a high degree of formal democracy can exist in any culture, whether self-expression values are strong or not. But when formal democracy exists in a culture with little emphasis on self-expression, the quality of the elites is usually very poor: translating the relatively high degree of formal democracy into a low degree of effective democracy. On the other hand, when formal democracy is present in an emancipative culture, the elite quality factor is usually very high, giving formal democracy its full effectiveness.

Precisely in those cases where the degree of effective democracy is much lower than the degree of formal democracy, it is because of a poor quality of the elites—in response to a weak emancipative culture. This can be demonstrated using the difference between formal democracy and effective democracy as a measure of façade democracy:

$$\text{Façade Democracy} = \text{Formal Democracy} - \text{Effective Democracy}$$

According to this measure, the degree of façade democracy is larger the more the level of formal democracy exceeds the level of effective democracy (the reverse case is impossible). In other words, façade democracy shrinks as the gap between formal and effective democracy closes. In the best case, the degree of façade democracy is zero.

Consider now Figure 6A. As this figure demonstrates, the degree of façade democracy shrinks systematically with the strength of self-expression values among publics. In other words, the stronger the emancipative imprint of a mass culture, the weaker the façade character of democracy. The only outliers in this respect are China and Pakistan who show a surprisingly low level of façade democracy given the weakness of emancipative values among their populations. This, however, is due to the fact that both China and Pakistan have very low levels of formal democracy, such that there can be no large gap between formal and effective democracy. Therefore, Figure 6B controls for the level of formal democracy. China and Pakistan are no longer outliers and the same finding occurs again: the degree of façade democracy shrinks systematically with increasing self-expression values among the masses.

According to these findings, rising self-expression values represent a social force that tends to close the gap between formal and effective democracy. There can be any level of formal democracy, irrespective of the strength of self-expression values among the population. But strong self-expression values among

Figure 6A. The Impact of Emancipative Values on Façade-Democracy

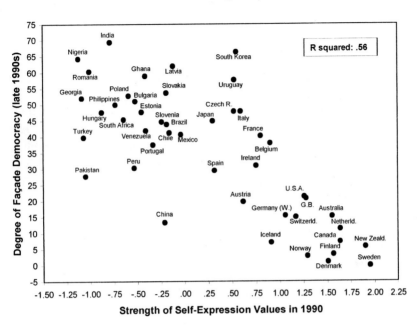

Figure 6B. The Impact of Emancipative Values on Facade Democracy
(Effect isolated from Levels of Formal Democracy)

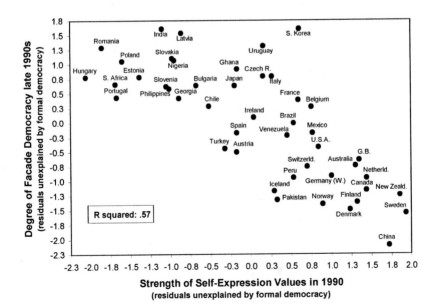

the masses are needed to produce the elite quality that makes formal democracy effective. Hence, effective democracy is much more closely linked to the emancipative force of self-expression values than is formal democracy. Formal democracy is a less systematic and more random phenomenon than effective democracy.

Conclusion

Although various factors play an important role in creating effective democracy, a major part of the story can be reduced to an emancipative sequence: (1) accumulated human resources on a mass-scale tend to strengthen people's emphasis on self-expression values; (2) mass-level self-expression values in turn fuel elite integrity and elite openness; (3) these elite characteristics converge in an joint factor of elite quality that increases the effectiveness of given levels of formal democracy.

　　Asking for the logic of this sequence, one can identify one underlying theme: Human Development. Following Welzel (2002), as well as Welzel, Inglehart, and Klingemann (2003), I conceptualize Human Development as the growth of human autonomy and choice in major aspects of people's lives. Available human resources are the most existential contribution to human autonomy and choice, providing people with the means and skills that widen the range of possible activities. If growing human resources reduce existential constraints on human autonomy and choice, people begin to place more emphasis on self-expression, giving rise to an emancipative culture in which human autonomy and choice are a highly valued. Rising self-expression values, in turn, fuel elite integrity and elite openness, since self-expression values are inherently linked with mass expectations that are targeted at making the elites responsive and inclusive. Elite integrity and elite openness converge in an efficacy factor: this factor makes effective the choices to which people are entitled by formal rights. This eventually results in effective democracy—the institutional reflection of growing human autonomy and choice among the masses.

　　In summary, mass-level human resources, self-expression values, the quality of elites, and effective democracy are linked through the emancipative logic of Human Development. With its common focus on human choice, this overarching process of Human Development champions an intrinsic value of human nature. For making choices is the most typical ability of the human species.

　　It reflects an existential logic that the sequence of Human Development starts with economic development. The economy signifies a society's patterns of physical subsistence. This is, without doubt, the sphere where the most existential conditions of a society originate. These existential conditions tend to be reflected in a society's culture. Self-expression values that emphasize human choice do not emerge in poor societies where scarce resources impose severe existential constraints on human choice. Although self-expression values manifest themselves in ways that reinforce their comfortable economic conditions, such reciprocal effects do not completely reverse the causal arrow. An emancipative culture is not completely derivative of advantageous economic conditions, but it is to a large degree.

Similarly, we consider it logical that our model assigns causal priority to culture over institutions. Culture includes the values and beliefs that define which sorts of institutions are more easily accepted and practiced. Hence, institutional designs (and even more so their efficacy) tend to reflect culture. This reflection, too, manifests itself in ways that reinforce its cultural conditions. But again, such reciprocal effects cannot completely reverse the causal arrow. Democratic institutions can be designed from scratch, but how they function is largely influenced by a culture's emancipative outlook. Unfortunately, the reverse way does not work: an emancipative culture that sustains democracy cannot simply be designed through institutional engineering. A well-written constitution is not enough to make it work, as the historical evidence of crumbling democracies has shown.

I do not claim that history has always followed a progressive path of Human Development, as described here. Quite the contrary, Human Development is a very recent phenomenon in history because it presumes mass-levels of human resources that have nowhere been reached earlier than after World War II. Although *formal* democracy is an older phenomenon, the levels of *effective* democracy that some countries, such as those in Scandinavia, reach nowadays are very recent—thanks to unprecedented levels of elite integrity and elite openness.

Public pressure on elites was probably never greater than nowadays. One should consider, in this context, the increasingly important role of the global information flow. Never before in history have ordinary people on almost any place on the globe had such easy access to performance evaluations, enabling them to criticize their elites, as soon as they fall short of international standards in human rights, fair elections, corruption, or gender empowerment. Given an increasing proliferation of international rankings, publics are more capable of measuring the quality of their elites against democratic standards. And, publics are more willing to apply these standards as they increasingly emphasize emancipative values.

APPENDIX

Table A1. Overview on Variables and Measurements

Names	Meaning	Scaling	Time	Sources
(1) Elite Integrity	Corruption Perception Scores, indicating the degree of corruption among political, bureaucratic and economic elites. Scale reversed such that it measures the degree of absence of elite corruption.	Scale from 0 to 100	Late 1990s	Transparency International, see http://www.transparency.org
(2) Elite Openness	Gender Empowerment Measure, indicating female representation among political, bureaucratic and economic elites	Scale from 0 to 1	Late 1990s	Human Development Report, see: http://www.undp.org
(3) Self-Expression Values	Dimensional summary of aggregated emancipative attitudes shown in Table 1	Factor scale with 0-mean and standard deviation 1	About 1990	European/World Values Surveys, data published in Welzel, Inglehart and Klingemann (2003)
(4) Formal Democracy	Scope of institutionalized freedom rights, calculated by adding civil and political rights scores	1-7 scales for civil and political rights reversed (such that larger scores indicate more rights) and added. Largest possible value (14=7+7) standardized to 100	Scores for 1999 and 2000 (added and averaged).	Freedom House, see: http://www.freedomhouse.org
(5) Elite Quality Factor	Elite Integrity + Elite Openness, indicating the overall quality of elites by summarizing their integrity and openness	Z-transformed scores for elite integrity and elite openness added. Maximum standardized to 1.0	Late 1990s	Variables (1) and (2) in this table

(Table 1 Con't on Next Page)

(Table 1 Con't)

Names	Meaning	Scaling	Time	Sources
(6) Effective Democracy	Formal Democracy * Elite Quality: weighting formal democracy by elite quality in order to measure the degree to which formal democracy is made effective by elites	Scores from 0 to 100 for formal democracy multiplied by scores from 0 to 1.0 for elite quality	Late 1990s	Variables (4) and (5) in this table
(7) Façade Democracy	Formal Democracy - Effective Democracy, indicates the degree to which level of formal democracy exceeds level of effective democracy	0-to-100 scores for formal democracy minus weighted 0-to-100 scores for effective democracy	Late 1990s	Variables (4) and (6) in this table
(8) Religious Tradition	Religious composition, weighted for its impact on elite quality: correlations between religious groups (Protestants, Catholics, Orthodox Christians, Muslims and "rest") and elite quality used as positive/negative weights in an addition of these religious groups' percentages; producing an index measuring the net impact of nations' religious compositions on elite quality	Factor scale	Late 1980s/early 1990s	Percentages of religious groups from Britannica Book of the Year 1998
(9) Democratic Experience	Number of years a country spent as a democracy from 1850 or its national independence until 1990, using the −10 to +10 autocracy-democracy index from Gurr and Jaggers (1995), calculating each year in which a nation reaches at least +6 as democratic	0 to 140 years	1850 until 1990	Polity 98-project (Gurr and Jaggers), see: http://www.bsos.umd.edu/cidcm/polity

(Table 1 Con't on Next Page)

(Table 1 Con't)

Names	Meaning	Scaling	Time	Sources
(10) Human Resources	Summary index for the accumulation and distribution of material, monetary and intellectual resources among the population	0 to 100 scale	Late 1980s	Vanhanen (1997)

NOTES

1   I conceptualize effective democracy in terms of a society's democratic performance, not its economic performance. One can consider economic development as a precondition or consequence of democracy, but not as a definitional part of it. Democracy is an inherently institutional phenomenon. Hence, effective democracy can only mean how effective a democracy's prime institutions are realized in practice. Freedom rights are among democracy's prime institutions, and elite integrity as well as elite openness are core indicators of how far these rights are set into practice.

2   Data and methodological report can be obtained from Transparency International's homepage: http://www.transparency.org.

3   Data from the first to the third wave of the World Values Surveys can be obtained from the International Consortium for Political Research (ICPSR) under the study-number 6160. Data from the fourth wave are not yet public domain. More detailed information on questionnaires, methods, and fieldwork can be obtained from the World Values Study Group's homepage: http://wvs.isr.umich.edu. For the data provided by the European Values Study Group, see http://evs.kub.nl and Halman (2001).

4   Although these items are taken from the postmaterialism scale (see fn. 3 in Table 1), I have reason to distinguish them as "liberty aspirations" from other components of postmaterialism, namely preferences for a "less impersonal society," "beautiful cities," and "a society in which ideas count more than money." The postmaterialist interpretation implies that these are "new" values that emerged only recently in postindustrial societies. I, however, believe this is not true in the case of liberty aspirations, which are historically related to the rise of prosperous "middle classes" as, for instance, in ancient Athens, in seventeenth century England, or in South East Asia during recent decades. This is argued in more

detail by Welzel (2002).

5   As noted by Barnes and Kaase et al. (1979), signing petitions is a low cost form of civic protest. Hence, a society with many people who sign petitions has a rich opportunity structure for low cost protest. This in turn implies that there must be many people who invest in the higher costs, which are necessary to create low cost opportunities for all.

6   All subsequent results referring to this elite quality factor have also been calculated using its two components, elite integrity and elite openness, separately. The results have been the same (not documented here).

7   Numbers after the country labels in Figure 3 indicate whether data are drawn from the third or fourth wave of the World Values Surveys.

8   Data are taken from the Britannica Book of the Year (1996) and refer mostly to the late 1980s and early 1990s.

9   "Other believers" include Hindus, Buddhists, Confucians, Taoists, Shintoists, and Animists.

10   These weights indicate the correlations between the elite quality factor and the percentages of the various religious groups. Using these correlations as weights for the religious groups, whose percentages are added after having been weighted, produces a religious composition factor that measures the impact of the nations' religious composition on the quality of elites.

11   These years haven been counted from the beginning of a nation's independence (or from 1850 onward in case of countries that have not been independent before 1850) until 1990. Countries that emerged from the dissolution of the Soviet Union and Yugoslavia have been coded like their former mother country as long as they belonged to it. A year has been counted as one under a democratic constitution, if a country obtained at least +6 points on the −10 to +10 "Autocracy-Democracy" index from Gurr and Jaggers (1995). I chose +6 because it marks the threshold from which a country is closer to the democratic pole (+10) than to the neutral point (0) on the −10 to +10 scale. This index is based on an analysis of constitutions considering the extent of restrictions on executive power and the dependence of legislatures and government from the electorate. Data and methodological description can be obtained from the homepage of the "Polity 98" project: http://www.bsos.umd.edu/cidcm/polity. I use these data here because they reach farther back in time than the scores from Freedom House and, therefore, are more adequate to measure the length of the democratic experience.

12   Vanhanen creates three subindices. The subindex of "physical resources" is generated from the share of family farms in the agricultural sector (weighted for the
agricultural sector's share in GDP) and the deconcentration of non-agricultural
resources (measured by 100 minus the share in GDP generated by the state, foreign enterprises, and large national trusts). The subindex of "intellectual resources" is measured by the number of students per 100,000 inhabitants and the literacy rate. The subindex of "occupational diversification" ("social complexity"
in my terminology) is produced from the proportion of the urban population and
the percentage of the non-agricultural work force. All component variables are
standardized before they are combined to the subindices. The three subindices
are each combined additively from their component variables, assuming that each
subindex represents a unique dimension. The same assumption then leads to a
multiplicative combination of the three subindices to create the overall index of
individual resources. This index is standardized to 100 as the maximum. For a
detailed description of scale construction, see Vanhanen (1997:42-63) and the
appendices of his book for extensive documentation of data sources.

13   The use of GDP can be misleading in the theoretical context of human development. For instance, by exploiting natural resources, some oil exporting countries
became extremely rich, showing exceptionally high figures of per capita GDP.
But people in these societies lack other resources that are important for human
autonomy and choice, including education and access to information.

14   As before, the religious tradition measures an "impact weighted" religious composition, using correlation coefficients as weights for religious groups whose
percentages are then added. Here, however, the dependent variable is not elite
quality but self-expression values. So I used the correlations between self-exp-

ression values and the religious groups: Impact weighted religious composition
= .58*%Protestants + .14*%Catholics - .30*%Orthodox - .46*%Muslims -
.28*%Other Believers. As before, this variable basically reflects a Western vs.
Non-Western religion factor, here measuring the impact of the nations' religious
composition on the self-expression values among their people.

15   In order to measure the scope of given freedom rights, I use scores for civil and
political rights from Freedom House (see Freedom in the World 2000). These
scores range from 1 to 7 on both scales, with 1 indicating the largest range and 7
indicating the lowest possible range of rights. I reversed these scores such that
higher values indicate a larger range of rights. Then I added the scores for civil
and political rights to create an overall index for the scope of freedom rights.
From the theoretical perspective of human development, this summation is appropriate since people need both "negative" freedom (i.e., civil rights protecting
their private choices) and "positive" freedom (i.e., political rights offering oppor-

tunities for public choice) in order to act as emancipated citizens. I standardized the additive civil and political rights scale, equating the highest possible value with 100 percent. And, I used the most recent scores for the years 1999 and 2000 (averaged), making sure that these measures are temporally subsequent to the self-expression values measure and contemporaneous to the measure of elite quality. For the research methods and scaling procedures of Freedom House see their homepage: http://www.freedomhouse.org. For an evaluation of the validity of these scales see Bollen and Paxton (2000).

REFERENCES

ALMOND, Gabriel A. and Sidney Verba.
    1963. *The Civic Culture: Political Attitudes in Five Western Democracies.* Princeton: Princeton University Press.
AXELROD, Robert.
    1980. *The Evolution of Cooperation.* New York: Basic Books.
BARNES, Samuel H. and Max Kaase et al.
    1979. *Political Action: Mass Participation in Five Western Democracies.* Beverly Hills: Sage.
BOLLEN, Kenneth and Pamela M. Paxton.
    2000. "Subjective Measures of Liberal Democracy." *Comparative Political Studies* 33(2):58-86.
BRINT, Steven.
    1984. "New Class and Cumulative Trend Explanations of the Liberal Political Attitudes of Professionals." *American Journal of Sociology* 90(1):30-71.
CASPER, Gretchen and Michelle M. Taylor.
    1996. *Negotiating Democracy: Transitions from Authoritarian Rule.* Pittsburgh: University of Pittsburgh Press.
DAHL, Robert A.
    2000. *On Democracy.* New Haven: Yale University Press.
DALTON, Russell J.
    1985. "Political Parties and Political Representation: Party Supporters and Party Elites in Nine Nations." *Comparative Political Studies* 18:267-99.
DONNELLY, Jack.
    1993. *Human Rights and World Politics.* Boulder: Westview Press.
ENCYCLOPAEDIA BRITANNICA.
    Various volumes. *Britannica Book of the Year.* London: Encyclopaedia Britannica.
FINER, Samuel E.
    1999. *The History of Government.* Vol. 1. Oxford: Oxford University Press.
FÖRSTER, Jens, E.T. Higgins, and L.C. Idson.
    1998. "Approach and Avoidance Strength during Goal Attainment: Regulatory Focus and the 'Goal Looms Larger' Effect." *Journal of Personality and Social*

Psychology 75:1115-1131.
FREEDOM HOUSE.
　　Various volumes. *Freedom in the World*. Lanham: University Press of America.
FUKUYAMA, Francis.
　　1989. "The End of History." *The National Interest* 16(Summer):4-18.
GASTIL, Raymond Duncan.
　　1993. "The Comparative Survey of Freedom: Experiences and Suggestions." Pp.
　　21-46 in *On Measuring Democracy: Its Consequences and Concomitants,* edited
　　by Alex Inkeles. New Brunswick: Transaction.
GURR, Ted R. and Keith Jaggers.
　　1995. "Tracking Democracy's Third Wave with the Polity III Data." *Journal of
　　Peace Research* 32(4):469-482.
HAAS, Michael.
　　1996. "Empirical Dimensions of Human Rights." Pp. 43-72 in *Human Rights and
　　Development*, edited by David Louis Cingranelli. Greenwich: JAI Press.
HALMAN, Loek, ed.
　　2001. *The European Values Study*. Tilburg: EVS, WORC, Tilburg University.
HELLER, Patrick.
　　2000. "Degrees of Democracy: Some Comparative Lessons from India." *World
　　Politics* 52(July):484-519.
HIGLEY, John and Richard Gunther, eds.
　　1992. *Elites and Democratic Consolidation in Latin America and Southern
　　Europe*. New York: Cambridge University Press.
HOFFERBERT, Richard I. and Hans-Dieter Klingemann.
　　1999. "Remembering the Bad Old Days: Human Rights, Economic Conditions,
　　and Democratic Performance in Transitional Regimes." *European Journal of
　　Political Research* 36(1):155-174.
HUMANA, Charles.
　　1992. *World Human Rights Guide*. 3d ed. New York: Oxford University Press.
HUNTINGTON, Samuel P.
　　1991. *The Third Wave: Democratization in the Late Twentieth Century*. Norman:
　　University of Oklahoma Press.
HUNTINGTON, Samuel P.
　　1996. *The Clash of Civilizations and the Remaking of the World Order*. New
　　York: Simon and Schuster.
INGLEHART, Ronald.
　　1997. *Modernization and Postmodernization: Cultural, Economic and Political
　　Change in 43 Societies*. Princeton: Princeton University Press.
INGLEHART, Ronald and Wayne E. Baker.
　　2000. "Modernization, Cultural Change, and the Persistence of Traditional
　　Values." *American Sociological Review* 65(February):19-51.
INGLEHART, Ronald and Pippa Norris.
　　2003. *Rising Tide: Gender Equality in Global Perspective*. New York: Cambridge
　　University Press.

IVERSEN, Torben.
1994. "Political Leadership and Representation in Western European Democracies." *American Journal of Political Science* 38:46-74.
JACKMAN, R.W. and R.A. Miller.
1998. "Social Capital and Politics." *Annual Review of Political Science* 1:47-73.
LINZ, Juan J. and Alfred Stepan.
1996. *Problems of Democratic Transition and Consolidation: Southern Europe, South America, and Post-Communist Europe.* Baltimore: Johns Hopkins University Press.
LIPSET, Seymour M. and Gabriel S. Lenz.
2000. "Corruption, Culture, and Markets." Pp. 112-124 in *Culture Matters: How Values Shape Human Progress*, edited by Lawrence E. Harrison and Samuel P. Huntington. New York: Basic Books.
MASLOW, Abraham.
1988. *Motivation and Personality.* 3d ed. New York: Harper and Row.
MULLER, Edward N. and Mitchell A. Seligson.
1994. "Civic Culture and Democracy: The Question of Causal Relationships." *American Political Science Review* 88(3):635-652.
O'DONNELL, Guillermo and Philippe C. Schmitter.
1986. "Tentative Conclusions about Uncertain Democracies." Pp. 1-78 in *Transitions from Authoritarian Rule*, vol. 4, edited by Guillermo O'Donnell, Philippe C. Schmitter, and Laurence Whitehead. Baltimore: Johns Hopkins University Press.
O'DONNELL, Guillermo.
1993. "On the State, Democratization and Some Conceptual Problems." *World Development* 21(8):1355-1369.
OLSON, Mancur J., Sarna Naveen, and Anand W. Swamy.
2000. "Governance and Growth." *Public Choice* 102:341-364.
PAXTON, Pamela.
2000. "Women's Suffrage in the Measurement of Democracy: Problems of Operationalization." *Studies in Comparative International Development* 35:92-111.
PUTNAM, Robert D.
1993. *Making Democracy Work: Civic Traditions in Modern Italy.* Princeton: Princeton University Press.
PYE, Lucian W.
1990. "Political Science and the Crisis of Authoritarianism." *American Political Science Review* 84(March):3-19.
RAWLS, John.
1993. *Political Liberalism.* New York: Columbia University Press.
ROSE, Richard.
2001. "A Divergent Europe." *Journal of Democracy* 12(1):93-106.
SEN, Amartya.
2001. *Development as Freedom.* New York: Knopf.
UNITED NATIONS DEVELOPMENT PROGRAM.

Various volumes. *Human Development Report.* New York: Oxford University Press.

VANHANEN, Tatu.

1997. *Prospects of Democracy: A Study of 172 Countries.* London: Routledge.

WEBER, Max

[1904] 1958. *The Protestant Ethic and the Spirit of Capitalism.* Boston: Allen and Unwin.

WELZEL, Christian.

2002. *Fluchtpunkt Humanentwicklung: Die Grundlagen der Demokratie und die Ursachen ihrer Ausbreitung* [*Focus Human Development: The Foundations of Democracy and the Causes of its Spread*]. Opladen: Westdeutscher Verlag.

WELZEL, Christian, Ronald Inglehart, and Hans-Dieter Klingemann.

2003. "The Theory of Human Development: A Cross-Cultural Analysis." *European Journal of Political Research* 42

ATTITUDES TOWARD DEMOCRACY: MEXICO IN COMPARATIVE PERSPECTIVE

Alejandro Moreno[*] and Patricia Méndez[**]

ABSTRACT

Mexico's gradual democratization had a critical point in 2000, when the presidential election brought about political alternation in that country. If democracy requires a compatible value system that helps such a system endure, how democratic are Mexicans today and what implications does this have for democratic consolidation in Mexico? This article examines new survey data to address this old question. Our findings reveal that the prevailing political culture in Mexico expresses comparatively low support for democracy and relatively high support for non-democratic government, on the one hand, and low interpersonal trust, low levels of tolerance, and a strong emphasis on deference, on the other. Education is an important determinant of democratic values, and individual variation is significant on a wide range of attitudes. Changes over time also indicate that Mexicans have reinforced both democratic and non-democratic values in the last few years, which makes it hard to assess whether, overall, Mexico's democratic values are expanding or shrinking.

Introduction

Mexico's gradual democratization came to a critical point in 2000, when the presidential election brought about political alternation in that country. After remaining in power for 71 years, the Institutional Revolutionary Party (PRI) was defeated at the polls. Vicente Fox, the National Action Party (PAN) candidate, became the first President from a party other than the PRI in Mexico's modern history. Three years earlier, the PRI had lost its majority in Congress, and the 1990s witnessed how opposition parties defeated the PRI in local and state-level elections, gradually ousting the PRI from office in every level of government. After all of these significant transformations, how democratic are Mexicans nowadays and how do they value democracy? This question derives from the early studies on political culture which stated that democracy requires a compatible value system that helps it endure (Lipset 1959; Almond and Verba 1963).

Our task in this article is to assess how Mexicans value democracy and to what extent they possess the elements of a democratic political culture. We do this by comparing Mexican democratic values with those of other regions of the world,

[*]   Department of Political Science, Instituto Tecnológico Autónomo de México, ITAM, Río Hondo No. 1, Tizapán-San Angel, México DF, 01000 México.
[**] Department of Survey Research, Reforma, Av. México Coyoacán No. 40, Col. Santa Cruz Atoyac, México DF, 03310 México.

and also by observing how Mexicans' democratic attitudes have changed in the last few years. We also look at the differences among Mexicans, focusing on education as an important predictor of democratic values.

Academic efforts to measure democratic values and support for democracy in Mexico are not new, but the 1990s brought a new wave of quantitative studies that used increasingly reliable and sophisticated opinion surveys based on national representative samples (Inglehart, Basañez, and Nevitte 1994; Domínguez and McCann 1996; Camp et al. 2001). These studies, as well as the surveys that provided the empirical evidence, reflect a period of profound political transformation. Moreover, Mexico included regularly national representative samples in international surveys that monitor, among other things, citizen support for democracy and the spread of democratic values. Both the World Values Survey, which serves as evidence to this article, and the Latinobarómetro surveys are good examples.

The literature on support for democracy in Third Wave democracies has recently raised interesting paradoxes. Let us mention three of them. First, democracy has nowadays a widespread legitimacy in the world, but trust in democratic institutions has declined (Diamond and Gunther 2001). Moreover, political participation has also lost the enthusiasm of the democratic honeymoon in third wave democracies (Inglehart and Catterberg 2002).

The second paradox is that, although open support for democracy is almost universal today, its measurement is not a precise indicator of how rooted democracy is in society (Inglehart n.d.). A very illustrative indicator is that democracy is highly valued in Islamic societies, but very few Islamic societies have functioning democratic regimes. Given the little difference in democratic principles and ideals between Islamic societies and the West, there is hardly a "clash of civilizations" in those terms (Norris and Inglehart 2002).

A third paradox is that today, when survey researchers measure support for democracy, they are measuring support for a socially desirable concept, and measurement validity only reflects overt support (Inglehart n.d.). The fact is that measures of overt support for democracy do not tell us how democratic societies are, or how tolerant. On the contrary, measuring tolerance may tell us how democratic a society is.

Support for democracy may erode, especially when the economic context may raise doubts about the functioning of democratic institutions. References to the Weimar Republic often illustrate this syndrome (Inglehart 1997). Support for democracy was not enough to allow democracy to endure in a profound economic crisis. Precisely, many third wave democracies have faced the challenge of economic transformation and recovery, and a decade ago some observers identified economic performance as one of the main obstacles to democratic consolidation (Przeworski 1991). Moreover, corruption and political scandals might bring disillusionment with democracy in newly democratic societies. In any case, good measurements of a democratic political culture are not limited to support for democratic rule—particularly when, today, survey responses on the issue are strongly subject to social desirability bias. Instead, such measurements should allow us to know something more than overt support for democracy; they should tell us something about tolerance, trust, and rejection of non-democratic forms of governance, for example.

Democracy and Political Culture in Mexico

Mexico's democratization was significantly achieved through electoral reforms and a gradual increase in political competition. The 1988 presidential election witnessed the first major electoral challenge to the Institutional Revolutionary Party, PRI, which was made possible thanks to a party split in 1987. Mexican opposition parties started to win elections earlier, especially at the municipal level. The first state governor from a party other than the PRI, in this case the National Action Party (PAN), was elected in Baja California, in 1989. The 1990s witnessed a more rapid increase in political competition thanks to further electoral reforms and both 1997 and 2000 were critical years in electoral terms. In 1997, the PRI lost its majority in Congress, obtaining only 39 percent of the national vote. The PAN and the PRD (Party of Democratic Revolution) obtained 27 and 26 percent of the national vote, respectively. In 2000, the PRI lost the presidency, obtaining 38 percent of the vote, whereas Vicente Fox, a candidate of the Alliance for Change (a coalition of PAN and the Greens) obtained about 43 percent. During the 1990s, the issue of democracy was the main determinant of party support and party competition. Those who favored a democratic transformation were more likely to support the PAN, whereas those who sought to keep the PRI in power expressed more authoritarian attitudes and values (Moreno 1998; Moreno 1999).

Recent surveys conducted in Mexico by government institutions have shown that a great majority of Mexicans support and value democracy. The results have been published with enthusiasm and optimism, speaking in favor of the strength of democratic values in that country. The simple fact that government institutions have polled Mexicans on this matter and published the results of their study shows an important change in Mexican political culture. Why would political elites do so under authoritarian rule? However, as a society, Mexico is far from having a very strong value system that is compatible with democracy. Comparatively, Mexicans show lower levels of tolerance and trust, and higher deference for authority and support for non-democratic rule than societies in other countries of the world. For example, Mexico's average score on a composite index of support for democracy is well under the average of 48 societies included in the 1995-1997 World Values Survey (Moreno 2001). This does not mean that democracy is not likely to endure in Mexico. It means that Mexicans are just starting to know democracy, both its virtues and its problems, and developing a real sense of it.

Our task in this article is to empirically answer the following questions:

How does Mexican democratic culture compare to democratic culture in other regions of the world? How have Mexican democratic values evolved in recent years? How diverse is democratic culture within Mexico? In a more rhetorical, less empirical sense: What implications are there for the consolidation of democracy in Mexico? By democratic culture we mean a set of values and attitudes that are compatible with democratic principles and practices, such as tolerance, interpersonal trust, emphasis on civil liberties and rights, political participation, support for democracy, and rejection of non-democratic forms of government. We are aware that our answers to these questions may not be definitive, but we hope that their empirical basis serves as a portrait of the Mexican political culture at the end of the twentieth and beginning of the twenty-first centuries.

Data Description

This article is based on data from the 1995-1997 and 2000-2001 World Values Survey (WVS), the third and fourth waves of the project, respectively. Our analysis of the WVS is mostly descriptive and, for illustration purposes, we decided to compare Mexico with regions of the world rather than with particular countries. The countries included in each region are the following: *Latin America and the Caribbean*: Argentina 1995 and 2000, Brazil 1995, Chile 1995 and 2000, Peru 1995, Puerto Rico 1995, Dominican Republic 1995, Uruguay 1995, and Venezuela 1995 and 2000. *Africa*: Ghana 1995, Nigeria 1995 and 2000, South Africa 1995 and 2000, Uganda 2000, Zimbabwe 2000. *East Asia*: China 1995 and 2000, South Korea 1995 and 2000, Japan 1995 and 2000, and Taiwan 1995. *South Asia*: Bangladesh 2000, Philippines 1995 and 2000, India 1995, Turkey 1995 and 2000, and Vietnam 2000. *Advanced Democracies*: West Germany 1995, Australia 1995, Canada 2000, Spain 1995 and 2000, United States 1995 and 2000, Finland 1995, Israel 2000, Norway 1995, Switzerland 1995, Sweden 1995 and 2000. *Post-Communist Societies*: East Germany 1995, Armenia 1995, Azerbaijan 1995, Belarus 1995, Croatia 1995, Slovenia 1995, Estonia 1995, Georgia 1995, Latvia 1995, Lithuania 1995, Moldavia 1995, Montenegro 1995 and 2000, Poland 1995, Russia 1995, Serbia 1995 and 2000, Tambov 1995, and Ukraine 1995. Mexico was analyzed separately from Latin America. The dataset with these countries has 97,643 respondents.

In this article we also use the National Survey of Political Culture and Citizen Practices (ENCUP 2001), a national representative sample of 4,183 adult Mexicans sponsored by the Interior Ministry of Mexico (SEGOB), and conducted by the National Institute of Statistics, Geography, and Information (INEGI). Fieldwork took place from November 4 to December 7, 2001. Our use of the ENCUP here is more analytical. We use multinomial logistic regression analysis and show the predicted probabilities from the models. The models based on the ENCUP are rather weak, but the differences by education show that there is a significant variation among Mexicans, as shown elsewhere (Moreno 2001). Also, by

looking at individual differences we recognize the problems of just reporting societal averages, as if each society was homogeneous (Knight 2001). We are well
aware that this is not the case.

Comparing Mexico's Democratic Culture

Comparisons always bring conceptual and empirical problems: what aspects
should be compared and how valid are the measurements in different national and
regional contexts? Trying to respond to the first part of the question, we identify
some of the main qualities considered as crucial factors in the flourishing of
democracy. Such factors are tolerance, trust, emphasis on civil rights and political
participation, and a general sense of subjective well-being (Inglehart n.d.).
Subjective well-being reflects the level of economic development in society,
which, according to several studies, is the basis of democratic development.
Rather than focusing on economic development and the sense of well-being, we
focus on tolerance and authority as elements of political socialization, on trust and
the openness to understand others' preferences, on support for democracy and
rejection of non-democratic rule, and on citizen evaluations of democratic performance and respect for human rights.

Tolerance and Obedience

A great deal of the literature on political culture follows the idea that political values are learned during the years of individual formation and socialization
(Segovia 1975; Moreno forthcoming). Without being a study of socialization, this
article shows some of the priorities that Mexican adults consider important in
children's education, and how they compare to other regions of the world. The
first and second columns of Table 1 show the percent of respondents in different
regions of the world that say that tolerance and obedience, respectively, are "very
important" to encourage among children. This combination of tolerance and obedience responds to the fact that tolerance is a favorable attitude towards democracy, while obedience reflects deference towards authority, not necessarily democratic. It is still common in Mexico to hear that children should be obedient, and
that a "good" child is the one who obeys his or her parents without questioning
them. The obvious translation into politics is that obedience reflects some subjec-
tion to political authority, and little questioning.

   According to the third and fourth waves of the World Values Survey, tolerance is considered a very important aspect to encourage among children in
advanced industrial democracies, where an average 81 percent of respondents
believe so. In contrast, post-Communist societies and East Asian countries
express the lower average levels of support for tolerance as a value that should be
taught to children. Comparatively, Mexico is slightly under the overall regional
average: 65 percent of Mexicans consider tolerance important for children, vis-à-

vis 67 percent expressed in all countries included in the analysis. On average, Latin American and Caribbean societies appear as more tolerant than Mexicans. Nonetheless, emphasis on tolerance in Mexico increased from 57 to 72 percent from 1997 to 2000. The 1997 survey was taken a few months before the PRI lost its majority in Congress in the mid-term 1997 elections. Perhaps the new political reality after 1997 contributed to the increase of the percent of Mexicans who consider tolerance important. Also, the Federal Elections Institute permanent media campaign of political values has placed an emphasis on political tolerance as well.

Table 1.
Measures of Democratic Attitudes: Tolerance, Obedience, and Interpersonal Relations

	Tolerance a	Obedience b	Trust c	Interpersonal relations d
	%	%	%	%
Advanced Democracies	81	29	41	64
Africa	67	62	16	61
East Asia	59	16	41	75
Latin America and the Caribbean	69	47	14	46
Mexico	65	54	24	41
Post-Communist Societies	62	30	23	59
South Asia	67	57	19	49
Mexico 1997	57	50	26	40
Mexico 2000	72	59	21	43

Source: 1995-2002 World Values Survey.
Notes: (a) The encouragement of tolerance in children is "very important"; (b) the encouragement of obedience in children is "very important"; (c) "most people can be trusted"; (d) "understanding others' preferences is more important than expressing one's own preferences in order to have successful human relations."

Mexicans are, on average, less interested in encouraging tolerance among children than other countries of different regions of the world, included Latin America. At the same time, they are more interested in promoting obedience. Only African societies consider obedience more important than in Mexico: 64 percent of the African publics surveyed emphasize obedience, vis-à-vis 54 percent of Mexicans. However, emphasis on obedience has increased in Mexico in recent years. In contrast, less than one-third (29 percent) of the publics in advanced industrial democracies, and about 16 percent of the East Asian publics emphasize obedience as an attribute that children should learn. In sum, Mexicans are more oriented towards promoting obedience and less towards expanding tolerance, in comparison to other regions of the world. The importance of tolerance increased in the last few years, but so did the importance of obedience.

Trust and Interpersonal Relations

Trust is a fundamental aspect in the functioning of democracy (Putnam 1991; Fukuyama 1995; Inglehart 1997). The combination of trust and tolerance reflects a will to understand others' preferences and aim at successful social relationships.

Table 1 shows the percent of respondents who express trust in people and who prioritize an understanding of others' preferences before the clear manifestation of one's own preferences.

In comparison to the levels of trust expressed in advanced democracies (41 percent, a similar percent to East Asia's), only 24 percent of Mexicans express trust in most people. The Latin American average level of trust is even lower, 14 percent, a lower level than the one registered in post-Communist societies, where the average trust is about 23 percent. Still, Mexico's level of trust is relatively low, in comparison to the one expressed in advanced democracies, and it decreased from 26 percent in 1997 to 21 percent in 2000.

Mexicans are, on average, less open to understand others' preferences. Only 41 percent place emphasis on the understanding of others' preferences in order to have successful human relations. This percentage is slightly lower than the Latin American average of 46 percent, and significantly lower than the percentage expressed in advanced democracies (64 percent) and in East Asia (75 percent). From 1997 to 2000, the percentage of respondents in Mexico who agree with the importance of understanding others' preferences was stable, only moving from 40 to 43 percent.

Comparatively, Mexican political culture is characterized by low levels of trust (or high levels of distrust, if preferable), and by low interest in other people's ideas and preferences. If these are parts of the social capital that make democracy work more efficiently, Mexicans lack a great deal of the lubricating factor for democracy: they seem to have a deficit of trust and are relatively closed to coexistence. Nonetheless, trust is not a trait of the majority, even in advanced democracies, where the overall average of trust is about 41 percent.

Support for Authoritarian Rule

The consolidation of new democracies requires that there are no real possibilities of an authoritarian regression, and that there is mass rejection to such possibilities. In Mexico, unlike other regions of the world, there is significant support for authoritarian forms of government, and even for military rule, which most living Mexicans have not experienced in their lifetime. Table 2 shows the percentage of respondents who say that having a strong leader who does not have to bother with Congress/Parliament and elections is good or very good, and the percentage of respondents who consider having the military rule as good or very good.

In Mexico, 41 percent of respondents support having a strong leader who does not bother with Congress and elections. This percentage is only outweighed by the one registered in South Asia, composed with countries such as India, Bangladesh, Turkey, Vietnam, and the Philippines. In that region, 52 percent of respondents say that this autocratic form of government is good. In contrast, 22 percent of the publics surveyed in advanced democracies support the idea of a strong leader. This is the lowest regional percent, but it is still a significant proportion: about one-fifth of those who live in stable industrial democracies are willing, at least in word, to accept a strong leader who does not bother with Congress and elections. The Latin American average of support for a strong leader is about 35 percent, similar to that of Africa (34 percent) and the post-Communist world (37 percent). Support for a strong leader grew in Mexico in the last few years from 39 percent in 1997, right before the first plural Congress came about, to 44 percent in 2000, right before Vicente Fox defeated the PRI candidate, Francisco Labastida, in the presidential election.

Table 2.
Support for Democratic and Non-Democratic Government

	Strong Leader a	Military government b	Support for democracy c	Democracies are indecisive d
	%	%	%	%
Advanced Democracies	22	6	86	47
Africa	34	22	72	41
East Asia	27	9	77	36
Latin America and the Caribbean	35	20	84	57
Mexico	41	25	65	46
Post-Communist Societies	37	10	70	48
South Asia	52	26	78	44
Mexico 1997	39	23	65	44
Mexico 2000	44	27	65	48

Source: 1995-2002 World Values Survey.
Notes: (a) Having a strong leader who does not have to bother with parliament and elections is "good" or "very good"; (b) having a military government is "good" or "very good"; (c) "Democracy is the best system," percent "agree"; (d) "Democracies are indecisive and have too much quibbling," percent "agree."

Most living Mexicans have not experienced military rule. In fact, the last president who had a military background after the Mexican Revolution, Manuel Ávila Camacho, ended his term in 1940, but his government cannot be characterized as a military rule. Despite this lack of military governments, today one out of four Mexicans thinks that having military rule is good. In South Asian societies, 26 percent of respondents support military rule, as well as 22 percent of the African publics. About 20 percent of Latin Americans say that military rule is something good, while only 6 percent of the publics in advanced democracies share that view. In sum, support for military government in Mexico is relatively higher than in other countries and regions, and it has increased in the last few years from 23 percent in 1997 to 27 percent in 2000.

Support for Democratic Governance

Today, overt support for democracy is high in most countries of the world, which means that having a simple majority or two-thirds of the public supporting democracy may be seen as a rather low score. Most Mexicans believe that democracy is the best system, but the percent in agreement with democracy is comparatively lower than the averages observed in most regions of the world. Moreover, overt support for democracy has not increased in Mexico in the last few years.

Table 2 shows the percent of respondents who agree that democracy is the best system, and the percent of respondents who agree that democracies are indecisive and have too much quibbling. About 86 percent of the publics in advanced democracies are convinced that democracy is the best system. Latin Americans (Mexico not included) are close to that level, with 84 percent; South Asia and East Asia have averages of 78 and 77 percent; African publics have an average 72 percent; and post-Communist societies 70 percent. Below all these averages of democratic support is Mexico, with about 65 percent. The same proportion was observed in 1997 and in 2000. This means that only two-thirds of Mexicans believe that democracy is the best system, and that proportion has not changed in the last few years. One-third of Mexicans are not convinced (or lack the information to say) that democracy is the best system.

Mexicans just started to live in a democracy and most of them just began to see their political system as such. According to a series of national polls conducted by *Reforma* newspaper in Mexico, fewer than half of Mexicans thought of their country as a democracy before the presidential elections of 2000. However, more than six out of ten Mexicans were convinced that Mexico was a democracy right after the presidential election (Moreno 2002).

Newly democratic experiences have brought different political dynamics to Mexicans' attention. After the 1997 mid-term elections, a plural Congress changed the balance of power in Mexico by changing the Executive-Legislative relations. Mexicans could watch on television or read in newspapers that democracy is an arrangement where disorder and lack of deference could be part of Mexico's institutional life without risking political stability. After the 2000 presidential election, Vicente Fox changed the style of the Mexican presidency in many ways, but perhaps the most significant change was not one of style, but of substance. The Mexican presidency has become more open and less effective. It is difficult for public policy and prospective legislation to move from a presidential initiative or good will to an actual government action or instituted law. The Indigenous Law in 2001, the Tax Reform in 2002, and the cancellation of a new airport construction in Mexico City in 2002, show how the new Mexican president has been unable to achieve his original goals.

Admitting that democracy may be slow and inefficient is not a signal of anti-democratic attitudes. Democracy implies that political outcomes are uncertain within institutional certainty (Przeworski 1991). Table 2 shows that most societies are divided along the idea that democracy is indecisive and has too much quibbling. About 57 percent of the Latin American societies share that view. In Mexico, that percentage is about 46 percent, similar to that of advanced democracies (47 percent) and post-Communist societies (48 percent).

Believing that a democracy is indecisive and troublesome is not an indicator of anti-democratic views. On the contrary, what is democracy if not an insti-

tutional arrangement that opens the possibility for different and generally opposing views and interests to be expressed, advanced, and negotiated? Tolerance of
homogeneity is a contradiction in terms. Tolerance has to do with diversity and
coexistence. Tolerance is tested precisely when political conflicts can be
processed through institutions with no need of violence. In Mexico, the belief that
democracy is indecisive and has too much quibbling increased from 44 to 48 percent from 1997 to 2000. Rather than being an increase in anti-democratic attitudes, this may be seen as a greater acknowledgement of some of democracy's
features. Unfortunately, this particular question has so much ambivalence that a
stronger conclusion cannot be reached.

Satisfaction with Democracy and Respect for Human Rights

Satisfaction with democracy and perceptions of how such a system guarantees
respect for human rights are important pillars in the way societies value democratic governance. Many of the new democracies had to build democratic institutions and develop mechanisms that changed the very fundamental relations
between government and citizenry. Some new democracies opened their past in
search of violations of basic human rights. What are the current perceptions of the
way democracy is developing and the way human rights are respected?

Table 3 shows the percentage of respondents who said they are "very" or
"somewhat" satisfied with the development of democracy in their country.
Comparatively speaking, the level of satisfaction is about 70 percent in South
Asia, 63 percent in advanced democracies, 53 percent in Latin America and the
Caribbean, and 50 percent in Africa. In East Asia, which includes China, the percentage of satisfaction with the development of democracy is about 45 percent. In
Mexico, only 37 percent say they are satisfied with the way democracy is developing in the country. This level is just above the percentage expressed in post-
Communist societies. It is clear that, before political alternation in 2000, Mexican
society was not very satisfied with the development of democracy in their country. The fourth wave of the WVS in Mexico was conducted in February 2000, four
and a half months before the presidential elections.

Table 3 also shows the percentage of respondents who believe that there
is a great deal or some respect for human rights in their country. About 74 percent
of the publics in advanced democracies think that there is respect for human rights
in their respective country. The average in East Asia is about 59 percent, in
Mexico it is 45 percent, in the post-Communist world 43 percent, and in Latin
America 41 percent. There are important episodes of violations to human rights
in Mexico, such as the student massacre in 1968, and the "Dirty War" in the early
1970s, just to mention two of the most important ones; and perceptions of respect
for human rights among the Mexican public are very similar to those in Latin
America and post-Communist societies. One should expect that an indicator of
how the public perceives respect for human rights not only reflects the authoritar-

ian past, but also the way newly democratic governments have dealt with the issue. The more respect for human rights, the higher the quality of democracy.

Table 3.
Satisfaction with Democracy and Perceptions of Respect for Human Rights

	Satisfaction with democracy a	Respect for Human Rights b
	%	%
Advanced Democracies	63	74
Africa	50	54
East Asia	45	59
Latin America and the Caribbean	53	41
Mexico	37	45
Post-Communist Societies	35	43
South Asia	70	53

Source: 2000-2002 World Values Survey.
Notes: (a) "Very" or "somewhat satisfied" with the way democracy is developing in the country; (b) there is "a lot" or "some" respect for human rights in the country.

The data shown in Table 3 suggest that Mexicans were comparatively unsatisfied with democratic development before political alternation, something that changed after the presidential elections. According to Moreno (2002), an index of satisfaction with democracy in Mexico, based on national representative samples shows that, on a weighted scale from 0 to 100, where 100 means very satisfied and 0 not at all satisfied, the average score obtained in October 1999 was 39. By August 2000, one month after the presidential election, the score increased to 60, and remained in the same level by November 2000. By November 2001, the average score was down to 50. Mexicans also share the lower positions in perceptions of respect for human rights.

With this descriptive account of democratic attitudes we conclude the first part of the article, which addressed the questions of how democratic Mexican political culture is, comparatively speaking, and how it has evolved in the last few years. The next part addresses a third question: how different are Mexicans among themselves, in terms of their democratic political culture? Before we move onto the second part, let us summarize our findings so far:

In comparison to the regional averages in the world, Mexicans encourage tolerance relatively less and obedience relatively more than most societies. In the last few years, emphasis on tolerance has increased in Mexico, but so has emphasis on obedience.

Mexicans are characterized by little interpersonal trust, which has in fact declined in the last few years. They are also relatively less open to understanding others' preferences in their human relations, an attitude that may hinder social and political coexistence in a heterogeneous society.

Mexicans show larger levels of acceptance of non-democratic forms of governance, such as autocracy and military rule, than in most regions of the world. Such acceptance has increased in the last few years.

Mexicans are comparatively less convinced that democracy is the best system. However, they are, as most societies, divided in the way they perceive democracy. Perceptions that such a system is indecisive and that it has too much quibbling are not indicators of anti-democratic attitudes, but an acknowledgment of those characteristics.

Mexicans were unsatisfied with the development of democracy until the 2000 elections. Fewer than half also considered that human rights are respected in that country. Both indicators show how perceptions about the quality of democracy in Mexico were at the end of the twentieth and beginning of the twenty-first centuries.

Internal Diversity: Findings from the National Survey of Political Culture

Which Mexicans are more likely to hold democratic values and attitudes? In this section we analyze the individual differences in support for democracy and tolerance among Mexicans. The analysis is based on multinomial logistic regression, and focuses on the predicted probabilities of holding one attitude or another with respect to democracy by levels of education. This variable has proved to be an important predictor of democratic attitudes.

According to the National Survey of Political Culture, conducted for the Interior Ministry (ENCUP 2001), 62 percent of respondents consider a democratic system preferable to any other form of government. This figure is consistent with the 65 percent of Mexican respondents of the 2000 World Values Survey that think democracy is the best system. In contrast, 9 percent of Mexicans polled by the ENCUP think that, under some circumstances, an authoritarian government is better than a democratic one.

As mentioned in the preceding section, the majority of Mexicans think democracy is the best system, but such a majority (62 to 65 percent, depending on the survey) represents a relatively low percentage in comparison to other regions of the world. Moreover, this majority is reduced to a plurality when respondents face some particular questions. What is more preferable: living under economic pressure without sacrificing civil liberties, or sacrificing civil liberties if that means not having economic pressures? About 47 percent of Mexicans would rather live under economic pressures without sacrificing civil liberties, whereas 32 percent think that civil liberties should be sacrificed in exchange for economic security. The distribution of responses to this question reveals that about one-third of Mexicans are willing, at least in word, to support suppression of civil liberties under economic pressures. Moreover, in terms of political tolerance, 52 percent of Mexicans disagree that television shows people with ideas politically different to their own, and about 35 percent agree.

Who is more likely to hold democratic attitudes? Who is more tolerant? Who is more likely to accept non-democratic forms of governance? Education and socioeconomic status are important predictors of pro-democratic attitudes in society, cross-nationally speaking (Moreno 2001). In order to show the impact of education and income, among other variables, we ran multinomial logistic regression models with different attitudes as dependent variables. The values taken by the dependent variables represented a pro-democratic position, a pro-authoritarian position, and an indifferent position. We used 6 different dependent variables with this coding. The model used gender, education, income, and region as independent variables. Additionally, we included economic retrospective evaluations, assuming that the most disaffected Mexicans would be more likely to reject democratic rule. The model is not an exhaustive one and has a relatively poor goodness of fit. The ENCUP survey did not offer any other independent variables (such as partisan orientations or left/right self-placement) that we think might improve the model. The only option we had was to include other attitudinal questions as independent variables, but this would have led us to a problem of endogeneity, so we decided not to include them. The analyses done in this section are unweighted. Let us now turn to the results.

Democracy and Political Effectiveness

Table 4 show the predicted probabilities derived from the multinomial regression model by education using dependent variables that represent support for democracy and attitudes toward political effectiveness. As stated earlier, education has a positive and significant impact on pro-democratic attitudes. The higher the respondent's education level, the more likely he or she will hold favorable attitudes toward democracy.

Table 4.
Democratic Attitudes in Mexico by Education, 2001.

	Citizen Preferences					
	(a) Democracy	Authoritarian government	(b) Heeding government	Effective government	(c) Civil liberties	No economic pressures
Education Level						
High	0.78	0.10	0.48	0.37	0.59	0.33
	0.72	0.10	0.43	0.40	0.54	0.35
	0.64	0.10	0.39	0.40	0.49	0.35
	0.56	0.10	0.34	0.40	0.43	0.34
Low	0.46	0.09	0.31	0.38	0.37	0.32

Source: National Survey of Political Culture (ENCUP), 2001. Author's calculations.
Entries are predicted probabilities from multinomial logit model described in text.
Notes: (a) Democracy over any other form of government vs. an authoritarian government under some circumstances; (b) A government that takes citizens into account even if it doesn't act when needed vs. a government that achieves its tasks but imposes its decisions; (c) living under economic pressure without sacrificing civil liberties vs. sacrifice civil liberties if that means living without economic pressures.

(Table 4 con't on next page)

Table 4 (cont.).
Democratic Attitudes in Mexico by Education, 2001

	Citizen Preferences					
	(a)		*(b) Different*	*Same*	*(c) Tolerance*	
	Democracy	*Dictatorship*	*values*	*values*		*Intolerance*
Education Level						
High	0.79	0.10	0.81	0.16	0.55	0.42
	0.70	0.13	0.76	0.19	0.44	0.49
	0.60	0.14	0.70	0.22	0.34	0.56
	0.48	0.15	0.62	0.25	0.25	0.59
Low	0.37	0.14	0.54	0.26	0.18	0.60

Source: National Survey of Political Culture (ENCUP), 2001. Author's calculations.
Entries are predicted probabilities from multinomial logit model described in text.
Notes: (a) Democracy even if it doesn't ensure economic security vs. a dictatorship that guarantees economic security; (b) people with different values and ideas vs. people with the same values an ideas; c) tolerance towards a person with different ideas to one's own in TV.

Generally, most Mexicans prefer democracy to authoritarianism, but such preference varies significantly by education. Eighty percent of the most educated Mexicans are likely to prefer democracy, whereas slightly over 40 percent of the least educated are likely to prefer democracy. Nonetheless, preferences for authoritarianism are not clearly related to education: the highly educated are as likely to prefer authoritarian governance under some circumstances as the least educated. This means that the lower the respondent's education, the more likely it is that he or she does not have a position towards either democracy or authoritarianism.

It has been demonstrated that Mexicans, as other Latin Americans, hold different concepts of democracy, and that education and the level of political sophistication make a difference on how democracy is perceived (Moreno 2001). The lower the level of education, the more likely it is that democracy is conceptualized in terms of elements that are not exclusively characteristic of democratic rule, such as fighting crime or maintaining order. Variables that represent levels of information and media consumption are even stronger predictors of the conceptualization of democracy than typical cultural variables, such as trust (Moreno 2001). Thus, political sophistication is positively related to support for democratic governance in Mexico.

However, education is a weaker determinant of the following attitude: what is better, a government that consults and takes citizen preferences into account even if it does not act when needed; or a government that acts effectively even if it imposes its decisions. Mexicans are clearly divided on this issue: fewer than half support the first position, and a similar proportion supports the second position. Table 4 shows that, as education increases, preferences for a government that consults citizens slightly increases. The differences, however, are not very significant. Even the most educated Mexicans are less than 50 percent likely to prefer a government that consults citizens to a government that imposes its decisions. The fact that the former option implies an ineffective government and the latter an effective one is causing this ambivalence. Citizens like to see government results.

Democracy and Economic Performance

The syndrome of the Weimar Republic represents the abandonment of democratic ideals and principles because of economic depression. How vulnerable are Mexican democratic values to economic adversities? Table 4 also shows that there are more Mexicans willing to live under economic pressure but without sacrificing civil liberties, than Mexicans who think the other way around. Moreover, as education increases, the desire to keep civil liberties, even in economically adverse times, also increases.

What about democracy vis-à-vis economic security? Table 4 shows that more Mexicans prefer democracy even if it does not ensure economic advancement to a dictatorship that guarantees economic security. Again, well-educated citizens express a higher preference for democratic rule. It is very noticeable, however, that one in ten Mexicans prefer a dictatorship that guarantees economic security. The question is hypothetical, since dictatorship does not necessarily "guarantee" economic security. Perhaps the "Asian Tigers" approach something similar to this situation, in which economic growth was significant under authoritarian rule. The current economic crisis in Argentina will show how rooted democratic values and attitudes are in that country.

Diversity and Tolerance

Table 4 shows that most Mexicans prefer that people have different ideas and values, but a considerable proportion prefers that people hold the same ideas and values. Support for diversity increases as education increases. Paradoxically, tolerance is not as widely shared as the taste for diversity, as shown in the same table. Although the majority of Mexicans prefers that people have different values and ideas, only a minority of them agree with television showing people with different and opposing ideas to their own. Even the most highly educated Mexicans seem clearly divided on this issue.

In sum, the data shown in this section indicate that Mexicans prefer democracy to authoritarianism, but are divided on the issue of effectiveness, suggesting that a government that imposes its decisions would be sometimes better than one who consults citizens but does not act when needed. There is a significant proportion of Mexicans who would be willing to sacrifice civil liberties if that means not living under economic pressures. Finally, most Mexicans prefer cultural diversity to homogeneity, but tolerance in practice is much more limited than such a preference for diversity would suggest. As noted earlier, tolerance of the homogeneous is a contradiction of terms. There is no ground for tolerance without diversity.

Conclusion

The presidential election of July 2, 2000 confirmed the completion of Mexico's transition to democracy. The question addressed here is how supportive Mexican political culture is of democracy. About two-thirds of Mexicans believe that democracy is the best system, but this is a comparatively small proportion if we take regional averages from other countries of the world. A good assessment of democratic values should not be limited to measuring overt support for democracy, because democracy has become a concept affected by social desirability bias. Even non-democratic societies express relatively high levels of support for democratic principles. Good measurements of democratic values should also include the elements that effectively contribute to make democratic life possible.

Focusing on Mexico from a comparative perspective, in this article we asked three central questions. How different are democratic attitudes in Mexico with those held in other societies? How have Mexican democratic attitudes changed in the last few years? How different are Mexicans amongst themselves in terms of their democratic attitudes? Data from the World Values Survey (WVS 1995, 2000) and the National Survey of Political Culture (ENCUP 2001) serve as the empirical evidence to provide some answers.

These data show that most Mexicans are convinced that democracy is the best system, but such a majority is, on average, a smaller proportion than in most regions of the world. Mexico's newly democratic experience is developing both different views of democracy and elements of judgment about it. Mexicans received democracy enthusiastically, according to opinion polls. Alternation in 2000 changed many of the citizen's disenchantment with the previous regime and increased trust in political institutions (Moreno 2002). Nonetheless, Mexican democracy and political culture are in a process of development, redefinition, and consolidation.

From a comparative perspective, tolerance and interpersonal trust in Mexico are more limited than in other regions of the world. Moreover, a significant proportion of Mexicans would be willing to sacrifice civil liberties in exchange for economic security. The proportion that thinks well of an autocratic government or a kind of military rule that has not even been witnessed by most living Mexicans is larger than in many other countries. Also, most Mexicans doubt that there is a widespread respect for human rights in their country. Such doubts obviously reduce favorable perceptions about the quality of democracy in Mexico.

Individual differences in the Mexican political value system are significantly explained by education. Less educated Mexicans are less likely to support non-democratic forms of governance or to be indifferent to democracy. The more educated Mexicans are, other things being equal, the more likely they are to hold democratic values and support democracy. Nonetheless, authoritarian and intolerant attitudes are observed among highly educated and non-educated Mexicans alike.

Asking whether Mexican political culture is compatible with democracy is an old question. Almond and Verba addressed it in the late 1950s, when they wrote *The Civic Culture*. Mexican political reality was different than it is today. However, these authors' statement that Mexicans were aspirational may have another meaning now. Mexicans may aspire not just to live in a democracy, as it was the case for a long time, but to live in a better, high-quality democracy. As they learn about it, we should expect changes in democratic values and attitudes in the future.

REFERENCES

ALMOND, Gabriel and Sidney Verba.
    1963. *The Civic Culture: Political Attitudes and Democracy in Five Nations.* Princeton: Princeton University Press.

CAMP, Roderic A., ed.
    2001. *Citizen Views of Democracy in Latin America.* Pittsburgh: University of Pittsburgh Press.

DIAMOND, Larry and Richard Gunther, eds.
    2001. *Political Parties and Democracy.* Baltimore: Johns Hopkins University Press.

DOMÍNGUEZ, Jorge I. and James A. McCann.
    1996. *Democratizing Mexico: Public Opinion and Electoral Choices.* Baltimore: Johns Hopkins University Press.

FUKUYAMA, Francis.
    1995. *Trust: The Social Virtues and the Creation of Prosperity.* New York: Free Press.

INGLEHART, Ronald.
    1997. *Modernization and Postmodernization: Cultural, Economic, and Political Change in 43 Societies.* Princeton: Princeton University Press.
    ———. n.d. "How Solid is Mass Support for Democracy and How Can We Measure it?" Unpublished manuscript.

INGLEHART Ronald, Miguel Basañez, and Neil Nevitte.
    1994. *Convergencia en Norteamérica: Comercio, Política y Cultura.* Mexico City: Siglo XXI.

INGLEHART, Ronald and Gabriela Catterberg.
    2002. "Transitions to Democracy: The Post-Honey Moon Decline in Political Participation." Paper presented at the Annual Meeting of the American Political Association, August 29-September 1, Boston.

KNIGHT, Alan.
    2001. "Polls, Political Culture, and Democracy; A Heretical Historical Look." In *Citizen Views of Democracy in Latin America*, edited by Roderic A. Camp. Pittsburgh: University of Pittsburgh Press.

LIPSET, Seymour M.

  1959. "Social Requisites of Democracy: Economic Development and Political Legitimacy." *American Political Science Review* 53:69-105.

MORENO, Alejandro.

  1998. "Party Competition and the Issue of Democracy: Ideological Space in Mexican Elections." In *Governing Mexico: Political Parties and Elections*, edited by Mónica Serrano. Macmillan-ILAS Series, Institute of Latin American Studies, University of London.

———. 1999. "Ideología y voto: Dimensiones de competencia política en México en los noventa." *Política y Gobierno* VI(1):45-81.

———. 2001. "Democracy and Mass Belief Systems in Latin America." In *Citizen Views of Democracy in Latin America*, edited by Roderic A. Camp. Pittsburgh, PA: University of Pittsburgh Press.

———. 2002. "La sociedad mexicana y el cambio." *Este País,* No. 136, April 2002.

———. Forthcoming. "Identificación partidista y socialización en México: Un análisis individual de padres e hijos." In *Los valores de los mexicanos, Tomo IV: Estabilidad y Cambio*, edited by Enrique Alduncin. Mexico City: Centro de Estudios Sociales de Banamex.

NORRIS, Pippa and Ronald Inglehart.

  2002. "Islam and the West: Testing de Clash of Civilization Thesis." Working Paper, RWP02-015, John F. Kennedy School of Government, Harvard University.

PRZEWORSKI, Adam.

  1998. *Democracy and de Market: Political an Economic Reforms in Eastern Europe and Latin America.* Cambridge: Cambridge University Press.

PUTNAM, Robert.

  1991. *Making Democracy Work.* Princeton: Princeton University Press.

SEGOVIA, Rafael.

  1975. *La politización del niño mexicano.* Mexico City: El Colegio de México.

INTERGENERATIONAL DIFFERENCES IN POLITICAL VALUES AND ATTITUDES IN STABLE AND NEW DEMOCRACIES

Renata Siemienska*

ABSTRACT

The examination of the intergenerational differences in two groups of democratic countries (traditional democratic countries and countries that began to establish democratic systems a little more than 10 years ago, when communist systems were overthrown in Central and Eastern Europe) shows growing similarities in attitudes and behaviors among young generations. The process is a consequence of cultural and economic globalization that encourages processes of change and adaptation in the new democracies.

Introduction

This article examines intergenerational differences in two groups of democratic countries: the long-established democratic countries, and those that began to build a democratic system about 10 years ago, when communist systems were overthrown in Central and Eastern Europe.

In the early nineties, there was an intensive debate about how likely the latter group of countries could create stable democratic systems—and who would best serve as mentors in the process of socialization in the new political and economic situation. More than 10 years have passed. It is now time to assess what changes have taken place in the prevailing values, attitudes, and behaviors in post-communist societies. We are particularly interested in whether generational changes are taking place in the attitudes and behaviors in post-communist countries and in stable democracies.

We will examine four basic hypotheses concerning forecasts related to the development of democratic systems. These hypotheses reflect the contradictory predictions that were made a decade ago about the emergence of democracy.

Thus:

(1)   *Post-communist countries have to go a long way before their societies become similar to stable, traditional democracies with regard to value systems, and they need to repeat their achievements (Dalton 1991), so one decade will not have brought massive changes.*

This hypothesis is consistent with the following:

*   Institute of Sociology - Institute for Social Studies, Warsaw University, Krakowskie Przedmiescie 3, 00-324 Warsaw, Poland.

(2)   *The young generation, although growing up in the new system, will be similar to the older generation because value systems change slowly.*

Inconsistent, particularly with the latter, are the following hypotheses:

(3)   *The young generation of post-communist countries will be significantly dissimilar from the older generations, since the speed of changes in the political and economic sphere will enforce adaptation of the young generation to the new requirements and mechanisms, leaving little space for inheriting what older generations, who adapted to a different system, could bequeath* (Ester, Halman, and de Moor 1993).

(4)   *The young generation of the post-communist countries becomes similar to the young generation of the traditional democracies with regard to values and attitudes, despite differences with regard to recent history.*

Inglehart (1997), as well as many other authors, underline that in most countries there is an observable trend toward an increasing emphasis on post-materialistic values, which is in turn part of a broader trend towards an emphasis on "self-expression values" and behaviors that are crucial characteristics of democratic countries.

In an attempt to check the effect of different conditions before and after 1990 in Central and Eastern European countries, we conducted a comparison of the different generations. Particularly, we were interested in the generation born between 1900 and 1926; persons born during 1967 to 1976, who were at least teenagers during the transformation; and persons who were children at the time.

Since changes, although not as rapid as in the post-communist countries, are experienced also in traditionally democratic countries, we conducted analogous analyses with democratic nations. The data for our detailed analysis are drawn from nine selected countries included in the 2000 World Values Survey. Three of them are postcommunist: Poland, Hungary, and the Czech Republic. They are Catholic or mainly Catholic. Poland is an almost exclusively Catholic country, and in the Czech Republic and Hungary the majority of society is Catholic. The three countries share, to a large extent, the same history as they were part of the Prussian, Austro-Hungarian, or Russian empires until the end of the World War I. The four Western European countries differ in many respects. First, Catholicism dominates only in France and Spain. The population of the western part of Germany is divided: part of the population is Catholic and part of the population is Protestant. Denmark and Sweden are Protestant. In the United States the above-mentioned religions are also dominant. Religion, according to Huntington (1996), Inglehart (1997), Norris and Inglehart (2002), and several other authors, plays an important role in shaping some social values and attitudes. The selection of countries was dictated by an assumption concerning the common roots of their cultures. In the analysis, the western part of Germany is treated separately because, as several studies show, East and West Germany differ considerably when attitudes and values are analyzed. In some analyses other countries are included to broaden the comparisons. In all cases data were collected on national representative samples.

Controversy Surrounding Socialization Factors and Mechanisms

Post-communist countries are undergoing economic and political transformations. In this context, some important questions arise: How, and to what extent, do young people differ from older generations and, further, are their attitudes and conceptions of life conducive to building a democratic system and a free market economy?

Several theories explain the mechanisms of change and intergenerational difference as the result of a whole series of factors, typical of a particular period or generation, as well as intergenerational interactions (for example, Mannheim 1960; Inglehart 1977, 1990). Mannheim (1960), in his theory of generational changes, states that the quicker the social changes occur, the more likely it is that young people will have a common culture, which is clearly different from the culture of the older generation. The rapidly changing situation forces young people to find new answers to adapt to new requirements, thus, the models of the older generation become obsolete. Inglehart demonstrated that "enduring intergenerational (value) differences reflect differences in the formative conditions that shaped the respective birth cohorts" (Inglehart 1990:137). His explanation of the Materialist/Postmaterialist is based on two hypotheses: "(1) 'a scarcity hypothesis' that one's priorities reflect one's socioeconomic environment so that one places greatest subjective value on those things that are in relatively short supply; and (2) 'a socialization hypothesis' that, to a large extent, one's basic values reflect the conditions that prevailed during one's preadult years" (Inglehart 1977:56; 1990:33). Inglehart's (1990) cohort analysis, based on data from 1970 through 1988 in six Western countries, "confirms the presence of substantial differences in the basic societal priorities of younger and older generations . . . this analysis demonstrates that as intergenerational population replacement has occurred, there has been a gradual but pervasive shift in the values of these publics" (p.56). In his opinion, and also the opinion of many other researchers (Jennings 1990), late adolescence is a time of special significance in political socialization. Over time, this value system dominates as systematic intergenerational change slowly takes place. The results of research conducted in ten Western European countries in 1981 and 1990 partially confirm the hypotheses presented above (Ester, Halman, and de Moor 1993).

Many researchers emphasize that family plays an important role in the process of socialization. The family creates the environment in which the individual grows up, as well as the broader social environment in which it is embedded. It was found that in American society, the environment in which the individual grows up is twice as important (in the sense of the exerted influence) as the environment in which the individual lives as a grown-up (Miller and Sears 1986). Some authors find that it is not socialization but the vertical and horizontal mobility of the individuals and the discrepancies in social status, which become a source of tension in the individuals, that cause them to become, for example, radically conservative or radically egalitarian. But the results of other studies suggest that the individual's attitudes and values in such cases are found to be "halfway" between what was taken from the environment of early socialization, and what is typical of the environment the individual has found him or herself in later on. Still other researchers (Jennings and Niemi 1974) stress that the relatively small similarity of attitudes and political orientations among the parents and their children is evidence of the lesser role of the parents in the socialization process than is usually assumed. It has, nevertheless, been shown that such a conclusion is only qualified when socialization is understood as the duplication of the knowledge and attitudes of the parents. It is necessary to take into consideration such situations in which (even if we assume that the parents fully and successfully control their children's socialization process) they might not want to pass their values on to them. In such a case, the socialization process, carried out according to the intentions, will demonstrate differences between the values of children and parents (Bronfenbrenner 1967; Inkeles and Smith 1974). Moreover, as Kagan (1962, 1969) shows, the persistence of certain traits from childhood to adulthood may take on various forms. Also, the appearance of the same behaviors in various periods of life may have a different meaning.

It seems intuitive that school should play an important role in socialization. It is an institution that, by definition, is convened in order to form the young generation by passing on a given amount of knowledge as well as given systems of values and life aspirations. Yet many studies show that its role is much more modest (Beck 1977) than one would think, both with respect to passing on attitudes, as well as information and abilities. Usually, the school prepares the young generation in a way that is in accordance with the expectations—as a rule—of the elite in the given society. In stable democratic societies where changes are taking place relatively slowly, expectations are usually consistent with the expectations of the majority of society. In a period of rapid and even violent changes, they may be to a significant extent divergent, which, as we will show later on, is the current situation in Poland.

An important role in the socialization process is played by the environment of peers, which is integrated by the similarity of problems, both with respect to the expectations of the older generation, as well as the adaptation to the conditions in which individuals growing up. But the direction of influence of peer groups is different in different countries. Sometimes they enforce the orientations and attitudes promoted by the school, at other times they offer completely different, evidently contradictory, models (Nathan and Remy 1977).

Various social groups and institutions may also ascribe to the various agents an excessive or insufficient role. For example, in situations where the authorities wish to abruptly break the society's cultural continuity, as was the case in Russia following the 1917 revolution as well as in other communist countries, they try to weaken the influence of the family, reinforcing at the same time the role of educational institutions controlled by them, for instance, the schools and youth organizations.

The role of certain agents of socialization may sometimes become particularly significant. For example in the 1970s and 1980s, Polish sociologists pointed to the enormous role of the family in the life of Polish society. The role of the Polish family was much greater than in Western countries. Its significance resulted from a situation where there were no institutions with which the people would be willing to identify, so the family became the basic reference and support group for the individual. A certain type of vacuum existed between the family and nation, thus, the family played a key role in the socialization process (Nowak 1979).

Globalization and its Consequences

Globalization has emerged as a major issue facing contemporary society. Some politicians and researchers are supporters of globalization while others protest very strongly, pointing out its negative effects both in developed and in poor countries, since it leads to further differentiation of the inhabitants of our planet, and it destroys the sense of security in the developed countries where social benefits, offered by the state, have been reduced throughout the last decades.

Globalization can be defined in many ways. Held (2000) proposes a definition that evinces the complexity of the concept: "Globalization connotes the stretching and intensification of social, economic, and political relations across regions and continents. It is a multidimensional phenomenon that embraces many different processes and operates on many different time scales" (p.395). Moreover, "political space for the development and pursuit of effective government and the accountability of political power is no longer coterminous with a delimited national territory. The growth of transboundary problems creates . . . 'overlapping communities of fate'; that is, a state of affairs in which the fortunes and prospects of individual political communities are increasingly bound together . . . Questions are raised both about the fate of the idea of the political community and about the appropriate locus for the articulation of the political good" (Held 2000:400). The issue is most apparent in the European Union where the limited autonomy of individual states may be observed. The problem, however, is not restricted to Europe.

Meyer (2000) points out that nowadays "the world polity and cultural system are relatively stateless, but they legitimate strong nation-state identities as the dominant actors. This produces very strong tendencies for the adoption of common models of modernity, despite extraordinary differences in resources and local culture" (p.233). As the author stresses, "national states now define their fundamental purposes as having to do with socioeconomic development or welfare and individual justice, rights and equality" (p.234) to meet common models of national state identity and purpose.

This new phenomenon, called "glocalization," is based upon celebrating the specificity of one's own heritage while accepting the standard models brought by globalization (Robertson 1994). At the same time, there is a need to ensure tolerance for those who are "different;" newcomers from more or less distant countries and/or members of groups characterized by different cultural patterns (Walzer 1995).

Many scholars (Putnam 1993; Coleman 1990) point to the role of "social capital," which is a special resource in democratic societies. Social capital is a resource that allows for the realization of the basic rules of democracy, that is, articulation of interests, participation of citizens in public life, and the things that make it easier to satisfy the needs of people. Putnam (1993) writes: "Social capital here refers to features of social organization, such as trust, norms, and networks, that can improve the efficiency of society by facilitating coordinated actions" (p.167). Analyzing the functioning of the democratic system in Italy, he concludes: "Spontaneous cooperation is facilitated by social capital" (p.167). In this situation, educational expansion around the world, which means increases in education and the dissemination of standardized qualities, helps individuals and societies survive in an unstable, rapidly changing world.

In this paper, we will analyze selected norms and values, involvement in the activities of formal and informal organizations, and interest in politics in selected countries in order to verify the hypotheses formulated above.

A comparison of different countries, however, requires caution. For example, the character and number of memberships in various organizations are conditioned on the culture and tradition of individual countries. Furthermore, membership in some organizations makes it impossible to belong to others in some countries (Milner 2002). Also, an interest in politics is not a simple function of the length of the period of existence of the democratic system in a country, it is often a condition of increasing social tension and significant events.

Our goal is to examine how, to what extent, and in what areas, the attitudes and opinions of younger and older generations differ. We also want to consider what factors may be more important than age in shaping the attitudes and values of societies in particular countries.

Important Characteristics in Raising Children

Significant differences exist among the traditionally democratic countries, as well as within the group of post-communist countries, in terms of which characteristics are important in raising children. These differences exist despite a frequently repeated assumption that each group of countries is homogeneous in this respect. The World Values Survey conducted in the early and mid-1990s (Inglehart 1997) and during 1999-2000 show the magnitude of the differences. The results of the 1999-2000 study are presented below.

Among the European Union countries, the importance attached to independence was between 1.196 (mean) in Denmark, 1.776 in Portugal, and slightly less in France (1.711) (the lower the mean, the more often a given characteristic was mentioned by respondents as important). In the group of post-communist countries, the lowest mean was in Lithuania (1.246), and the highest in Poland (1.779). In both groups of countries there is more unanimity with regard to the importance attached to responsibility, and there are no significant differences between groups. In Denmark, the greatest importance is attached to teaching children responsibility (mean 1.192), while in Ireland (mean 1.468) and North Ireland (mean 1.466) this value is regarded as the least important. In Central and Eastern Europe, respective countries are Estonia (mean 1.217) and Romania (mean 1.408). Even more important for the inhabitants of the EU countries is tolerance; it is most important in Sweden (mean 1.075), and relatively least important in W.Germany (mean 1.267). On the other hand, in the post-communist countries tolerance is regarded as important less often; the greatest importance is attached to it in Poland (mean 1.203), and the least in Romania (mean 1.444).

Unselfishness is perceived as an important characteristic much less often. In the European Union countries, unselfishness is listed as important most often in Great Britain (mean 1.403), and least often in W. Germany (mean 1.938). In the post-communist countries, unselfishness is regarded as even less important and differences between countries are smaller. It is listed as important most often in Slovenia (mean 1.624) and almost equally often in the Czech Republic. The smallest number of respondents listed it as important in Romania (mean 1.935). Among the analyzed features, imagination was listed least often in both groups of countries. In the European Union countries, imagination was listed as important most often in Sweden (mean 1.596) and least often in Italy (mean 1.876). In the post-communist countries it was listed most often in Romania (mean 1.871) and Poland (mean 1.872), and least often in Slovakia (mean 1.973).

Direction of Changes in Intergenerational Comparisons

The analysis shows that the directions of changes in the level of acceptance of individual characteristics that should be taught are different. Here we will limit ourselves to discussing one of them in detail: tolerance.

In France, tolerance is traditionally very highly accepted by society. However, the youngest respondents perceive it as an important characteristic less often (by several percentage points) than the older respondents.

In West Germany, where the acceptance of tolerance is generally lower than in France, it is higher among the younger age groups than among the oldest respondents. The middle-agers (those born in years 1947 to 1956) most often regarded tolerance as important. In Germany, the importance attached to tolerance by the oldest respondents is among the lowest of the compared countries of Western Europe.

In Spain, while the level of acceptance for tolerance is similar in all age groups, it is highest among the youngest respondents.

In Denmark, differences in the perception of tolerance as an important characteristic between particular age groups are much greater than, for example, in Germany. Among the oldest respondents it is similar to Germany. Among the youngest respondents it is high (87.5 percent). However, as in Germany, the highest percentage of those accepting tolerance can be found among those born between 1947 to 1956 (92.3 percent).

Swedish society attaches the greatest importance to tolerance among all compared Western democracies: more than 90 percent in all age groups.

The three post-communist countries also differ in the degree of perceived importance of tolerance. In the Czech Republic and Hungary, in all age groups, low importance is attached to tolerance, when compared with other analyzed countries. In Poland, as in the two countries mentioned above, as well as in Germany and Denmark, the oldest respondents relatively least often perceive tolerance as a desired value (slightly above 60 percent). However, younger respondents in Poland differ much from older ones; more often perceiving tolerance to be among the most important characteristics (about 80 percent).

Figure 1. Tolerance as an Important Feature in Children's Socialization

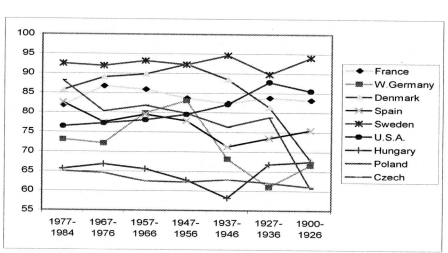

To recapitulate, attitudes towards tolerance have been changing in various ways in different countries. In some of them, the youngest respondents less often perceive it as important. In the largest European countries (France, W. Germany), among the youngest respondents, tolerance has fewer supporters than in other age groups. As for the correctness of the hypothesis with regard to the influence of the political system upon popularization of tolerance, it turns out that this pertains only to Poland, when we analyzed the post-communist countries.

Dynamics of Attitudes Towards "Others"

In the World Values Survey, attitudes toward those who are different with regard to race, religion, and culture (i.e., Muslims, Jews, immigrants) are measured by the extent to which respondents accept members of these groups as neighbors. In the Western European countries it is a constant trend: the younger respondents accept "others" more often. In all examined countries, except for Spain, the oldest respondents are ready to accept "others" *fairly* often.

The youngest generation (born in years 1977 to 1984) in France, Germany, and Spain are, on average, two times more accepting than the oldest generation. In Sweden and Denmark the attitudes of the youngest generation are three times more tolerant than the oldest. However, the youngest are slightly more xenophobic than the middle-generation.

The three post-communist countries we compared differ very significantly from each other, both with regard to the level of xenophobia and intergenerational differences. In Hungary, the level of xenophobia is very high and the intergenerational differences are relatively low. In the Czech Republic the intergenerational differences are relatively low as well, but in general the level of xenophobia is similar to the levels in some Western countries. In Poland the intergenerational differences are extremely high; they are at the level of one to five between the youngest and the oldest. The level of xenophobia among the youngest group is similar to some Western countries. In the case of Poland, we can say that the new situation has caused a rapid change in ways of perceiving "others."

In Western countries only a few respondents in all age groups (especially among the younger inhabitants) would not like to live next door to immigrants. The societies of the post-communist countries (especially Hungarians) are more hostile towards immigrants and the attitude varies more among generations. Undoubtedly, the difference in the degree of tolerance between the two groups of countries is caused by the different experiences of the societies. For example, the lack of mobility between countries and competition for scare resources, characteristic of communist countries for decades, fostered xenophobia and left people and institutions unprepared for contact with different cultures.

The post-communist countries differ significantly from the others in their eagerness to protect their own labor market against foreigners. There is a far-reaching dislike to employ them, common for all generations in these countries. The dislike for foreigners is slightly lower in Poland than in the other post-communist nations, especially among the youngest respondents. In the EU countries, especially in Germany, France, and Denmark, the younger generations are more eager than the older generations to accept foreigners into the labor market.

Figure 2. Immigrants as Disliked Neighbors

Figure 2. Immigrants as Disliked Neighbors

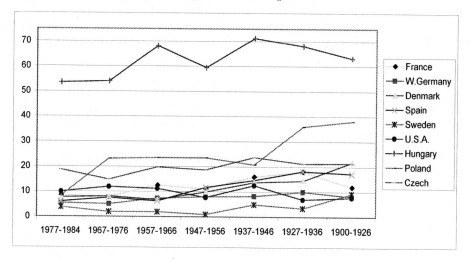

Figure 3. Priority of Own Nationality when Jobs are Scarce

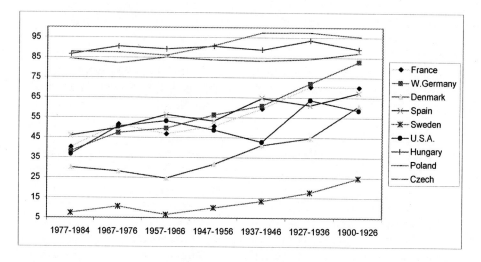

Attitude Towards Equality of Men and Women in the Labor Market

It is clear that societies differ in their attitudes towards the equality of men and women. The differences are significantly larger among the older respondents than among the youngest when countries are compared. The findings confirm observations that globalization causes a universalization of attitudes and encourages similar cultural models based on similar rationality (Inglehart 1997; Meyer 2000). In all societies, younger generations are more open than older cohorts to new models of social roles and human rights. They adjust much easier to labor market conditions shaped by the globalizing economy.

The significant differences among older age cohorts demonstrate the role of different cultural models in societies. The experiences of the Central and East European countries have been shaped by the communist system where the situation for women was differently defined than in the West. A lack of opportunities to create women's (or, to be more specific, feminist) grassroot organizations, mobilization of women as a labor force by government after World War II (Siemienska 1990, 1999), and accompanied by strong state propaganda proclaiming gender equality led to a social belief of "too much gender equality" in the communist countries. Women felt burdened by the combination of housework and professional careers. The societies believed that the change of political and economic systems in the early 1990s would allow women to improve their situation by staying at home, while men would again become the main bread-winners for families. Consequently, this led to a belief that men should have a privileged position in the labor market. Thus, the observed differences between Central/East European countries and Western European countries are related to two different models of women's entrance into public life several decades ago. In the communist countries there is what may be termed the "other-directed model," while in the West there is the "inner-directed model." The first one has emerged chiefly because of sudden and rapid changes in life circumstances that forced women to go beyond accepted, traditional patterns of behavior and adjust to a new macrostructural situation. The institutionalized external pressure in relation to the individual was crucial in this case. In the latter model, changes in women's own ideas concerning their role in social life prompted them to seek opportunities to be active outside their family life.

Figure 4 : Men have more Rights to Job Opportunities than
Women (% of those who disagree)

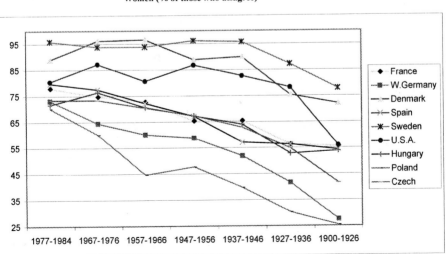

Civic Duties

Expectations towards citizens of democratic states are based on the assumption that citizens identify themselves with the state, and thus are aware of their duties that they regard as legitimate. They are willing to respect these duties, which is expressed in their behaviors. Among these is participation in public life, which is expressed in interest in politics, participation in elections, activities of formal organizations, and abiding by the law. We will discuss some of these below.

Interest in Politics

In accordance with the Putnam model, we assume that citizens should be interested in politics since this will enable them to understand and take part in local and national decisions; more generally, to competently act within the public sphere.

The hypothesis that traditional democracies host a larger share of citizens seriously interested in politics than new democracies was not confirmed in previous surveys (WVS 1990-1993). Rather, it might be that citizens' periodically become active, especially when they are dissatisfied with the political regime. Surveys from the early 1990s have shown that in South Korea, South Africa, Lithuania, Bulgaria, and Poland more respondents reported that politics plays a "very important" or "quite important" role in their life than, for example, in Switzerland, Austria, France, Italy, or Belgium, not to mention the relatively new democracies of Spain and Portugal. For example, the Polish society was highly politicized during the 1980s. This period started with the creation of Solidarity and ended with the 1989 Parliamentary elections. It led to a change of the political system. This development started a phase in which politics did not matter as much as it did before; in 1990, 42 percent of the respondents indicated that politics plays a "very important" or "important" role in their lives, while in 1997 their share decreased to 30 percent. This was also reflected in the frequency of discussions on political issues among peers (in 1990, 83 percent of the respondents said that they frequently discussed political matters with friends, while in 1997 only 18 percent did so). The decrease was also reflected in the level of the respondents' interest in politics. For instance, in 1990, 49 percent reported themselves to be "very interested" or "somewhat interested" while their share decreased down to 42.1 percent in 1997, and down to 42.8 percent in 1999. This development was mirrored in other post-communist countries (between 39.5 percent in Romania and 58 percent in Slovakia) with considerably lower levels of interest in politics than in traditional democracies (between 64.2 percent in the United States and 77.9 percent in West Germany). Apparently, an interest in politics springs from various sources. Sometimes it is a result of a current economic and/or political situation; sometimes it is a persisting element of a long tradition of political culture.

Interest in politics depends mainly on the respondent's level of formal education and gender. Respondents with a higher level of formal education expressed higher levels of interest in politics (male respondents with a post-materialist orientation, rather older, less religious, expressed higher levels of interest). The respondents' economic situation (determined on the basis of the declared saving capacity) did not play a part here.

A detailed analysis of similarities and differences between individual age groups in the nine countries shows that, in accordance with the research conducted in years 1999-2000, the younger generations are the least interested in politics. There is a dramatic difference between the younger cohort and the next age group, which in many countries is closer with regard to the interest level of the older generations. It can be said that young people in the post-communist countries are rapidly becoming similar in their lack of interest in politics to the young people in the Western countries. In all countries, respondents born in between 1927 to 1946 least often show complete lack of interest in politics.

Figure 5. Interest in Politics (not at all)

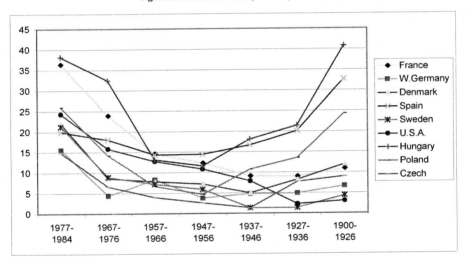

Abiding by the Law

The basis for analysis were responses to the following questions: "Whether you think it can always be justified, never be justified, or something in between . . . (on a 10-point scale, where 1 means "never justifiable," 10 means "always justifiable" in the following situations: "claiming government benefits to which you are not entitled," "avoiding a fare on public transport," "cheating on taxes if you have a chance," and "someone accepting a bribe in the course of their duties."

The level of abiding by the law differs for various issues and countries. However, everywhere the youngest are the least abiding. In West Germany, France, United States, Sweden, and Denmark the youngest respondents (born in years 1977 to 1984) are less abiding than the slightly older cohort (born in years

1967 to 1976). Among the post-communist countries, differences between the age groups mentioned above are similar to those in Western democracies, except for Hungary, where citizens have similar opinions, almost regardless of age. However, the level of abiding with the issues mentioned is slightly lower in the post-communist countries than in Western democracies. This is probably associated with the belief, present for decades, that the existing state was an imposed formation, and most citizens did not identify themselves with it.

Trust

Trust in mutual relations is regarded as a very valuable resource that makes cooperation between people possible and easier (e.g., Putnam 1993; Inglehart 1990, 1997; Dalton 2002; Milnar 2002). The countries in our sample can be divided into three groups: (1) post-communist countries, which are characterized by a low level of trust in people in all age groups, (2) Western Europe countries, where the level of trust is slightly higher than in the previous group, and (3) Scandinavian countries (Denmark and Sweden).

In most countries (6 out of 9), the youngest show the lowest level of trust in people. However, they are not much different from the oldest group. This phenomenon can be observed in countries with different histories. Only in Hungary, West Germany, and France can we talk about an intergenerational increase of trust. Trust in people is a cultural trait, characteristic of some societies. In some societies, it is definitely low (for example Poland, Czech Republic, and France in all age groups). In others, it is very high (Scandinavian countries). However, in all countries the pattern of intergenerational differences is similar.

Figure 6. Trust

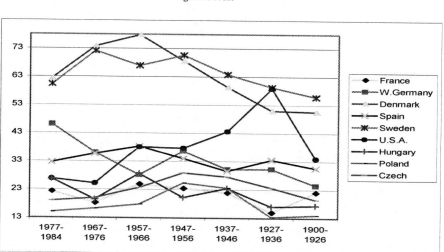

Activity in Voluntary Organizations

The existence of a civic society plays a key role in the promotion and shaping of a democratic system. It is sometimes defined—accordingly with the widest meaning of the concept—as various activities that fill the space between the operation of the "state" and "economy" (for instance, Habermas 1984; Young 1999; Walzer 1995). They are a form of, and a result of, the self-organization of the members of the society. These activities differ in their character and function from those characteristics of the state and the economy. Moreover, they potentially influence the power of institutions and actors who operate within them. They cause an increase of social justice by identifying social problems that are typical for certain groups by articulating them and exerting pressure in order to make sure that certain solutions are applied. These activities often pertain to groups that can be found on the margin of institutions. It is argued, that activities which occur within the "free space" between the state and the economy are favorable for democratization of the system.

As Putnam points out while observing how local and regional Italian societies function, their development and the extent to which they fulfill the needs of its members was dependent upon the existence and type of civic culture. Wherever this culture was absent, or marginal, realization of the objectives mentioned above is difficult.

> The success in overcoming the dilemmas of collective action and the self-destruction of opportunism, which are revealed by these dilemmas, depend upon the wide social context, within which a specific game is played. Voluntary cooperation is easier within a society, which has inherited a significant social capital in the form of norms of mutuality and a network of civic involvement . . . It pertains to such features of social organization as trust, norms and relations, which may increase the effectiveness of the society, making it easier to coordinate action. (Putnam 1993:258)

Moreover, Etzioni-Halevy points out another aspect of the functioning of a democratic society:

> The ultimate test of the importance of the public in a democracy is its ability to make elites responsive to its own wishes . . . Elite autonomy cannot ensure such responsiveness. But the elite rivalry it entails increases the likelihood that elites will need the support of the public for the maintenance of their positions and for the achievements of their goals. (Etzioni-Halevy 1993:108)

Research shows that the systems of values of elites are somehow correlated with systems of values of society members, though they are not identical. Elites are products of the societies from which they have originated, but their systems of values are not copies of the values of the "average" citizen (Inglehart 1990; Siemienska 2000).

In this article, we are dealing only with several types of actions taken by members of the societies. At the same time, we want to show that a high level of mobilization in the 1980s did not turn, after the economic and political transformation in Poland, into a high level of involvement in the types of activities characteristic of democratic societies. Moreover, in some respects it is lower than in countries that have had a similar history, as well as in stable democracies.

Communal Activity

As Dalton (2002) writes, and he does not stand alone in this matter, "The essence of grassroots democracy is represented in communal activity . . . The existence of . . . autonomous groups and independent action defines the characteristics of a civic society . . . The communal mode shifts control of participation to the public and thereby increases the citizenry's political influence" (pp. 43-44). At the same time, observers of American life state that (however, this pertains also to other countries) a change of lifestyle that takes place under the influence of the mass media (i.e., television and the Internet) causes people to get less involved in various common actions, especially of the "traditional" type (e.g., gatherings of inhabitants). At the same time, new interest groups are created, such as groups of women or organizations focusing on environmental protection.

Some societies or regions have a long tradition of acting on behalf of community, while others lack communal activity. This phenomenon and its consequences are discussed in detail by Putnam (1993). The situation of the post-communist countries is distinct. The centralized totalitarian system, which then moved to authoritarianism, excluded the possibility of grassroot organizations that are often the result of civic activity. The ones that existed were established through decisions from above and were controlled by the authorities. Political opposition and its organizations (e.g., "Solidarity" in Poland in the 1980s and Charter 77 in Czechoslovakia in the 1970s) were not legal parts of the system. Thus, when we compare levels of participation in voluntary organizations, we must consider differences between countries with communist and non-communist pasts. In the newly created conditions in post-communist countries, civic involvement has gained a new, special meaning.

In the Western democracies compared here, involvement in the activities of voluntary organizations is high in all age groups (measured by the number of organizations in which people participate). For example, in the United States and Sweden the number of people claiming the lack of any activity in any voluntary organizations is low. It is interesting to note that post-communist countries are similar on this point. There is no uniform pattern with regard to intergenerational similarities and differences. In the post-communist countries, the youngest are less active than older people. But the phenomenon of decreased activity in voluntary organizations among youngsters is even stronger in many traditional democracies. It should be added, though, that the measurement tool used here—the index of number of organizations in which the respondents participate—is not ideal, since some people can be very involved in the activity of a single organization and spend more time with it than people who are less active while belonging to a greater number of organizations.

Figure 7. Absence of Unpaid Voluntary Work (Index)

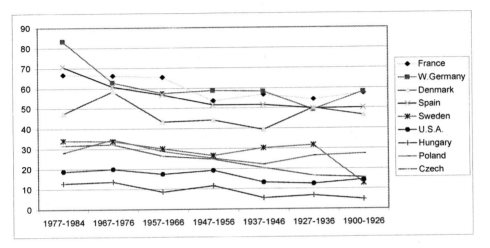

Other activities that meet the needs of individuals include participating in sport organizations and church services/events. Activity in sport clubs is least popular in Poland and Hungary, and a little bit more popular in the Czech Republic. However, in all these countries it is less popular than in the Western countries, especially Denmark. The younger people, more often than the older people, are engaged in such activities; an exception here are older Americans who are more active than members of all age groups in their own society, as well as in the other societies.

Figure 8. Spend Time at Sport Clubs (at least once a week)

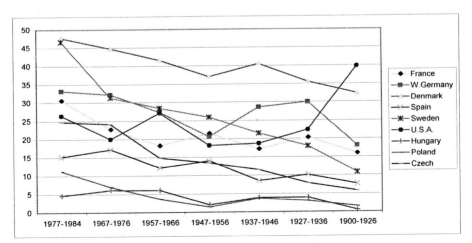

Spending time in church differentiates the societies of the United States, Poland, and Spain from other countries; the oldest (persons born before 1946) attend church services significantly more often than their peers in other countries. In the other countries, all generations rarely go to church. Poland is the only country in which the youngest generation goes to church most often; much more often than the older ones. A similar trend, but to a much lesser extent, can be observed in Hungary and France. In the United States and Spain, the church service attendance rates of the younger generations were similar to the attendance rates of their parents and grandparents.

Figure 9. Spend Time in Church (once a week or more)

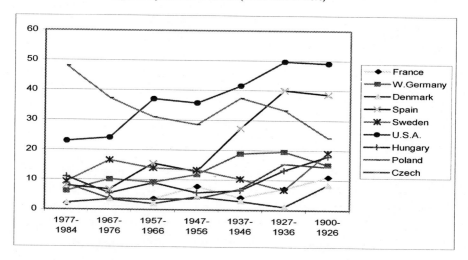

Satisfaction with Democracy

A significant question for researchers and politicians was how the younger generation would adapt to change (i.e., globalization and increasing unemployment) when the intergenerational transfer of democratic values is eroded. However, it turns out that the youngest respondents in France, West Germany, Denmark, and the United States are satisfied to the same extent as the older members of the society. In Spain, they are slightly less satisfied. In Hungary, the Czech Republic, and particularly in Poland, they are more satisfied. These results appear to contradict the thesis that young people cannot quickly be socialized into, or adapt to, the conditions and requirements of democracy.

Age and Other Factors Differentiating Attitudes and Behaviors

Multiple regression analyses were performed to establish the role of age as a differentiating factor of attitudes and behaviors in comparison to other demographic, as well as social and cultural, characteristics of respondents in different countries (macrostructural factors were not included in the analyses). The assumption was that the different sets of factors could play different roles in shaping attitudes and behaviors of members of particular societies.

A multiple regression analyses, where the dependent variables were the opinions and attitudes discussed above, showed that (Tables 1 and 2 are examples of the analyses):

(1) the same independent variables are not always statistically significant factors which explain variation in the same attitudes or behaviors in various countries; and

(2) age is not always a significant factor.

The attitudes and behaviors are often more differentiated by education and an interest in politics, showing that changes in the social structure (which are, to a large extent, a result of changes in education) will play an important role in the future as a factor in decreasing differences between the societies of the new and old democracies. The same pertains to the sense of satisfaction with the standards of living.

To recapitulate, the changes that take place make the societies of young democracies similar to those of the old democracies. The comparison shows growing similarities more in attitudes and less in behavior especially in young generations. The process is a consequence of cultural and economic globalization, which speeds processes of change and adaptation in the new democracies. The findings also demonstrate that the existence of established democratic systems per se differentiate, only to some extent, the behaviors of the societies in our sample.

The speed of the changes does not only depend on a communist or noncommunist past. The post-communist countries vary in this respect. Among three post-communist countries of Central Europe, the greatest changes are occurring in Poland where the youngest generation differs greatly from the older ones in many values and attitudes. Further analyses should help to explain the differences.

ANNEX

Interest in Politics (Index):

The index of interest in politics, is constructed on the basis of the following questions: "When you get together with friends, would you say you discuss political matters" (1) frequently? (2) occasionally? "How interested would you say you are in politics?" (1) very interested (2) somewhat interested. "How often do you follow politics in the news on television or on the radio or in the daily press?" (1) every day (2) several times a week. Minimum (not at all)- 0, maximum –3.

Unpaid Voluntary Work (Index):

The index includes organizations and activities focused on (1) social welfare, (2) religious and church organizations, (3) education, cultural activities, (4) labor unions, (5) political parties, (6) local community action on issues like poverty, (7) Third World development or human rights, (8) conservation, environment, (9) professional associations, (10) youth work, (11) sports and recreation, (12) women's groups, (13) peace movement, (14) voluntary organizations concerned with health. Minimum (not at all)- 0, maximum- 14.

Children's Desired Modern Qualities (Index):

The index includes: independence, responsibility, imagination, tolerance, and unselfishness. Minimum (any of the qualities is not mentioned) – 0, maximum –5.

Attitudes Toward "Others" (Index):

The index based on lack of acceptance as neighbors: people of different race, Muslims, immigrants, Jews. Minimum (the most positive) - 0, maximum (the most negative) – 4.

Materialist/Postmaterialist orientation:
    Selection of the following goals as the most important:
    (1) Materialist: "maintaining order in the nation" and "fighting rising prices";
    (2) Mixed between Materialist and Postmaterialist;
    (3) Postmaterialist: "giving people more say in important government decisions" and "Protecting freedom of speech."

Left-right orientation (10 point scale):
    Left 1 (1-4), Center 2 (5-6), Right 3 (7-10).

Religiosity (index 100-point scale):
    The index includes:
    Importance: "How important is God in your life." (% "Very" scaled 6-10).

    Comfort: "Do you find that you get comfort and strength from religion?"

    Identify: "Independently of whether you go to church or not, would you say you are . . . A religious person, not a religious person, or a convinced atheist?" (% Religious).

    Believe: "Do you believe in God?" (%Yes).

    Attend: "Apart from weddings, funerals and christenings, about how often do you attend religious services these days?" (% Once a week or more).

    Life: "Do you believe in life after death?" (% Yes)

Source: Inglehart and Norris (2003).

Table 1. Multiple Regression Model: Children's Desired Qualities-Index (Betas)

	U.S.	Spain	France	W. Germany	Denmark	Sweden	Hungary	Poland	Czech
Constant	3.626	2.393	1.476	1.959	2.468	2.667	1.326	2.153	1.490
Religiousity-index	-.251***	-.109***	-.097***	-.067*	-.092***		-.199****	-.167****	-.055*
Proud to be (nationality)			.091***	.060*	.126****			.063	
Identity with geographical group	.059*		.144****				.095**	.058	.087****
Satisfaction with democracy						.061*			
Mat/postmat (4 item index)		.133****	.165****	.136****	.128****	.131****	.125****	.065	.175****
Child quality index									
Decision-making freedom				.058*	.077*	.060*	.064		.047*
Education		.072*	.073**	.082***			.140****		
Age		-.088**	-.062*	-.190****	-.098**	-.208****		-.170****	-.054*
Employment status			-.063*		-.099**				-.047
Gender	.119****		.132****	.049	.125****	.095****	.060		.083***
Interest in politics (index)		.064*	.117****	.111****	.176****	.076**	.089**	.132****	.080***
Left-right self placement	-.113****		-.153****	-.114****	-.105***	-.048			
Family savings past year									
Trust –index	-.134****	-.116****				-.145****			
Adjusted R square	.107	.090	.195	.146	.167	.123	.118	.098	.070

$* p < .05.$ $** p < .01,$ $*** p < .001,$ $**** p < .000.$

Table 2. Multiple Regression Model: Attitudes Toward "Others"-Index (Standardized Coefficients Beta)

	U.S.	Spain	France	W. Germany	Denmark	Sweden	Hungary	Poland	Czech
Constant	-6.375E-03	.956	.473	.424	-.3.264E-02	.102	2.048	.113	.911
Religiousity-index				-.071*					
Proud to be (nationality)			-.072**		-.082**			-.085**	
Identity with geographical group							-.060		
Satisfaction with democracy			.083**	.090***	.164****	.060*	.073*	.123****	.091****
Mat/postmat (4 item index)			-.136****	-.069**	-.080*				-.105****
Child quality index	.050		-.080**	-.057*		-.055*	-.104**	-.076*	-.080***
Decision-making freedom		-.059*		-.105****					-.055*
Education							-.079*		
Age		.075*	.073**	.064*	.146****	.109****	.109**	.173****	
Employment status									.068**
Gender			-.047			-.087***			-.078***
Interest in politics (index)		-.105 ***			-.076*	-.081**	-.064		
Left-right self placement		.107***	.103****	.136****	.121****	.126****	.075*	.062	
Incumbent satisfaction		.076*				-.061*			
Confidence l-index		-.098**							
Family savings past year									
Trust –index	.089**					.100****			
Adjusted R square	.008	.043	.065	.064	.085	.056	.055	.072	.045

$* p < .05.$ $** p < .01,$ $*** p < .001,$ $**** p < .000.$

REFERENCES

BECK P.A.
1977. "The Role of Agents in Political Socialization." In *Handbook of Political Socialization,* edited by S.A. Renshon. New York, London: The Free Press.
BRONFENBRENNER, U.
1967. "Response to Pressure from Peers vs. Adult Among Soviet and American School Children." *International Journal of Psychology* 2:199-207
COLEMAN, J.
1990. *Foundations of Social Theory.* Cambridge, MA: Harvard University Press.
DALTON, R.
2002. *Citizen Politics. Public Opinion and Political Parties in Advanced Industrial Democracies.* New York, NY: Seven Bridges Press.
ESTER, P., P. Halman and R. de Moor eds.
1993. *The Individualizing Society. Value Change in Europe and North America.* Tilburg: Tilburg University Press.
ETZIONI-HALEVY, E.
1993. *The Elite Connection: Problems and Potential of Western Democracy.* Oxford: Blackwell Publishers Polity Press.
HABERMAS, J.
1984. *Theory of Communicative Action Vol.2.* Boston, MA: Beacon Press.
HELD, D.
2000. "Regulating Globalization? The Reinvention of Politics." *International Sociology.* 15(2):394-408.
HUNTINGTON, S.
1996. *The Clash of Civilizations and the Remaking of World Order.* New York, NY: Simon and Schuster.
INGLEHART, R.
1990. *Culture Shift in Advanced Industrial Society.* Princeton, NJ: Princeton University Press.
INGLEHART, R.
1997. *Modernization and Postmodernization.* Princeton, NJ: Princeton University Press.
INGLEHART, R. and P. Norris.
2003. "Religion, Secularization and Gender Equality." Unpublished manuscript.
INKELES, A. and D.H. Smith.
1974. *Becoming Modern: Individual Change in Six Developing Countries.* Cambridge, MA: Harvard University Press
JENNINGS, M.K.
1990. "The Crystallization of Orientations." In *Continuities in Political Action,* edited by M.K. Jennings and J.W. van Deth. Berlin, New York: Walter de Gruyter & Co.
JENNINGS, M.K. and R.G. Niemi.
1974. *The Political Character of Adolescence. The Influence of Families and Schools.* Princeton, NJ: Princeton University Press.
KAGAN J.

1969. "Three Faces of Continuity in Human Development." In *Handbook of Socialization Theory and Research,* edited by D.A. Goslin. Chicago, IL: Rand McNally

KAGAN, J. and H. Moss.
1962. *From Birth to Maturity.* New York, NY: Wiley.

MANNHEIM, K.
1960. *Ideology and Utopia.* London, England: Routledge and Kegan Paul.

MEYER, J.W.
2000. "Globalization. Sources and Effects on National States and Societies." *International Sociology* 15(2):233-248.

MILLER A.H. and D.O. Sears.
1986. "Stability and Change in Social Tolerance: A Test of the Persistence Hypothesis." *American Journal of Political Science* 30:214-236.

MILNER, H.
2002. *Civic Literacy. How Informed Citizens Make Democracy Work.* Hanover, NH: University Press of New England.

NORRIS, P. and R. Inglehart.
2002. "Islam & the West: Testing the 'Clash of Civilizations' Thesis." *Comparative Sociology.* December (forthcoming)

NATHAN, J.A. and R.C. Remy.
1977. "Comparative Political Socialization: A Theoretical Perspective." In *Handbook of Political Socialization,* edited by S.A. Renshon. New York-London: The Free Press.

NOWAK, S.
1979. "Przekonania i odczucia wspólczesnych (Beliefs and Feelings of the Contemporary People)." In *Polaków portret wlasny (Poles' Own Portrait)* collective work, Cracow.

PUTNAM, R. D.
1993. *Making Democracy Work. Civic Traditions in Modern Italy.* Princeton, NJ: Princeton University Press.

ROBERTSON, R.
1994. "Glocalization: Space, Time and Social Theory." *Journal of International Communication* 1(1).

SIEMIENSKA, R.
1990. *Plec, Zawód, Polityka (Gender, Occupation, Politics).* Warsaw: Institute of Sociology, Warsaw University.

SIEMIENSKA, R.
1999. "Elites and Women in Democratising Post-Communist Societies." *International Review of Sociology* 9(2):197-219.

SIEMIENSKA, R.
2002. "The Political Culture of Elites and the Public: Building Women's Political Representation in Post-communist Poland." In *Social Change. Adaptation and Resistance,* edited by: T. Klonowicz and G. Wieczorkowska. Warsaw: Warsaw University - Institute for Social Studies Press.

YOUNG, I. M.
1999. "State, Civil Society, and Social Justice." In *Democracy's Value,* edited by I. Shapiro and H.C. Casiano. Cambridge, MA: Cambridge University Press.

WALZER, Michael.
1995. "The idea of civil society." In *Towards a Global Civil Society,* edited by Michael Walzer. Providence: Bergham Books.

GENDER, AGING, AND SUBJECTIVE WELL-BEING

Ronald Inglehart[*]

ABSTRACT

Previous research has consistently found that men and women have similar levels of happiness, life satisfaction, and other global measures of subjective well-being. This article demonstrates that significant gender-related differences in subjective well-being exist—but tend to be concealed by an interaction effect between age, gender and well-being. Women under 45 tend to be happier than men; but older women are less happy. Thus, in a pooled sample of 146,000 respondents from 65 societies, among the youngest group, 24 percent of the men and 28 percent of the women describe themselves as very happy; but among the oldest group, only 20 percent of the women describe themselves as very happy, while 25 percent of the men do so. The relationship between gender and well-being reverses itself, moving from a female advantage of 4 points to a deficit of 5 points. Given the huge sample size, these differences are highly significant.

The aspiration-adjustment model implies that, despite their continuing disadvantages in income, status, and power, women of today should show higher levels of subjective well-being than men. A global women's movement has been pushing for gender equality throughout the world, with some success, so that currently, women's achievement tends to be above traditional aspiration levels. But this is offset by a systematic tendency to devalue older women. This tendency is particularly strong in advanced industrial societies where women have made the most progress—but where the mass media and advertising convey the message that only young women are beautiful and devalue the social worth of older women (Bluhm 2000). This produces an interaction between gender, age, and well-being that conceals statistically significant and theoretically interesting gender differences in subjective well-being.

Introduction: Happiness and Aspiration-Adjustment

Are men happier than women? Almost every study that has addressed this question has found only minimal gender-related differences in subjective well-being. This might seem surprising. In almost every society on earth, men have higher incomes, more prestigious jobs, and more authority than women—all of which are linked with relatively high levels of subjective well-being. The obvious expectation would be for women to show lower levels of happiness than men. Nevertheless, surveys carried out in many countries have consistently found that men and women have similar levels of happiness, overall life satisfaction, and

[*]   Institute for Social Research, University of Michigan, 3067 ISR, Ann Arbor, Michigan, 48106-1248, USA.

other global measures of subjective well-being.

Previous studies have found that differences in income, education, occupation, gender, marital status, and other demographic characteristics explain surprisingly little of the variation in people's levels of subjective well-being. As one would expect, those with higher incomes report somewhat higher levels of happiness and life satisfaction than those with lower incomes, but the differences are small, generally explaining no more than 4 percent of the variation—and education, occupation, age, religiosity, and gender explain even less—with gender showing particularly small effects (Andrews and Withey 1976; Barnes et al. 1979; Inglehart 1990; Myers and Diener 1995). This persistent finding has been explained in terms of "aspiration adjustment" (Campbell, Converse, and Rodgers 1976; Andrews and Withey 1976) and "set-point" (Lykkens and Tellegen 1996) models, both of which postulate that: (1) recent changes, such as receiving a raise or losing one's job, can have a major impact on an individual's well-being—but that people's aspirations adjust to their level of achievement. After some time, they report about the same level of well-being as they did before the change, returning to the individual's normal "set-point;" but (2) different individuals have different set-points. Year after year, some people display higher levels of well-being than others (Costa, McCrae, and Zonderman 1987).

Thus, although in the short run, a raise in salary, or a promotion to a more prestigious job has the effect one would expect (tending to bring higher levels of happiness and life satisfaction), in the long run, people adjust their aspiration levels to their attainment level. After some time, one returns to one's normal baseline level of subjective well-being. Aspiration adjustment also works in the opposite direction. Negative changes bring lower levels of happiness and life satisfaction in the short run, but in the long term, one adjusts one's aspiration level to the new conditions and eventually experiences about the same level of well-being as before.

Consequently, within any given society, subjective well-being varies surprisingly little across any stable characteristic such as gender (a life-long characteristic for most people). An individual's income may vary a good deal over time, so happiness does vary according to one's income if it has recently changed; but one's gender is a permanent characteristic, which means that when they are surveyed, most people have long since adapted to the advantages and disadvantages of being male or female.

Subjective well-being levels do vary a good deal cross-culturally: given that societies are characterized by relatively high or low baseline levels of happiness and life satisfaction which are reasonably stable over time (see Diener and Suh 2000). But within any given society, one generally finds only minor differences between the happiness levels of men and women. Thus, Inglehart (1990) analyzed data from all Euro-Barometer surveys carried out from 1980 through 1986 in twelve West European countries, plus the 1981-1982 World Values Survey data from the United States, Canada, Hungary, and Japan. He found that overall, men and women showed almost exactly the same levels of life satisfaction and happiness. Two societies were anomalous: in Ireland and Japan, women showed higher levels of well-being than men, with women being more satisfied than men by margins of 5 and 4 points, respectively; and women being happier than men by margins of 9 and 4 points, respectively. Normally, differences of this size would attract little attention, but they stand out in comparison with the negligible gender-related differences found elsewhere. Inglehart attributed the relatively high levels of well-being among Japanese and Irish women to the fact that, starting from positions of relatively great deprivation, women in both countries have made substantial strides toward equality in the last decade or two. Although women remained disadvantaged in comparison with men, they had experienced an upward shift, raising their perceived situation relative to their aspiration level (Inglehart 1990):

> We find that Japanese women are significantly *more* satisfied with their lives than men. This might seem almost incredible from a common-sense viewpoint, but it is in perfect accord with the aspiration-adjustment model. For centuries, Japanese women have had a position of extreme subordination—to their fathers, in childhood, to their husbands during marriage, and to their sons in later life. Their aspiration levels reflected this fact. Even today, the opportunities available to women in Japan are much more limited than in most Western societies. Nevertheless, there has been a *relative* improvement in the position of Japanese women within recent years—one that is far more dramatic than that which has taken place in the West, because it started from a much lower base line. The phenomenon of recent improvement—even though it still falls far short of equality—seems to have produced relatively high satisfaction levels.
>
> The Republic of Ireland resembles Japan in this respect. Culturally, Ireland has been an extremely conservative society, in which both divorce and the sale of contraceptives remained illegal until recently, and when a woman married she was virtually obliged to give up her career. Since Ireland's entry into the European Community, both legislation and social norms concerning women have been changing at a relatively rapid rate. This may account for the fact that Irish women currently show significantly higher levels of subjective well-being than Irish men. (Pp.222-223)

This article suggests that we may be overlooking significant gender-related differences in subjective well-being: they are there but they are concealed. The aspiration-adjustment model implies that, theoretically, we should be finding significant differences between the happiness levels of men and women in the contemporary world—with women showing *higher* levels of subjective well-being than men. For the past few decades, a global women's movement has been pushing for gender equality throughout the world. Although progress has been slow, in recent years this movement has had considerable impact in many countries. In business, social, and political life, women have been moving into desirable careers and other opportunities that once were available only to men. One indicator of the fact that the world is changing is the dramatic increase in the percentage of women who are members of parliament in countries around the world. According to Inter-parliamentary Union estimates, in 1987 women made up only 9 percent of the membership of the world's parliaments. By 2002, this figure increased to 14 percent (Interparliamentary Union 2002). There has been much more progress in some regions than in others. In the Nordic countries in 2001, 43 percent of the members of the lower house were women. In Arabic speaking countries, on the other hand, less than 5 percent of the elected representatives were women. Although women are still heavily underrepresented in most countries, they are experiencing positive changes, which theoretically should shift the aspiration-adjustment balance in a positive direction.

But the impact of these positive changes is partly offset by another factor that works in the opposite direction: a systematic tendency to devalue the social worth of older women. This tendency is particularly powerful in precisely those advanced industrial societies where women have made the most progress in the last decade or two. In these societies, the mass media and advertising emphasize a cult of youth, conveying the message that only young women are beautiful and, with various degrees of subtleness, devaluing the social worth of older women (Bluhm 2000). Mature males may be depicted as attractive because of their power and experience, but older women are shunted aside—except in so far as they can manage to retain the appearance of youth. The cosmetics industry and plastic surgery have profited immensely by projecting this message with massive assistance from the entertainment industry.

Does this culturally defined devaluation of older women actually have an impact on the subjective well-being of older women? A massive body of empirical evidence suggests that it does. As this article will demonstrate, surveys from scores of advanced industrial societies demonstrate that women under the age of 45 tend to be significantly happier than men; but women above this age are less happy than men. This interaction between gender, age, and subjective well-being tends to conceal the fact that there are substantial differences between the subjective well-being of men and women. When we combine all age groups, the fact that younger women are happier than men, is largely offset by the fact that older women are less happy—reducing the overall size of the gender difference to a level small enough to be dismissed as due to sampling error. The evidence suggests that the recent trend toward gender equality, incomplete as it is, may have had a positive impact on the subjective well-being of women in many countries. But a culturally defined tendency to devalue the social worth of older women seems to work in the opposite direction, tending to obscure the existence of significant gender-related differences in subjective well-being levels unless one differentiates between what is happening among younger and older women.

Method and Database

As the aspiration-adjustment model implies, the gender-related differences in happiness and life satisfaction that we find tend to be of modest size. In any one national sample, they might seem to reflect nothing more than normal sampling error. For that reason, our analysis will be based on a large database containing scores of surveys. Even if the differences are modest in any given sample, if we find a consistent pattern, in survey after survey, in which women show higher levels of subjective well-being than men, we can be confident that the finding is reliable. Moreover, we suspect that there are important cross-cultural differences in the strength of the tendency to downgrade the social value of women as they age. Consequently, we will examine gender-related differences with a cross-cultural perspective. In order to obtain a large database, and in order to capture cross-cultural differences, our analysis will be based on the World Values Surveys, which have carried out three waves of representative national surveys, from 1981 to 1999, in more than 60 societies on all six inhabited continents. These societies range from low income societies to advanced post-industrial societies, cover almost all major cultural zones, and include more than 75 percent of the world's population. A total of almost 150,000 respondents were interviewed in these surveys, which are available from the ICPSR survey data archive. We will use self-reported levels of happiness and satisfaction with one's life as a whole as our indicators of subjective well-being. Previous research has established that these are two particularly sensitive indicators of overall well-being, emerging as the highest loading items in factor analyses based on dozens of indicators of subjective well-being (Andrews and Withey 1976; Inglehart 1990). Utilizing these indicators, we will compare the subjective well-being of men and women of various age groups, in order to determine whether the hypothesized interaction between gender, age, and well-being exists; and how pervasive it is across various cultures.

Figure 1 shows the percentage of men and women who described themselves as "very happy" in 122 representative national samples in the World Values Surveys from 19981 through 1997. When this pooled sample is analyzed according to both age and gender, clear evidence of the hypothesized interaction effect emerges: among the three youngest age groups, women are more likely to describe themselves as "very happy" than are men. But the gender-related difference disappears among the 45 to 54 year old group, and among those aged 54 and older, men report higher levels of happiness than women. These gender-related differences are not large. Among the youngest group, 24 percent of the men and 28 percent of the women describe themselves as very happy—but because of the huge sample size, this four-point difference is significant at a high level. At the opposite end of the age continuum, we find a contrasting difference: only 20 percent of the women describe themselves as "very happy," while 25 percent of the men do so. The relationship between gender and well-being has reversed its polarity and, given the huge sample, the five-point difference is highly significant. This massive body of cross-sectional evidence suggests that women experience declining levels of happiness as they age, while the happiness levels of men are stable or even rise slightly. Consequently, the gender gap in happiness shifts from +4 in favor of women to –5; a net shift of 9 percentage points in the expected direction.

Figure 1. Happiness by Age and Gender in 65 Societies

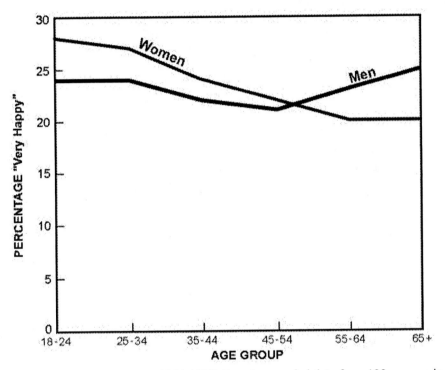

Source: World Values Surveys, 1981-1997. Based on pooled data from 122 surveys in 65 societies on all six inhabited continents, containing 70,192 men and 76,079 women. Overall, 23 percent of the men and 24 percent of the women describe themselves as "very happy."

Figure 2 shows the interaction between gender, age, and well-being based on our other indicator of global well-being, overall life satisfaction. The pattern is similar to that in Figure 1. Among the three youngest age groups, women report higher levels of life satisfaction than men, but there is a cross-over when we reach the 45 to 54 year old group. Among the three oldest groups, men report higher levels of life satisfaction than do women. Again, the differences are modest but statistically significant. Among the two youngest groups, women are more satisfied with their lives as a whole by margins of 1.5 and 3 percentage points, respectively. Among the two oldest groups, men are more satisfied with their lives than women, by margins of 3 and 6 points, respectively. Here, again, the relationship

Figure 2. Life Satisfaction by Age and Gender in 65 Societies

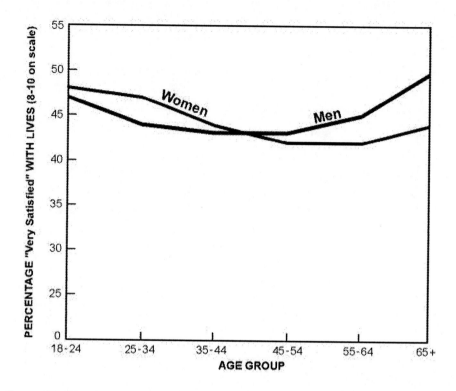

Source: World Values Surveys, 1981-1997. Based on pooled data from 122 surveys in 65 societies on all six inhabited continents, containing 71,690 men and 77,301 women. Overall, 45 percent of the men and 45 percent of the women describe themselves as "very satisfied" with their lives as a whole (choosing points 8-10 on a ten-point scale).

between gender and well-being reverses its polarity as one moves from younger to older respondents, with a net shift in the gender gap of about 8 percentage points.

Is this pattern universal—perhaps determined by biological factors inherent in human nature? Or do gender-related differences vary from one society to another, suggesting that they are shaped by cultural and historical factors? Table 1 shows the size of the overall gender gap in happiness across the societies included in the World Values Surveys (more than one survey is available for many of these societies, and where this is the case, we use the pooled surveys for that country for the sake of reliability).

As is immediately apparent, the size and the polarity of the gender gaps vary considerably. There is no iron law that men are happier than women or vice versa. As the aspiration adjustment hypothesis implies, the gender-related differences are generally rather small. Only 17 countries show gender gaps of more than

Table 1. Happiness by Gender
(Percentage describing Self as "Very happy")

Country	Men	Women	Gap	Country	Men	Women	Gap
Turkey	33	42	9	Britain	35	36	1
Japan	20	28	8	India	26	27	1
Ireland	38	46	8	Moldova	3	4	1
Australia	37	44	7	U.S.	38	39	1
Iceland	40	47	7	Latvia	4	5	1
New Zealand	29	36	7	Armenia	6	6	0
Dominican.Rep.	28	35	7	Belarus	5	5	0
Northern Ireland	39	45	6	Belgium	39	39	0
Sweden	34	40	6	East Germany	16	16	0
Netherlands	39	44	5	Estonia	5	5	0
Nigeria	50	55	5	Georgia	11	11	0
Uruguay	18	23	5	Lithuania	4	4	0
Canada	35	39	4	Poland	15	15	0
Colombia	45	49	4	Portugal	15	15	0
Switzerland	36	40	4	Serbia	13	13	0
Taiwan	24	28	4	South Korea	11	11	0
Bangladesh	15	18	3	Spain	20	20	0
Chile	31	34	3	Austria	34	33	-1
Finland	22	25	3	Czech Republic	10	9	-1
Norway	28	31	3	Italy	16	15	-1
Peru	27	30	3	Macedonia	14	13	-1
Philippines	38	41	3	Romania	6	5	-1
South Africa	36	39	3	Slovakia	8	7	-1
Argentina	27	29	2	Ukraine	6	5	-1
Bulgaria	7	9	2	Venezuela	56	55	-1
China	20	22	2	Albania	4	2	-2
Croatia	10	12	2	Azerbaijan	12	10	-2
Denmark	38	40	2	Brazil	22	20	-2
France	26	28	2	Russia	7	5	-2
Hungary	12	14	2	El Salvador	57	54	-3
Mexico	38	40	2	Pakistan	31	25	-6
Slovenia	12	14	2	**Mean:**	**25**	**26**	**1**
West Germany	15	17	2				
Bosnia	14	15	1				

Source: World Values Survey / European Values Survey.

3 percentage points but in 16 of these 17 cases, women show higher levels of happiness than men (Pakistan is the only country showing a large deficit in women's happiness). Japan and Ireland rank high on this table, as they did in Inglehart's (1990) analysis, but now they are joined by a number of additional countries. Moreover, most of the 16 countries where women are happier than men are

defined by the World Bank as "high income" countries (Japan, Ireland, Australia, Iceland, New Zealand, Northern Ireland, Sweden, Netherlands, Uruguay, Canada, and Switzerland). This first look at the evidence tends to support the claim that at this point in history, women show higher levels of well-being than men, especially in advanced industrial societies.

But, as we have argued, lumping together both older and younger respondents in national samples such as these may conceal much of what is really going on. Table 2 focuses on the younger respondents—the segment of the population in which the new pattern should manifest itself most clearly. Table 2 reveals some striking findings. First, the new pattern of women being happier than men is much more clearly evident. It appears in about 80 percent of the societies in Table 2, and in fully 31 cases, women are happier than men by a margin of 4 or more percentage points. Only two societies (Pakistan and Brazil) show the opposite tendency, with men being happier than women by margins of 4 or more points. Furthermore, positive gender gaps tend to be found in the more developed societies. Fully 21 of the 24 "high income" countries (shown in bold face type in Table 2) show happiness gaps of +4 or more points (Portugal, Spain, and Italy are the only high income countries that fail to do so). It is not surprising that economic development is conducive to relatively high levels of subjective well-being—but why does it seem to be especially conducive to high levels of happiness among *women*? Our interpretation is that at this phase of history, economic development and the rise of the knowledge society are producing much greater changes in the role of women than in the role of men; introducing a greater degree of gender equality than has existed ever before in history.

But it is not simply a matter of economic development. For many decades historically Protestant societies have led the way toward gender equality. Most Protestant countries adopted women's suffrage by about 1920; a milestone that came considerably later in most non-Protestant countries. Even today, as Table 3 demonstrates, Protestant countries tend to have higher percentages of women in parliament than countries with other cultural traditions. If it is true that progress toward gender equality tends to raise the subjective well-being of women, then one would expect historically Protestant societies to show relatively large positive gender gaps in Table 2. This expectation is amply supported. *All* of the Protestant countries that have not experienced communist rule (these countries are indicated by an asterisk in Table 2) show positive gender gaps of four or more points. East Germany (which has experienced communist rule) also falls into this category. Progress toward gender equality is closely linked with democratic institutions, which permit movements seeking social change to express themselves politically.

Although the leaders of communist societies sometimes gave lip service to gender equality, in practice they were generally authoritarian and patriarchal. Like other autonomous social movements, the women's movement was relatively weak in communist countries and the rise of gender equality was slow. Accordingly, only two of the 24 ex-communist countries show a positive gender

**Table 2. Happiness by Gender among Respondents Under 45 Years Old
(Percentage "Very Happy")**

Country	Men	Women	Gap	Country	Men	Women	Gap
Australia*	34	48	14	Bulgaria	8	11	3
North Ireland*	39	50	11	Moldova	3	6	3
Sweden*	34	45	11	Serbia	13	16	3
Iceland*	39	50	11	Spain	21	23	2
Dominican Rep.	26	37	11	India	27	29	2
Japan	19	29	10	China	21	23	2
Turkey	32	42	10	Portugal	18	20	2
France	25	34	9	Latvia*	4	6	2
Netherlands*	38	47	9	Philippines	40	42	2
Uruguay	16	24	8	Georgia	12	14	2
New Zealand*	27	35	8	Bangladesh	15	17	2
Germany (W.)*	12	19	7	Macedonia	14	16	2
Ireland	40	47	7	Croatia	12	14	2
Britain*	33	39	6	Slovakia	7	9	2
Denmark*	38	44	6	Italy	17	18	1
Hungary	14	20	6	Mexico	40	41	1
Chile	30	36	6	Belarus	5	6	1
Canada*	35	40	5	Lithuania	5	6	1
Norway*	29	34	5	Peru	28	29	1
Argentina	28	33	5	South Korea	11	11	0
Finland*	23	28	5	Estonia*	6	6	0
Switzerland*	37	42	5	Ukraine	7	7	0
Nigeria	50	55	5	Russia	7	7	0
Germany (E.)*	13	18	5	Romania	6	5	-1
Belgium	40	44	4	Venezuela	58	57	-1
U.S.*	35	39	4	Albania	4	3	-1
Slovenia	13	17	4	El Salvador	59	57	-2
Taiwan	26	30	4	Azerbaijan	13	11	-2
Austria	36	40	4	Armenia	8	5	-3
Bosnia	15	19	4	Brazil	23	18	-5
South Africa	34	37	3	Pakistan	30	25	-5
Poland	16	19	3	Mean	25	28	3
Czech	9	12	3				

Notes: "High income" countries (as defined by the World Bank in 2001) are shown in bold face.
* Indicates historically Protestant countries. Ex-communist countries are shown in italic type (East Germany, Latvia and Lithuania are ex-communist and historically Protestant).
Source: World Values Survey / European Values Survey.

gap of 4 or more points (the exceptions are East Germany, which is a high-income country with a Protestant heritage, and Slovenia, the only other high-income ex-communist country). Most of the 24 ex-communist countries (shown in italic type) rank in the lower half of Table 2. Communist rule, apparently, was not conducive to the changes that have produced the relatively high levels of happiness found among younger women in most societies. But does this phenomenon reflect the communist experience itself, or the economic decline that has characterized most former communist countries during the past 15 years? We suspect that it is the latter. Severe economic decline tends to bring lower levels of well-being, but we see no reason why it would have a greater impact on women than on men. Moreover, the evidence in Table 3 suggests that communist societies have been far less conducive to gender equality than Protestant societies—at least in so far as the proportion of women in parliament is an indicator. Among the historically Protestant societies in Table 3, the median percentage of women in the lower

Table 3. Women in Parliament
(Percentage of Women in the Lower House of Parliament, among Countries in WVS)

Country	% of Women in Lower House	Country	%
Sweden	**43**	Slovakia	14
Denmark	**38**	**U.S.**	**14**
Finland	**37**	Moldova	13
Norway	**36**	Slovenia	12
Netherlands	**36**	Uruguay	12
Iceland	**35**	Ireland	12
Germany	**32**	Colombia	12
New Zealand	**31**	France	11
Argentina	31	Romania	11
South Africa	30	Lithuania	11
Spain	28	Azerbaijan	11
Austria	27	Belarus	10
Bulgaria	26	Italy	10
Australia	**25**	Venezuela	10
Belgium	23	El Salvador	10
Switzerland	**23**	India	9
China	22	Hungary	8
Canada	**21**	Ukraine	8
Croatia	20	Russia	8
Poland	20	Japan	7
Portugal	19	Georgia	7
Peru	18	Yugoslavia	7
Great Britain	**18**	Bosnia	7
Estonia	**18**	Brazil	7
Philippines	18	Macedonia	7
Latvia	**17**	Korea (South)	6
Dominican Republic	16	Albania	6
Mexico	16	Turkey	4
Czech Republic	15	Nigeria	3
		Bangladesh	2

Source: Inter-Parliamentary Union Web site, http://www.IUP.org
Historically Protestant countries are in bold face type.

house of parliament is 32 percent. Among the former communist societies, the figure is only 11 percent (Islamic societies rank even lower, with a median figure of 3 percent).

High levels of per capita GNP, a Protestant historical tradition (even in countries where Protestant church-attendance has largely died out today), and the absence of communist rule, are all linked with relatively high levels of happiness among younger women (as compared with men of their age) and they overlap to a considerable extent. Now, let us examine the gender-related differences in subjective well-being at the other end of the age continuum—among those more than 54 years of age.

Table 4 shows the gender gaps in happiness, with the polarity reversed in comparison with Table 2. The countries with the largest *negative* gaps now appear at the top (we arbitrarily define gaps where women are happier than men as "positive," and the opposite situation as "negative"). Among those over 54 years of age, the countries that show the largest deficits tend to be the rich, Western societies that showed the largest positive deficits in Table 2. Nine of the eleven countries in which women lag behind men by margins of six or more points are "high income" countries as defined by the World Bank (these countries are shown in bold face type). Australia, which ranked at the top of Table 2, with a positive happiness gap of 14 points among younger respondents, now shows a gap of - 9 points. Similarly, France and The Netherlands, which both showed positive gaps of 9 points in Table 2, now show gaps of –9 points. And Britain, which showed a positive gap of 6 points, now has a negative gap of 11 points. Although both younger and older women rank lower than men in some societies such as Macedonia and Pakistan, the richer societies tend to show a relatively strong positive gender gap among younger respondents—which becomes negative among older respondents. The presence of a negative well-being gap among older groups is not a universal pattern. In some countries, older women show *higher* levels of happiness than their male peers. In South Africa, Nigeria, Brazil, Uruguay, Peru, the Philippines, Japan, and Ireland, older women are happier than men by margins of six or more points—but only two of these countries are rich post-industrial societies and interestingly enough, they are Japan and Ireland, the two societies in which women showed exceptionally high levels of well-being in Inglehart's (1990) analysis. At the other end of the scale, India, Taiwan, and Pakistan are the only non-Western societies in which older women are less happy than their male peers by margins of two or more points. The presence of high positive gender gaps in well-being among younger respondents, linked with negative gaps among older respondents, is largely a phenomenon of rich Western societies.

We have identified several factors that are related to different levels of well-being in men and women. Now let us try to sort out their effects in multivariate analysis. Tables 1 through 5 showed the percentage of people saying they are "very happy," which has an intuitively clear meaning that is useful for illustrating the differences between various groups. In the following analyses, our

Table 4. Happiness by Gender
among Respondents over 54 years old
(Percentage "Very Happy")

Country	Men	Women	Gap	Country	Men	Women	Gap
Macedonia	17	5	-12	Mexico	37	38	-1
Britain	43	32	-11	Slovenia	11	10	-1
France	26	17	-9	Latvia	6	5	-1
Netherlands	43	34	-9	Estonia	5	4	-1
Australia	44	35	-9	Ukraine	4	3	-1
Austria	35	26	-9	Croatia	8	7	-1
Belgium	40	32	-8	Sweden	36	36	0
Denmark	38	32	-6	Finland	23	23	0
Spain	22	16	-6	Korea (S.)	11	11	0
Germany (E.)	21	15	-6	Romania	5	5	0
Bosnia	10	5	-6	China	20	20	0
Germany (W.)	19	14	-5	Portugal	9	9	0
India	23	18	-5	Azerbaijan	6	6	0
Moldova	6	1	-5	Bangladesh	17	17	0
Serbia	15	11	-4	Hungary	11	12	1
Italy	14	11	-3	Bulgaria	5	6	1
North. Ireland	44	41	-3	Turkey	38	39	1
U.S.	43	40	-3	El Salvador	51	52	1
Norway	29	26	-3	Venezuela	51	52	1
Argentina	27	24	-3	Armenia	3	4	1
Switzerland	35	32	-3	New Zealand	35	36	1
Chile	34	31	-3	South Africa	37	41	4
Georgia	9	6	-3	Brazil	22	26	4
Canada	39	37	-2	Uruguay	17	23	6
Iceland	45	43	-2	Philippines	36	42	6
Poland	13	11	-2	Ireland	35	42	7
Belarus	6	4	-2	Japan	21	28	7
Czech	9	7	-2	Peru	31	42	11
Pakistan	29	27	-2	Nigeria	39	55	16
Taiwan	19	17	-2	Mean	23	20	-3
Lithuania	4	2	-2				
Russia	6	4	-2				
Albania	2	0	-2				
Slovakia	6	4	-2				

Source: World Values Survey / European Values Survey.
"High income" countries (as defined by the World Bank in 2001) are shown in bold face type.

dependent variable is an index of well-being based on each respondent's mean scores on both happiness and overall life satisfaction. Although the mean scores on this index have no intuitive meaning, this is a broader-based and more reliable measure of subjective well-being than the simple percentage that is "very happy."

The aspiration adjustment and set-level hypotheses both imply that recent *changes* play a major role in shaping distinctive levels of well-being within given societies. So far we have found that the tendency for women under 45 to show higher levels of happiness than their male peers is largely a phenomenon of *rich* societies. We suggested that this may reflect progress toward gender equality, which in recent years has been moving at a far more rapid pace in developed societies than in less developed ones. But if economic development is indeed conducive to rising gender equality (which tends to bring a positive gender gap), then an indicator of recent economic *change* should provide an even more direct measure of the underlying causal process than an indicator of relative economic levels. We test this idea in Table 5 using each society's mean rate of economic growth from 1985 to 1995 as an indicator of recent economic change. As Model 1 indicates, relatively high rates of economic growth are indeed linked with relatively large positive gender gaps among people under 45 (and the correlation is even

Table 5. The Well-being Gap among those under 45 years old:
The Impact of Economic and Historical Factors
(Dependent Variable: Mean Score on Well-Being Index among Women under 45,
minus Mean Score among Men under 45)

	(Model 1)	(Model 2)	(Model 3)	(Model 4)	(Model 5)
Mean growth in GNP/capita, 1985 – 1995	.022** (.008)	.028** (.008)	.031** (.008)	.031** (.008)	.032** (.008)
Historically Protestant (1=Protestant, 0=not)	—	.146 (.086)	.263* (.121)	.153 (.086)	.135 (.089)
Percentage of women in lower house	—	—	-.008 (.005)	—	—
PPP estimates of GNP/capita in 1995 ($1,000s)	—	—	—	.0007 (.007)	—
Years of Communist rule	—	—	—	—	-.0013 (.002)
Adjusted R2	.17	.20	.19	.18	.19
N	57	57	57	57	57

Note: Figures are unstandardized OLS regression coefficients, with their standard errors shown in parentheses. * $p < .05$, ** $p < .01$.
The dependent variable is based on the given group's mean score on the overall life satisfaction scale, minus two times its mean score on the happiness scale (which has opposite polarity). Thus, one case is the mean score on this index for French women under 45, minus the mean score for French men under 45.

stronger than that with GNP/capita). The relationship between economic growth and a positive gender gap is significant at the .01 level and explains 17 percent of the total variance. When we add a dummy variable that taps a Protestant histori-cal tradition (see Model 2), the explained variance rises to 20 percent, although the Protestant variable does not quite reach the .05 significance level. Model 3 adds the percentage of women in the lower house of parliament to the regression equation; this variable may not be a good indicator of gender equality—at any rate, it does not show a significant effect on the size of the gender gap. But a soci-ety's growth rate continues to show a highly significant effect, and the indictor of a Protestant historical tradition now rises above the .05 level of significance. Model 4 tests the impact of a society's level of wealth (as indicated by the World Bank's purchasing power parity estimates of real GNP per capita in 1995). Although this variable does show a significant zero-order correlation with the dependent variable, it has no significant effect when we control for economic growth and the presence of a Protestant historical tradition (both of which are linked with high levels of GNP/capita). Finally, Model 5 tests the impact of com-munist rule. Although the number of years of communist rule that a society expe-rienced has a significant zero-order correlation with the dependent variable ($r = -.46$), it explains no additional variance when we control for recent economic growth, which has a strong negative correlation with communism ($r = -.76$). The emergence of a positive gender gap (that is, relatively high levels of feminine well-being among those under 45 years of age) seems to be linked with high lev-els of economic development. It also tends to occur in societies with a Protestant cultural tradition that is favorable to the trend toward gender equality.

A rather different set of factors is linked with the negative gender gap among older groups. As Table 6 demonstrates, neither economic growth nor a Protestant cultural tradition show significant effects on subjective well-being among those over 45 (Model 1). A history of communist rule and a high level of development, however, do: communist rule is significant at the .01 level, and GNP/capita is just below the .05 level in Model 2, which also includes the soci-ety's growth rate. When the latter is dropped from the regression equation (Model 3), the explained variance rises to 17 percent, and both GNP/capita and years of communist rule show statistically significant impacts on the gender gap. In both cases, this impact is negative: older women tend to be *less* happy than their male peers in richer societies, and societies that have experienced communist rule. The percentage of women in the lower house of parliament has no significant impact and explains no additional variance in Model 4. Our best model is Model 3.

The contrasting gender gaps among older and younger groups seem to reflect different causal factors. Although high levels of economic *growth*, togeth-er with a Protestant cultural tradition, are conducive to a positive gender gap among younger respondents, the emergence of a negative gender gap among older respondents is linked with high levels of *wealth* and a history of communist rule. Not all communist societies show this negative gender gap, however. In China (as

**Table 6. The Well-being Gap among those 45 and older:
The Impact of Economic and Historical Factors
(Dependent Variable: Mean Score on Well-Being Index among Women 45 and older,
minus Mean Score among Men aged 45 and older)**

	(Model 1)	(Model 2)	(Model 3)	(Model 4)
Mean growth in GNP/capita, 1985 – 1995	.016 (.124)	-.011 (.015)	—	—
Historically Protestant (1=Protestant, 0=not)	.087 (.123)	—	—	—
PPP estimates of GNP/capita in 1995 ($1,000s)	—	-.015 (.008)	-.013* (.006)	- .015* (.007)
Years of Communist rule (USSR=2,Other=1,else=0)	—	-.009** (.003)	- .007** (.002)	-.007** (.003)
Percentage of women in lower house	—	—	—	.0045 (.005)
Adjusted R2	.10	.15	.17	.14
N	57	57	60	60

Note: Figures are unstandardized OLS regression coefficients, with their standard errors shown in parentheses. * $p < .05$, ** $p < .01$
The dependent variable is based on the given group's mean score on the overall life satisfaction scale, minus two times its mean score on the happiness scale (which has opposite polarity).

well as Japan and Taiwan) older women show *higher* scores than men on the well-being index. It is primarily in Western communist societies, and especially the Soviet successor states, that we find a negative gender gap among older women. The negative gender gap among older women is mainly a phenomenon of rich Western societies.

Conclusion

The aspiration-adjustment model implies that, at this point in history, we should be finding significant differences between the happiness levels of men and women in the contemporary world—with women showing *higher* levels of subjective well-being than men. For the past few decades, a global women's movement has been pushing for gender equality and this movement has had considerable impact, especially in the more developed countries. In so far as it has improved the status of women, this should raise their subjective well-being. Even though their objective conditions remain less favorable than men's, the model implies that positive changes should produce a positive gap between women's aspirations and achievements.

Empirical evidence from scores of countries demonstrates that among the more developed societies, women do indeed tend to show higher levels of life satisfaction than men. But this phenomenon is largely offset by a tendency for women to suffer a declining sense of well-being as they age. So that while younger women currently show higher levels of well-being than men in most Western societies (and in *all* historically Protestant societies, where women have made the most progress toward equality), this pattern tends to reverse itself among the older age groups. In precisely those rich Western societies where younger women show substantially higher levels of happiness than their male peers, older women tend to be *less* happy than men of the same age. This happiness deficit among older women does not seem to be an inherent part of the human condition. It is absent in many Asian, African, and Latin American societies, and in some of them, older women show *higher* levels of subjective well-being than men do. We believe that these relatively low levels of happiness among older women reflect a culturally defined tendency to devalue the social worth of older women; a tendency that is particularly powerful in economically developed societies. We have data from 24 countries that the World Bank defines as "high income." Without a single exception, every one of these societies currently shows a positive gender gap in subjective well-being among those under 45 years of age, with women being happier than men. But 18 of these 24 societies show a negative gender gap (and only three show a positive gender gap) in happiness among those who are 45 and older.

Causality is always difficult to demonstrate, and we are not able to do so in the present case. We would need data concerning perceptions of recent changes in the status of women, and the extent to which perceptions of women's beauty and social value, impact on women as they age. Neither the World Values Surveys, nor any other surveys we are aware of, provide such evidence in a broad global perspective. But the findings presented here are consistent with the hypothesis that recent improvements in the status of women (which have been especially large in the economically most developed societies) have tended to raise the happiness levels of women in these societies—but that this trend has been largely offset by a tendency to devalue the social worth of older women in precisely those rich societies in which women have otherwise made the most progress. This results in an interaction between gender, age, and well-being: younger women tend to be happier than men (especially in richer countries) is offset by the evidence that older women tend to be *less* happy than men in these same societies, producing very small overall gender differences. This interaction tends to conceal statistically significant and theoretically interesting gender differences in subjective well-being.

Causality is difficult to demonstrate, but the empirical evidence is compatible with this interpretation. This, or some other combination of factors, has brought about a situation in which today, younger women are happier than men in literally all of the rich countries; but older women are *less* happy than men in most of these same societies. This pattern is not universal; it seems to reflect societal causes rather than anything genetically determined. These causes seem to have an important impact on human happiness—and merit further research.

REFERENCES

ANDREWS, Frank M. and Steven B. Withey.
    1976. *Social Indicators of Well-being: Americans' Perceptions of Life Quality.* New York: Plenum.
BARNES, Samuel et al.
    1979. *Political Action: Mass Participation in Five Western Democracies.* Beverly Hills: Sage.
BLUHM, Sheila M.
    2000. *Aging Beauty: The Adaptive Reconstruction of the Aging Process in Women.* Ph.D. dissertation, Department of Sociology, Western Michigan University.
CAMPBELL, Angus, Philip E. Converse, and Willard L. Rodgers.
    1976. *The Quality of Life.* New York: Russell Sage.
COSTA, P.T., R.R. McCrae, and A.B. Zonderman.
    1987. "Environmental and Dispositional Influences on Well-being: Longitudinal Follow-up of an American National Sample." *British Journal of Psychology* 78:299-306.
DIENER, Ed and Eunkook M. Suh, eds.
    2000. *Subjective Well-Being Across Cultures.* Cambridge MA: MIT Press.
EBSTEIN, R.P. et al.
    1996. "Dopamine D4 Receptor (D4DR) Exon III Polymorphism Associated with the Human Personality Trait of Novelty Seeking." *Nature Genetics* 12:78-80.
HAMER, D.H.
    1996. "The Heritability of Happiness." *Nature Genetics* 14:125-126.
INGLEHART, Ronald .
    1990. *Culture Shift in Advanced Industrial Society.* Princeton: Princeton University Press.
INGLEHART, Ronald.
    1997. *Modernization and Postmodernization: Cultural, Economic and Political Change in 43 Societies.* Princeton: Princeton University Press.
INTERPARLIAMENTARY UNION
    2002. "Women in Parliaments (Percentage of Women in each National Parliament)." Retrieved March 15, 2002 (http://www.ipu.org/wmn-e/classif.htm).
LYKKEN, D and A. Tellegen.
    1996. "Happiness is a Stochastic Phenomenon." *Psychological Science* 7:186-189.
MYERS, David G. and Ed Diener.
    1995. "Who is happy?" *Psychological Science* 6:10-19.

WHY ARE SOME WOMEN POLITICALLY ACTIVE? THE HOUSEHOLD, PUBLIC SPACE, AND POLITICAL PARTICIPATION IN INDIA

Pradeep Chhibber*

ABSTRACT

Women in India do not participate in political life to the same extent as men. While a fair number of women turn out to vote they have little representation in legislative bodies at the national and state level. This paper attributes the limited presence of women in legislative bodies to the fact that many women are still confined to the household. Evidence to support this claim comes from an analysis of a survey that was conducted in a state of Northern India to assess which women have been able to take the opportunity to join local bodies where, one-third of all seats, are now reserved for women. The analysis suggests that even after controlling for demographic factors, only those women who have an identity that is independent of the household are likely to avail the opportunity to contest elections for local bodies. The paper then extends the findings from the Indian case to other nations by analyzing the World Values Survey and finds that similar patterns exist globally. It is women who have an identity outside the household who are more likely to be politically active.

Introduction

While major changes have occurred in the status of women in some parts of the world in recent decades, the role of women continues to be home-centered, thus, excludes public activities and political life. In the contemporary world, some regimes have enforced this principle most severely (the Taliban in Afghanistan, for example), but it is also a powerful factor in many other countries such as Japan (where there is still a strong expectation that when women marry, they will leave full-time employment outside the home).[1] Moreover, the impact of home-centered roles for women is not restricted to non-Western countries. The view that "a woman's place is in the home" prevailed in Western societies well into the twentieth century and, as this article will demonstrate, it still bears significant influence. In so far as such roles, which include the constellation of norms, values, beliefs, attitudes, and actions are accepted, they will continue to inhibit women from participating in politics.

In India, a large number of women do not work and, by implication, spend much of their time at home. In 1991, only 22 percent of the women were in the workforce as compared to 52 percent of the men. In 1961, only 28 percent of the

* Department of Political Science, University of California, Berkeley, 210 Barrows Hall #1950, Berkeley, CA 94720-1950, USA.

women were in the workforce (Gopalan and Shiva 2000:119). Many of the women in 1991, however, worked in the unorganized sector and did not have regular employment. While 28 percent of the men were employed with "casual wages" (i.e., did not have a permanent job), 39 percent of the women were casual wage employees (Gopalan and Shiva 2000:119). In the organized sector, where there is greater job security, the proportion of women employed to total employment was only 16 percent in 1996, up from 11 percent in 1961 (Gopalan and Shiva 2000:344). Given that few women are in the workforce, women's participation in political life is fairly limited (Burns, Scholzman, and Verba 2001). While a large enough proportion of women turn out to vote and the gender gap in turnout has dropped to single digits in the 1990s (from almost 20 percent in 1971), women still are not well represented in political life which requires them to be active in the public sphere—such as membership in Parliament and in State Legislative Assemblies. To redress the low level of participation by women in deliberative bodies, the government of India amended the constitution in 1992 (73rd and 74th amendments) so that a third of the seats in the *Panchayats* (local governments), including the chairpersonship of these local bodies, would be reserved for women. As this constitutional amendment mandates that women be elected to local office, it offers us a chance to assess which women become politically active.[2]

This constitutional amendment has indeed brought women into local bodies (Gopalan and Shiva 2000), but which women have been able to take advantage of their new entitlements? Are women aware of the changes that were introduced by the central government? Further, are there significant inter-community differences in terms of awareness and responsiveness to these changes? The answers to these questions are interesting from a theoretical standpoint. Prominent arguments, both in India and elsewhere, have suggested that women's participation is generally lower either because they have been "socialized" differently (especially as far as marriage, motherhood, employment, and property ownership are concerned), or because they have fewer resources (Schlozman, Burns, Verba 1994; Verba, Burns, and Schlozman 1997; Burns, Schlozman, and Verba 1997b). An implicit assumption in these sets of arguments is that the lower level of participation of women is mostly the result of a process of socialization that leads them to think of political activity in a different way than men. In other words, women don't take as active a part in political life because they don't think (as autonomous actors) that political participation is important. An implication that follows from this line of reasoning is that women do not think that entering political life would necessarily be advantageous. If they did, they would participate as autonomous actors.

This paper suggests that a far less benign interpretation may account for the lower level of political participation by women in India.[3] It observes that women are aware of the advantages that politics brings, but are still not active participants in political life. This lower level of participation is not only a consequence of the resources that women possess, it is also a result of the role of women in the family. It is argued that those women who can negotiate independent space for themselves within the household are more likely to participate in political life. This factor (the ability to negotiate within the household), the paper will argue, retains its significance, even controlling for the societal and individual characteristics that explain participation such as a respondent's socioeconomic status.

The paper begins by describing the position of women in public political life in India—particularly in their virtual absence in legislative bodies—at the state and at the national level. It is surprising that the proportion of women in the legislature remains low even in those states where women have a better quality of life in terms of access to education and life expectancy (Kerala, for example). Since women in India have little place in the public arena, they also express less faith in the political process. The second part of the paper discusses the findings from a six-state post-election survey conducted in 1996, and a survey of women in a northern Indian state that assesses women's involvement in political life subsequent to the adoption of the constitutional amendments guaranteeing women a third of all places in local bodies. The third section outlines the argument that describes the link between political activity and status within the household. The next part analyzes a survey designed specifically to assess which women are contesting elections for local bodies seven years after the amendment (which gives women guaranteed seats in local bodies) was adopted by the national government. This section observes that five years after the adoption of the amendment, women's participation in local politics remains below that of men and that women were not even aware of their new entitlements. Further, neither a woman's caste affiliation nor socialization could adequately account for their low level of awareness of the 73d amendment. Whether women knew of the amendment or not was largely determined by their levels of education, family income, and whether they belonged to a "political family" (i.e., someone in their family had partaken in electoral politics). The more important finding relates to which women choose to contest elections. Whether a woman contests local elections or not depends, in addition to socioeconomic status, on her position in the household. Women who can negotiate independent space for themselves are more likely to be active participants in the political process. The penultimate section of the paper examines whether these findings are unique to India or if similar phenomenon can be detected in other parts of the world as well. The paper concludes with some caveats and suggestions for future research.

Women in the Indian Legislatures

As in other parts of the world, few women in India find a place in the lower house of parliament—the *Lok Sabha* in India. The *Lok Sabha* in 2002 had 8.8 percent women placing India 82nd of the 180 countries for which data on women in the lower house is reported by the Inter-Parliamentary Union.[4] There is also gender gap in national elections in India, just as there is in countries like the United

States. Women have also turned out at lower rates than men for elections to the *Lok Sabha*. As Table 1 indicates, in all elections in Independent India, women have consistently turned out to vote less than men, though the gap has become lower in the last two decades. Similarly, the presence of women in parliament has remained remarkably stable at 5 percent until the 1990s when it averaged around 8 percent.

Table 1.
Women's Representation in Parliament
(Turnout differential and the percentage of women in the *Lok Sabha*)[5]

Year	Turnout Differential between men and women	Percent women in the *Lok Sabha*
1952		4.4
1957		5.4
1962	17	6.7
1967	11	5.9
1971	21	4.2
1977	11	3.4
1980	9	5.1
1984	10	7.9
1989	9	5.3
1991	10	7.9
1996	9	7.3
1998	8	7.9
1999	8	8.8

The smaller proportion of women who have a place in the *Lok Sabha* is replicated in the *Vidhan Sabhas* (state legislative assemblies) as well. Table 2 reports the number of women who are members of the legislative assemblies. It is clear that the proportion of women who find a place in these legislatures is low and remains in the single digits for almost every state. What is remarkable about this very low level of representation for women is that it occurs even in states like Kerala, which have been hailed for their favorable treatment of gender concerns. While women indeed have achieved almost universal literacy in Kerala and are far more active in the labor force, their political presence in the legislative bodies is remarkably low. This difference, by itself, should give pause to arguments that seek to link women's education and employment to a place in public political life axiomatically.

Table 2 provides evidence that Indian electoral politics is still the domain of men.[7] Evidence from post-election national surveys confirms this understanding. Table 3 reports the results of an analysis of a national post-election survey conducted in 1971. The table suggests that women were far less likely to say that elections influenced the government than men. More than half of the men in a post-election survey said that elections could influence the government, whereas less than one-third of the women thought similarly. These differences held up when respondents were asked whether voting has any effect on government action. Finally, women also felt that they had less say in the government than men.

Table 2.
Women's Participation and Representation in State Assemblies[6]

State	Election Year	Turnout - Men	Turnout -Women	Percentage of Women in the State Legislature
Andhra Pradesh	1999	72.07%	66.24%	9
Arunachal Pradesh	1999	72.38%	73.58%	3
Assam	2001	77.23%	71.82%	8
Delhi	1998	50.89%	46.41%	13
Bihar	2000	70.71%	53.28%	6
Goa	2002	69.90%	68.23%	3
Gujarat	1998	63.34%	55.03%	2
Haryana	2000	69.97%	67.85%	4
Himachal Pradesh	1998	70.26%	72.21%	9
Jammu & Kashmir	1996	60.57%	46.08%	2
Karnataka/Mysore	1999	70.62%	64.58%	3
Kerala	2001	74.39%	70.67%	6
Madhya Pradesh	1998	66.45%	53.53%	8
Maharashtra	1999	63.62%	58.03%	4
Manipur	2002	90.09%	91.07%	2
Meghalaya	1998	74.20%	74.83%	5
Mizoram	1998	76.42%	76.22%	0
Nagaland	1998	80.65%	77.07%	0
Orissa	2000	63.63%	54.25%	9
Punjab	2002	65.92%	64.27%	7
Pondicherry	2001	69.51%	70.70%	0
Rajasthan	1998	67.45%	58.88%	7
Sikkim	1999	84.36%	79.10%	3
Tamil Nadu	2001	61.30%	56.83%	11
Tripura	1998	81.96%	79.65%	3
Uttar Pradesh	2002	56.75%	50.33%	6
Uttaranchal	2002	55.96%	52.89%	6
West Bengal	2001	77.83%	72.53%	9

Table 3.
Gender and the Influence of Elections on the Government

Issue	Women answering Yes	Men Answering Yes
Do you have a say in government	23	39
Do elections influence the government	32	53
Voting has an effect on government action	38	59

Source: 1971 Center for Developing Studies post-election survey.

The 73d amendment to the Indian constitution was introduced in 1992 with the ostensible purpose of giving women a larger voice in the political process. The amendment would reserve at least one-third of the total number of seats to be filled by direct election in every *Panchayat* for women. It would also ensure that one-third of the chairmanships of the *Panchayats* would be reserved for women.[8] Insofar as the 73d amendment also required that states hold elections to the *Panchayats*, and as the amendment was adopted in 1992, the amendment could have influenced the extent of political participation by women almost instantaneously.

Has the amendment changed the gendered nature of participation in India? Evidence that this is not the case comes from a survey conducted in 1996 in six states: Maharashtra, Gujarat, West Bengal, Andhra Pradesh, Karnataka, and Uttar Pradesh. There is considerable variance in the role of local government in these states. In Gujarat, Maharashtra, and West Bengal, local government has been extremely important, whereas it has been less significant in Andhra Pradesh and Karnataka. In Uttar Pradesh, on the other hand, local government is almost non-existent. The position of women in these states is also different. The female-male ratio varies from 972 in Andhra Pradesh to 879 in Uttar Pradesh, while female literacy varies between 52 percent in Maharashtra to 25 percent in Uttar Pradesh. The states also differ in economic indicators and party strength. Their per capita income in 1990 to 1991 ranged from Rs.7,316 (in Maharashtra) to Rs.3,516 in Uttar Pradesh. Per capita domestic product in 1986 to 1987 varied between Rs.1,039 (Maharashtra) to Rs.607 (Uttar Pradesh). The political landscape of the states was also different with diverse party system configurations in each region. The right wing Hindu party, the Bharatiya Janata Party (BJP), has a significant presence in Uttar Pradesh, Maharahstra, and Gujarat; the Communist Party of India (Marxist) rules West Bengal; the Congress party is still an important electoral force in Gujarat, Maharashtra, Andhra Pradesh, Karnataka, and West Bengal; while a regional party, the Telugu Desam, governs Andhra Pradesh. Within each state, five to nine districts (based on the population proportions) were randomly selected. Within these districts, 96 assembly constituencies were picked. A total of 2,850 interviews were conducted.

Respondents were asked a series of questions on their participation in the local political process. They were asked if they attended *panchayat* and party meetings; if they, along with their neighbors, participated in a protest; if they contacted either bureaucrats or party leaders; and if they took part in campaign activities. On all scores women's participation was significantly lower than that of men with well over four in five women saying that they had never partaken in such activities. Most telling was that 85 percent of the women, four years after the adoption of the 73d amendment, said they had not participated in any *panchayat* meetings. Further support for the continued lack of participation by women came from the responses of women and men to questions about their interest in local elections. 36 percent of women said that they were not interested in local elections at all, in contrast to 21 percent of men who felt similarly.

The various participation measures were combined into one measure of participation (after a factor analysis yielded only one factor) and regressed on gender and a variety of controls. Gender retains its significance in explaining political participation even controlling for income, caste, education, age, and the state in which a respondent resided. In other words, women are still not active participants in the local political process despite the constitutional amendment that requires active participation by women in the electoral process.

Table 4.
Gender and Local Political Participation
(percent who had not participated at all)

Arena	Male	Female
Panchayat Meetings	61	85
Party Meetings	75	90
Campaign	80	90
Contact with bureaucrats	66	82
Party Leaders	72	87

Source: 1996 post-election study conducted by OASES.

Being Public: Stepping Outside the Household and Political Participation by Women

This paper builds on this existing research and suggests that the lower levels of participation of women in political life can also be accounted for by their role in the household. In particular, this paper argues that women who can exercise autonomy in and from the household are more likely to be active participants in political life. Political activity takes place in the public sphere. Political participation is fundamentally a public act—for men and for women. In many parts of the world, however, the public space is still inhabited and dominated by men. For instance, political demonstrations in many parts of the world are still the domain of men, as are legislatures. Women do not have a place in the public space. For women to be politically active they need to be in the public arena. For this to happen, women need to be able to "step out of the household." Women must have an existence autonomous of the household. Hartmann (1981) notes (perhaps echoing Aristotle), households are still the sphere of male dominance.[9] As long as women are confined to the home and they do not have an identity independent of the household, their levels of political participation will necessarily be lower than men's because they cannot be in the public space. Or, a theory of political participation of women in a family needs to address their place inside and outside the home (Okin 1998).

Are there other factors that prevent women from entering the public arena? One set of explanations suggests that women participate at lower levels than men since there are far more demands on a woman's time including housework and child rearing (South and Spitze 1994). Burns et al. (2001) find that men indeed do spend more time on paid work and wives more on housework, but both men and women have similar amounts of free time and that "leisure has no systematic impact on political participation" either by men or women (Burns et al. 2001:257). Another reason for why women are not politically active is that they are actively discriminated against—legally or otherwise. This is a difficult topic to research since direct evidence for discrimination is not often available.[10] The Indian case offers an opportunity to examine what factors influence political activity by women controlling for discrimination. In India the 73rd amendment, as we noted above, reserved a third of all seats in local elected bodies for women. In other words, there is a policy that *favors* political activity by women. Since the law favors women's activity in local bodies and does not discriminate against them, the events following the 73rd amendment offer us a chance to examine what else influences a woman's participation in political life. What we find is that not all women are politically active. Why, despite a proactive policy to bring women into political life, do only some women entertain that possibility? Is it that the only women who participate are those who can step out of the household?

Stepping into the Public: Which Women in India Participate in Politics?

While political participation by women in the state and national legislative bodies remains low, and women still do not actively participate in political life, almost a third of the seats in local bodies and the chairpersonship of these bodies are now with women (Gopalan and Shiva 2000:141-142). Which women are willing to take an active part in local bodies? To answer this question a survey was conducted in rural areas in the North Indian state of Haryana. This geographically concentrated survey was conducted so that context specific influences on participation could be controlled for. It has been argued that the standard individual focused models of political participation are inadequate for there are strong contextual influences on participation. To control for such context effects we conducted a survey in the rural areas of one state. Since state politics is important in India, and rural and urban women differ in terms of the opportunities available to them, a survey conducted in the rural areas of one state allows us to control for the most salient context effects that could have a bearing on who participates in politics. A total of 980 women were interviewed by female investigators in 40 villages that fell in 5 districts: Sonepat, Kurukshetra, Rewari, Rohtak, and Hissar.

The survey revealed, surprisingly, that most women did not know about the reservations for them in local elections. Only 44 percent of them knew of the reservations; of these 44 percent, most (almost two-thirds) did not know what the extent of the reservation was. Only one-fourth could correctly identify the percent reserved for them was one-third (Table 5).

This lack of awareness of the extent of the reservations for women does not mean that women are not aware of the influence of politics in their lives. A majority of them said that political participation would be good for them, partic-

Table 5.
Women, Political Participation, and Social Attitudes

Issue	Percent saying yes
Do you know of reservation for women	44
Will participation in elections solve women's problems	72
Will participation in elections raise the social status for women	97
Can women taking part in elections look after family and children adequately	84
Can women complete their responsibilities after winning elections	55
Is reservation a sham? Men will never allow equality for women	60
Do women participate on behalf of some man	55
Does the lack of cooperation of men hinder women's development	56
Should women stay in the four walls of the house	00
Are you in favor of self sufficient women	100
Can independent women be capable housewives	92
If women are given work, jobs, and education will that increase their self-confidence and self-reliance	100
Is there *purdah* in this area	100
Do you have a voice in the matters of marriages?	83
Is marriage mostly within your caste?	100
Is marriage within the village?	0
Do women help in purchases?	47
Do men and women have different wage rates?	98

Source: 1998 Survey of Women and Political Participation in Haryana.

ipation would solve the problems faced by women, and it would also raise their social status. More importantly, most women also did not see entering political life as disrupting any other facet of their life, such looking after family and children, in a significant way. Furthermore, the voice for equality, self-sufficiency, and education was almost unanimous among the women interviewed. This unanimity persisted, despite that in Haryana most women still practice *purdah* and are living in an area characterized by village exogamy. That women are quite expressive about equality raises doubts about theories that say women are not aware of their rights and buy into the dominant male social and political discourse. Agarwal (1992) uses Bourdieu's (1990) notion of *doxa* to suggest that women in India accept the dominant male ideology. This way of reasoning would suggest that rural Indian women are accepting of their position because they do not question some facets of their life, especially their relationship to men. Most women (56 percent), when asked whether men are responsible for their lack of social mobility, answered in the affirmative. This question, and the response of women to the question, provides some evidence that Indian women have not internalized their positions as non-participants in the political process as the exponents of *doxa* would suggest.

Studies either of participation by women in the political process or their attitudes towards social issues in India have pointed to the critical role of caste. It has been suggested that that a respondent's caste influences the attitudes of women, and that forward caste women are more likely to be conservative and adopt positions similar to those of men. Lower caste women are, on the other hand, more independent and it is assumed that there is a freedom associated with marginality that lower caste women may enjoy. In Haryana, however, caste did not influence the attitudes of women on a whole range of issues. Women, either *dalit* or belonging to the backward or forward castes, thought similarly about whether participation would be good for them or not; what the major problems faced by women were; whether men could be held partly responsible for these problems; and their role at home (Table 6).

Table 6.
Does Caste Influence a Woman's Attitude?

Issue	Dalit	Backward	Forward
Do you know of reservation for women	35	46	48
Will participation in elections solve women's problems	75	77	68
Will participation in elections raise social status for women	96	97	97
Can women taking part in elections look after their family	78	87	84
Is reservation is a sham - men will never allow equality	60	56	61
Do women participate on behalf of some man	57	52	56
Major Problem faced by women – economic	19	10	5
Major Problem faced by women – education	66	76	75
Can men be held responsible (partly) for these problems	64	77	71
Do women help in purchases	42	49	46
Do you have as much respect in society as you expected	69	65	67
Are you busy at home all day	59	55	67
Do you have a desire to work outside of the home	69	55	47

Source: 1998 Survey of Women and Political Participation in Haryana.

What Explains a Woman's Knowledge and Participation?

The data presented in Tables 5 and 6 provide clear evidence that despite the reforms introduced by the constitutional amendments of 1992 many women in rural areas are not aware of these reforms. Why, however, are a substantial proportion of women unaware of these reforms? Is the awareness of women a function of their caste, their socialization, their personal educational and income levels, or their family status? To determine which of these factors is important, a multivariate statistical model was estimated. The dependent variable is whether the respondents are aware of the reforms or not. A number of independent variables, each addressing key theories on the participation of women in the literature, comprise the model.

The first set of variables includes a respondent's demographic characteristics: the educational level of the respondents, their family income, age, and caste. A second argument suggests, in consonance with the models of participation that link income and education to political activity (Verba and Nie 1972), that since men and women have differential access to socioeconomic resources and since socioeconomic status influences political participation, women are less politically active than men. In India, women have less education than men and since they are also less likely to be in the workforce, women may be less politically active than men (Gleason 2001). Since most of the respondents are housewives, there is no reason to introduce occupation as a control. In addition, a whole set of attitudinal variables that approximate socialization are also incorporated into the model. Women were asked if they were busy at home all day and we could expect those who answered in the affirmative to have lower levels of participation. A similar set of expectations could be held for those women who thought that women's participation was a sham and that women would never be made equal; that in contesting these local elections women were really assisting males. On the other hand, women who expressed that taking part in elections would solve women's problems could be expected to be more active participants in the political process.

Another set of variables included in the model dealt with the relations between men and women. Respondents were asked whether they helped in shopping (a proxy variable for their ability to travel to the market) and if their progress was halted by a lack of help from men. In an open-ended question respondents expressed detailed reasons for how men thwarted their progress. These responses were recoded into three categories. First, those who said that the division of labor kept them preoccupied with housework all day; second, they were made to stay at home; and third, open expression was not permitted in the household. These three sets of responses are included in the final model as dummy variables. The final variable added to the model was whether the respondent belonged to a family in which someone had contested elections prior to the local elections. Given the well-known importance of political families in India, we can expect women from more active political families to be more aware of any policy changes that would affect their chances to win office or gain access to resources. Whether a respondent belongs to family with someone in political life or not has been used as an indicator of socialization by Burns et al. (2001).

The results reported in Table 7 yield interesting patterns. The only demographic variables that seem to influence a respondent's awareness of the amendment are those related to the economic position of the respondent—education and family income. The caste of the respondent, once controlled for education, income and attitudinal variables, did not have a significant influence on whether they were aware of the amendment or not. The variable with the largest impact on the respondent's knowledge of the amendment was whether someone in the family had contested elections or not. Those who come from "political families" are more likely to be aware of these changes.

While socioeconomic status, especially income and education, influence a woman's knowledge of the 73rd amendment, do the same variables have a bearing on which women contested local elections? Do demographic variables continue to retain their significance in explaining which women contested local elections as models of participation would suggest? The results reported in Table 8 point out that the explanation for which respondents contested elections is different from whether they are aware of the amendment or not. The dependent variable in Table 8 is whether a person contested the elections (0) or did not (1). Hence, a negative sign on the coefficient of an independent variable indicates that the variable did have a positive influence on a respondent's participation in local elections, whereas a positive sign suggests that the variable had a negative impact on a woman's contesting local elections.

Table 7.
Who Knows About the 73d Amendment
(Logit Model with knowledge of the Amendment as the Dependent Variable)

Variables	Coefficient	Standard Error
Education	1.044**	0.12
Dalit	-0.433*	0.25
Forward Caste	0.060	0.23
Family monthly income	0.159**	0.06
Busy at home all day	-0.005	0.19
Women's participation is a sham	0.174	0.25
In competing women are helping a man	0.342	0.26
Participation is good for women	-0.036	0.19
Do you help in shopping	-0.271	0.18
Women's progress is thwarted by men	0.449	0.96
Busy with housework all day	0.650	0.97
Have to stay at home	0.152	0.98
Cannot express myself openly	1.441	0.99
Family members in politics	1.613**	0.27
Constant	-1.232	2.18

$^*p < .10$
$^{**}p < .05$

N: 820
chi^2 240.29
Prob > chi^2 0.0000
Log Likelihood -1104.454
Percent Correctly Predicted 75

These results provide more support for the socialization models. They suggest, quite clearly, that demographic factors are not the only important factors in determining whether a woman contests local elections or not. Respondents with higher family income, as expected, are more likely candidates. Higher education levels, while they predict the awareness of the respondents of the 73d amendment, do not explain who is a candidate. In fact, quite unexpectedly, most of the candidates are those with higher levels of education but come from less wealthy families.[11]

The more interesting facet of these results is the significant impact of the attitudes of the respondents on whether they were candidates or not. Candidates, quite obviously, did not think women's participation was just a show. But, those who spent less time shopping, were forced to stay at home, spent a fair bit of time working in the home, and were not allowed open expression, were not candidates for local elections. Women's socialization was important in determining whether they contested elections or not. Those who are able to disengage themselves more from household activities are more likely to be candidates in the local elections. Whether there is an expansion of women's participation or not, then, depends upon their role in the household. *If women are less constrained in the household, they are more active participants in the political process.*

Table 8.
Who Participates in Local Elections
(Logit Model—Participation as a Candidate in Local Elections as the Dependent Variable)

Variables	Coefficient	Standard Error
Education	-0.423**	0.17
Dalit	0.501	0.34
Forward Caste	0.123	0.29
Family monthly income	0.194**	0.06
Women's participation is a sham	1.714**	0.39
In Competing women are helping a man	0.305	0.40
Participation is good for women	-0.415	0.33
Do you help in shopping	-1.183**	0.26
Women's progress is thwarted by men	-1.851*	0.99
Busy with housework all day	-2.322**	1.01
Have to stay at home	-2.349**	1.04
Cannot express myself openly	-2.336**	1.05
Constant	3.422	2.24

$^*p < .10$
$^{**}p < .05$

N: 820
chi^2 166.91
Prob > chi^2 0.0000
Log Likelihood 684.585
Percent Correctly Predicted 89

Women and Political Participation: The Indian Experience Generalized

In order to assess whether constraints in the household influence the political participation of women elsewhere (in countries other than India), the World Values Survey of 2000-2001 was analyzed. The World Values Survey offers a unique opportunity to test whether arguments that are generated from specific circumstances have validity beyond the area in which they were first generated. The survey (Table 9) reveals quite clearly that there are significant differences among the interest shown by men and women in politics. The survey asked respondents how interested they were in politics. The responses were coded into two categories: those who were interested and those who were not. There is a difference between the level of political interest shown by men and women across the globe. Thirty-nine percent of the women had an interest in politics, whereas 52 percent of the men did. This difference was statistically significant. The difference in interest is not characteristic of all nations. In Argentina, the Philippines, and Tanzania men and women were equally interested in politics.

Men and women also participate differentially in political life.[12] The World Values Survey asked whether a respondent had taken part in political activities such as signing a petition, or taking part in a demonstration. Responses in the affirmative to these three questions were coded such that if a respondent had undertaken even one of these activities the respondent was considered to have participated in politics. Those who did not take part in any of the activities were classified as non-participants. Once again, 30 percent of the men were participating in political life, whereas only 24 percent of the women engaged in political activity (Table 9). The difference is statistically significant. In not all nations, however, do men and women participate at differential rates. In the United States, Canada, Sweden, Argentina, South Korea, Israel, Tanzania, Vietnam, and Egypt the differences between men and women's participation rates were not significant.

Table 9. Political Interest and Political Action by Gender

Country	Political Interest			Political Action		
	Female (Mean)	Male (Mean)	Significance Level	Female (Mean)	Male (Mean)	Significance Level
Spain	.2353	.3648	.000	.3007	.4032	.000
USA	.6168	.6927	.006	.8292	.8020	.224
Canada	.4260	.5454	.000	.7350	.7384	.867
Japan	.5656	.7159	.000	.5802	.5719	.756
Mexico	.3068	.3762	.004	.1356	.1915	.003
South Africa	.4313	.5835	.000	.3059	.3577	.003
Sweden	-	-	-	.8961	.8700	.196
Argentina	.1800	.1874	.731	.2646	.2644	.992
South Korea	.3943	.6010	.000	.5017	.5265	.390
Puerto Rico	.3890	.4803	.018	.2009	.3098	.001
Nigeria	.4429	.6062	.000	.1192	.2723	.000
Chile	.2061	.3028	.000	.2124	.2947	.001
India	.2806	.5640	.000	.1746	.3993	.000
China	.6232	.7879	.000	0	0	-
Turkey	.3172	.4855	.000	.1147	.1953	.000
Peru	.4314	.5233	.000	.2552	.3315	.001
Venezuela	.2104	.2777	.007	.1563	.2264	.002
Zimbabwe	.2552	.3786	.000	.0341	.1134	.000
Philippines	.4839	.5138	.302	.0732	.1662	.000
Israel	.6459	.7658	.000	.4294	.4519	.437
Tanzania	.7183	.7127	.836	.3340	.3441	.718
Bangladesh	.2304	.5484	.000	.0745	.1944	.000
Indonesia	.2954	.4465	.000	.1080	.1520	.000
Vietnam	.7186	.8753	.000	.0553	.0777	.157
Uganda	.4140	.6032	.000	.1591	.3107	.000
Serbia	.3103	.4587	.000	.2853	.3958	.000
Montenegro	.3510	.5536	.000	.1962	.3486	.000
Egypt	.3029	.5433	.000	.2082	.1896	.202
Morocco	.1289	.2676	.000	.1195	.2145	.000
Iran	.5116	.5989	.000	0	0	-
All	*.3909*	*.5327*	*.000*	*.2482*	*.3058*	*.000*

Source: World Values Survey, 2000.

What accounts for the fact that some women are interested and active in politics are others are not? Can the argument developed from the Indian case be applied to other circumstances? In other words, are women who have an active life outside the household more interested and more active in politics even when controlling for their demographic characteristics and other explanations for participation? To assess this question, two logit models were estimated—one to determine why some women are interested in politics and the other to assess why some women are more politically active (Tables 10 and 11). The analysis is conducted only with female respondents.

The World Values Survey does not offer the same set of questions to assess a woman's role outside the household as the survey of women in India. It does, however, ask respondents how often they meet with their friends. It can be assumed that those women who meet their friends more often are more likely to have a life independent of the household than those who do not. This variable—meeting with friends—becomes the key independent variable in the analysis. And, if women who have a life outside of the household are more interested in politics and more politically active, this variable should be significant even when controlling for other factors that could influence whether a female respondent is interested in politics and politically active. In the Indian state of Kerala it has been found that women who contested elections to the local bodies often said that they did so at the urging of friends (Sooryarmoorthy 2000).

A number of other factors too could influence a woman's interest and participation in politics. First and foremost, as Table 9 reveals, there are significant inter-country differences between the level of interest and participation in political life by women. Seventy-one percent of the women interviewed expressed an interest in politics in Tanzania and Vietnam, whereas only 12 percent of the women in Morocco felt the same. Similarly, large variances can be found in the extent of political participation by women—89 percent of the women in Sweden were participants in political life, whereas only 3 percent of the women took part in some political activity in Zimbabwe. The logit models, therefore, had to control for the country of a respondent. In addition to the national origin of the respondent, other demographic factors could influence participation. It is well acknowledged that more educated women, those who are employed, women of higher social standing (social class), and urban women are more likely to be interested in politics and are more politically active. Similarly, those women who belong to any secondary association could be expected to be more active politically while housewives should be less politically active.

The World Values Survey has data on all these attributes. The socioeconomic status of a respondent is determined by the their education as well as their self-reported social class. Whether a person is an urban resident or not is ascertained by whether the interview was conducted in a city or not. Women who worked either for themselves, part-time, or full-time were categorized as employed. The survey also records whether respondents belonged to a number of organizations or not (respondents were asked whether they belonged to any of thirteen associations). If a respondent said that she belongs to even one of those organizations, she is coded as belonging to an organization. Those who do not belong to any associations are coded as non-members. Finally, respondents were asked whether they found being a housewife fulfilling. Those who agree strongly or agree are grouped together and differentiated from those who do not think so.

Table 10 reports the results of the analysis for why some women are more interested in politics. As expected, there are strong and significant country specific effects. Further, women who are more educated, live in cities, and are of

Table 10.
Why do some Women express an Interest in Politics?

	Logistic Regression Coefficient	Standard Error
USA	-1.411**	.137
Canada	-.453**	.139
Mexico	-.998**	.124
Puerto Rico	-.954**	.134
Nigeria	-1.148**	.144
Chile	-.296*	.120
India	-1.735**	.141
Venezuela	-.984**	.128
Zimbabwe	-1.836**	.142
Philippines	-.504**	.131
Bangladesh	-1.502**	.141
Indonesia	-1.160**	.145
Serbia	.737**	.148
Montenegro	-1.086**	.134
Egypt	-.898**	.143
Morocco	-.844**	.109
Jordan	-1.755**	.144
Education	.113**	.010
Employed	-.015	.047
Social Class	-.109**	.024
Urban	.120*	.053
Meeting Friends	.180**	.046
Associational Membership	.552**	.056
Being a Housewife is fulfilling	-.122	.064
Constant	-.395*	.159

Dependent variable is political interest.
*$p<.05$; **$p<.01$
N: 11488
chi^2 1394.786
Prob > chi^2 0.0000
-2 Log Likelihood 13219.367
Percent Correctly Predicted 68

higher social class (the variable for social class goes from upper to lower class which is why the sign is negative) are more interested in politics, as are women who are members of associations. Whether or not a woman is a housewife or employed has no bearing on her interest in politics. The variable assessing whether a woman has a life outside the household or not, or whether a woman met with her friends often, had a significant and positive impact on the level of political interest.

What about political activity? Why are some women more politically active? Are those women who have a place outside the household also more politically active. Table 11 reports the results of the analysis that seeks to understand why some women are more politically active. In Table 11, "political interest" was added as a control variable, as women with political interest are more likely to be politically active. Burns et al. (2001) have used political interest as proxy for the

Table 11.
Why are some women Politically Active?

	Logistic Regression Coefficient	Standard Error
USA	2.419**	.245
Canada	3.994**	.260
Mexico	3.735**	.243
Puerto Rico	1.296**	.260
Nigeria	1.162**	.261
Chile	1.041**	.252
India	1.790**	.250
Venezuela	1.964**	.247
Zimbabwe	1.177**	.258
Philippines	.093	.280
Bangladesh	.614*	.281
Indonesia	.839**	.278
Serbia	-.100	.305
Montenegro	2.055**	.247
Egypt	1.503**	.261
Morocco	2.118**	.234
Jordan	1.460**	.268
Education	.124**	.012
Employed	.242**	.057
Social Class	.013	.030
Urban	.130	.066
Meeting with Friends	.258**	.056
Associational Membership	.547**	.067
Being a Housewife is fulfilling	.053	.082
Political Interest	.710**	.056
Constant	-4.654	.284

Dependent variable is political action.
*$p<.05$; **$p<.01$
N: 11488
chi^2 3194.492
Prob > chi^2 0.0000
-2 Log Likelihood 9260.987
Percent Correctly Predicted 83

different socialization of men and women in order to argue that women have lower levels of political interest and, thus, are not as politically active.

Once again, there are clear and significant country specific effects. As expected women who are more educated, are employed, and belong to associations are more likely to be politically active. Whether a woman lives in an urban area or not and her social class has no effect on whether she participates or not. Of course, women who are more interested in politics are more politically active. Once again, the variable of theoretical interest for this paper—the degree to which a woman associates with friends—has a significant and positive impact on why some women participate and others do not.

While independence from the home is significant and important for women, independence from the household does not have the same resonance for political activity by men. The reason for this, as suggested above, is the gendered nature of the household. To determine the influence of activity outside the household for the levels of participation by men, an analysis exactly the same as Table 11 for women was conducted.

It was found that meeting with friends did not have a significant influence on whether a man was politically active or not once we controlled for the other factors that could influence political participation. The coefficient was .065 with a standard error or .059 and did not approach acceptable levels of significance.

Conclusion

In examining political participation by women, this paper has noted that levels of participation in India are low. The 73d amendment gave them new opportunities. Many women are, however, still not aware of the reservations made for them in local elections. While a woman's socioeconomic status has a bearing on her interest in politics and political activity, the impact of a woman's position in the household cannot be denied. Whether a woman can negotiate space for herself independent of the household is an important determinant of whether she is an active participant in politics or not. This claim highlights the fact that political participation is a public act and that for women to be equal participants in the public arena they need to be able to step outside the household—a sphere of male dominance in many parts of the world. What determines which women can make independent space for themselves is beyond the scope of this paper and is a task left for future research.

NOTES

1   See Brinton (1993) for a carefully done analysis of the career patterns of Japanese women. Even in the United States there is mounting evidence that women are returning to the "home" especially when children need to be raised.

2   See Nussbaum (2002) for a discussion of changes in the status of women in
        India.

3   Basu (1992) and Ray (1999) offer pioneering studies of women's movements in
        India. Both of them note that political parties in India limit women's participa-
        tion.

4   The data are available at http://www.ipu.org/wmn-e/clasify.htm. India had more
        women in Parliament than Japan, Greece, Russia, and Sri Lanka and fewer than
        Rwanda, Uganda, the Philippines, Chile, and Malaysia.

5   Data available at the Election Commission of India web site
        http://www.ec.gov.in/.

6   Data from the Election Commission of India at http://www.ec.gov.in/.

7   Women, not surprisingly then, also have lower levels of identification with polit-
        ical parties. In 1971, 74 percent of women did not identify with any political par-
        ty in contrast to only 55 percent of the men who felt similarly. In 1989, men too
        were as likely not to identify with a political party—70 percent of them said so
        whereas 79 percent of women did not identify with a party. As it is men whose
        identification with political parties has dropped the largest, an insofar as this lack
        of attachment to a party is a key element of the contemporary deinstitutionaliza-
        tion of the Indian Party System, that deinstitutionalization emerges as gendered.

8   The amendement said that "Not less than one-third of the total number of seats
        reserved . . . shall be reserved for women belonging to the Scheduled Castes or,
        as the case may be, the Scheduled Tribes [and that] not less than one-third
        (including the number of seats reserved for women belonging to the Scheduled
        Cases and the Scheduled Tribes) of the total number of seats to be filled by direct
        election in every Panchayat shall be reserved for women and such seats may be
        allotted by rotation to different constituencies in a Panchayat." Further, it said
        that "that not less than one-third of the total number of offices of Chairpersons
        in the Panchayats at each level shall be reserved for women . . . provided also that
        the number of offices reserved under this clause shall be allotted by rotation to
        different Panchayats at each level."

9   Burns et al. (2001) examine the role of gender in terms of power relations with-
        in the household and attempt to determine who makes decisions in the household,
        and they seek to determine whether the gender gap in participation would be lin-
        ked to who makes decisions in the household. They do not find clear support for
        such a hypothesis.

10   One way of determining the impact of discrimination is to examine a corollary

to the discrimination argument, which states that women who do participate should do so because of a consciousness of the discrimination that they face in the political world. For this claim see (Miller, Gurin, Gurin, and Malanchuk 1981; Gurin 1985; and Young 1994).

11   For an indepth study of women candidates in Panchayat elections in Haryana, see Arora and Prabhakar (1997).

12   The concept of political participation was limited to "activity that has the intent or effect of influencing government activity" (Burns et. al. 2001:4). Strikes were not included as only women who work could strike and that would limit the range of political activity for housewives and the self-employed.

REFERENCES

AGARWAL, Bina.
       1994. *A Field of One's Own*. Delhi: Cambridge University Press.
ARORA, Subhash C. and R.K.Prabhakar
       1997. "A Study of Municipal Council Elections in India: Socioeconomic Background of Women Candidates in Rohtak, Haryana." *Economic and Political Weekly* XXXVII(10):918 -926.
BASU, Amrita.
       1992. *Two Faces of Protest: Contrasting Modes of Women's Activism in India*. Berkeley: University of California Press.
BOURDIEU, P.
       1977. *An Outline of a Theory of Practice*. Cambridge: Cambridge UniversityPress.
BRINTON, Mary.
       1993. *Women and the Economic Miracle: Gender and Work in Postwar Japan*. Berkeley: University of California Press.
BURNS, Nancy, Kay Lehman Scholzman, and Sidney Verba.
       1997. "The Public Consequences of Private Inequality: Family Life and Citizen Participation." *American Political Science Review* 91(2):373-389.
BURNS, Nancy, Kay Lehman Scholzman, and Sidney Verba.
       2001. *The Private Roots of Public Action: Gender, Equality, and Political Participation*. Cambridge, Harvard University Press.
GLEASON, Suzanne.
       2001. "Female Political Participation and Health in India." *Annals of the American Academy of Political and Social Science* 573:105-126.
GOPALAN, Sarla and Mira Shiva, eds.
       2000. *National Profile on Women, Health and Development: Country Profile—India*. Delhi: Voluntary Health Association of India and World Health Organization.
GURIN, Patricia.
       1985. "Women's Gender Consciousness." *Public Opinion Quarterly* 49:143-63.

HARTMANN, Heidi.
    1981. "The Family as the Locus of Gender, Class, and Political Struggle: The
    Example of Housework." *Signs* 7:366-394.
MILLER, Arthur H., Patricia Gurin, Gerald Gurin, and Oksana Malanchuk.
    1981. "Group Consciousness and Political Participation." *American Journal of
    Political Science* 25:494-511.
NUSSBAUM, Martha C.
    2002. "Sex, Laws, and Inequality: What India can teach the United States."
    Daedalus 131(1):95-106.
OKIN, Susan Moeller.
    1998. "Gender, the Public, and the Private." In *Feminism and Politics*, edited by
    Anne Phillips. Oxford: Oxford University Press.
RAY, Raka.
    1999. *Fields of Protest: Women's Movements in India*. Minneapolis: University of
    Minnesota Press.
SCHLOZMAN, Kay Lehman, Nancy Burns, and Sidney Verba. 1994. "Gender and the
    Pathways to Participation: The Role of Resources." *Journal of Politics* 56(4):
    963-990.
SOORYARMOORTHY, R.
    2000. "Political Participation of Women: The Case of Women Councilors in
    Kerala, India." *Journal of Third World Studies* 17:45-60.
SOUTH, Scott J. and Glenna Spitze.
    1994. "Housework in Marital and Nonmarital Households." *American
    Sociological Review* 59:32-47.
VERBA, Sindey, Nancy Burns, and Kay Lehman Schlozman. 1997. "Knowing and Caring
    About Politics: Gender and Political Engagement." *Journal of Politics* 59(4):
    1051-1072.
YOUNG, Iris Marion.
    1994. "Gender as Sexuality: Thinking about Women as a Social Collective."
    Signs 19:713-738.

DATE DUE

Printed in the Unite
44182LVS00005B/

969 870777